T0316394

Measuring Public Pension Liabilities in the European Union

Sozialökonomische Schriften

Herausgegeben von
Bert Rürup und Werner Sesselmeier

Band 42

PETER LANG

Frankfurt am Main · Berlin · Bern · Bruxelles · New York · Oxford · Wien

Olaf Weddige

Measuring Public Pension Liabilities in the European Union

PETER LANG
Internationaler Verlag der Wissenschaften

Bibliographic Information published by the Deutsche Nationalbibliothek
The Deutsche Nationalbibliothek lists this publication in the Deutsche Nationalbibliografie; detailed bibliographic data is available in the internet at http://dnb.d-nb.de.

Zugl.: Freiburg (Breisgau), Univ., Diss., 2010

D 25
ISSN 0172-1747
ISBN 978-3-631-60273-7

© Peter Lang GmbH
Internationaler Verlag der Wissenschaften
Frankfurt am Main 2011
All rights reserved.

www.peterlang.de

Für Julia und Jonathan

Die vorliegende Dissertation entstand während meiner Zeit als wissenschaftlicher Mitarbeiter am Forschungszentrum Generationenverträge der Albert-Ludwigs-Universität Freiburg. Sie wurde im November 2009 vom Promotionsausschuss der Wirtschafts- und Verhaltenswissenschaftlichen Fakultät angenommen. Ich möchte allen danken, die diese Arbeit möglich gemacht haben.

Mein besonderer Dank gilt meinem Doktorvater Prof. Dr. Bernd Raffelhüschen für das in mich gesetzte Vertrauen und die fachliche Unterstützung während der vergangenen Jahre. Ebenfalls danken möchte ich Prof. Dr. Heinz Rehkugler für die Übernahme des Zweitgutachtens.

Da diese Arbeit auf einer Studie für die Europäische Zentralbank basiert, welche am Forschungszentrum Generationenverträge in Gemeinschaftsarbeit durchgeführt wurde, gilt mein weiterer Dank meinen Kollegen Christoph Müller und in besonderem Maße Matthias Heidler, der gerade zu Beginn des Projekts entscheidende Impulse gab. Weiterhin danken möchte ich Stefan Moog für seine wertvollen Ratschläge und Christian Hagist für seine nie enden wollende Diskussionsbereitschaft und das gründliche Korrekturlesen.

Meinen Eltern gebührt Dank für all die Jahre meiner Ausbildung, in denen sie mich tatkräftig unterstützt haben. Und zum Abschluss möchte ich mich bei den wichtigsten Personen in meinem Leben bedanken: Julia, ohne Deine Hilfe und Motivation wäre diese Arbeit nicht fertig geworden! Und Jonathan, Du hast durch Deine anstehende Geburt dafür gesorgt, dass ich den Abgabetermin nicht mehr verschieben konnte! Vielen Dank Euch beiden Süßen!

Freiburg, im Juli 2010

Olaf Weddige

Contents

Contents

Contents

List of tables

List of tables

List of tables

List of figures

List of figures

List of abbreviations

ABM	Automatic balance mechanism
ABO	Accumulated benefit obligations
ADL	Accrued-to-date liabilities
AdL	Alterssicherung der Landwirte (German old age security pension scheme for farmers)
AOW	Algemene Ouderdomswet (Dutch basic pension scheme)
AT	Austria
BG	Bulgaria
BGN	Bulgarian Lev (national currency of Bulgaria)
bn.	billion
CGA	Caixa Geral de Aposentações (public employee pension scheme in Portugal)
CMFB	Committee for Monetary, Financial and Balance of Payments statistics
COLA	Cost of living adjustment
CPI	Consumer price index
CSSA	Czech social security administration
CZ	Czech Republic
CZK	Czech Koruna (national currency of the Czech Republic)
DB	Defined Benefit
DE	Deutschland (Germany)
DRV	Deutsche Rentenversicherung (German statutory pension insurance administration)
ECB	European Central Bank
EMU	European Economic and Monetary Union
ERM	European Exchange Rate Mechanism
ES	Espana (Spain)
EU	European Union
EUR	Euro
FDC	Financial defined contribution
FER	Pension scheme for farmers in Poland
FI	Finland
FN	Footnote

List of abbreviations

FR	France
FUS	Fundusz Ubezpieczen Spolecznych (Polish social insurance scheme)
GBP	Pound Sterling (national currency of the United Kingdom)
GDI	Gross disposable income
GDP	Gross domestic product
GR	Greece
GRV	Gesetzliche Rentenversicherung (statutory pension insurance scheme)
HU	Hungary
HUF	Hungarian Forint (national currency of Hungary)
IAS	Indexante de Apoios Sociais (measure of social support in Portugal)
IMF	International Monetary Fund
IBO	Indexed benefit obligations
IPD	Implicit pension debt
IPL	Intertemporal public liabilities
IT	Italy
KELA	Pension regulation for employees of the social insurance institution Finland
KiEL	Evangelical-Lutheran church pensions act
KuEL	Local government pensions act Finland
LT	Lithuania
LTL	Lithuanian Litas (national currency of Lithuania)
LUTUL	Farm closure allowance act Finland
LV	Latvia
LVL	Latvian Lats (national currency of Latvia)
m.	million
MEL	Seamen's pensions act Finland
MIG	Minimum income guarantee
MISSOC	Mutual Information System on Social Protection
MPC	Minimum period of contribution
MT	Malta
MYEL	Farmers' pensions act Finland
NDC	Non-financial defined contribution; notional defined contribution

NL	Netherlands
NSSG	National statistical service of Greece
OADR	Old-age dependency ratio
OECD	Organization of Economic Co-Operation and Development
OSGL	Open-system gross liabilities
OSNL	Open-system net liabilities
PAYG	Pay-as-you-go
PBO	Projected benefit obligations
PIA	Primary insurance amount
PL	Poland
PLN	Polish Zloty (national currency of Poland)
PROST	Pension Reform Option Simulation Toolkit
PT	Portugal
RCG	Research Center for Generational Contracts (Freiburg University)
SE	Sweden
SEK	Swedish Krona (national currency of Sweden)
SG	Sustainability gap
SHIW	Survey on Household Income and Wealth (Italy)
SK	Slovakia
SKK	Slovakian Koruna (national currency of Slovakia before January 1st, 2009)
SNA	System of national accounts
SOEP	Socio-Economic Panel Study (Germany)
SS	Seguridad Social (Spanish social security system)
SVB	Soziale Verzekeringbank (administrative body of the Dutch AOW)
SVR	Sachverständigenrat zur Begutachtung der gesamtwirtschaftlichen Entwicklung (The German Council of Economic Experts)
TyEL	Employees pensions act Finland
UK	United Kingdom
VaEL	State employees' pensions act Finland
VBL	Versorgungsanstalt des Bundes und der Länder (supplementary pension scheme for public employees not being civil servants)

List of abbreviations

| YEL | Self-employed persons' pensions act Finland |
| ZUS | Zaklad Ubezpieczen Spolecznych (Polish social insurance institution) |

1 Introduction

Demographic developments present a major future risk for the public pension systems of most developed countries. Continuously increasing life expectancy and large age groups of the so-called baby-boomer generation in combination with low fertility rates since the mid-1970s will cause considerable enhancements of old-age dependency ratios. This means that public pension systems organized on a pay-as-you-go (PAYG) principle will be forced to either raise contribution rates or taxes, shorten future replacement rates, or enforce a combination of both. Due to this development, measuring future pension payments has become an important aspect of economic research. In this regard, two important issues have to be addressed:

The first issue refers to the question of measuring the public pension entitlements of private households until today. From a fiscal perspective, these entitlements are equal to the accrued-to-date liabilities (ADL) of a public pension system. These liabilities are not an indicator of fiscal sustainability, but they display the implicit pension debt which the government owes to private households. The extent of these liabilities has an impact on the saving behaviour of private households. Thus, it seems reasonable to measure the ADL of a pension scheme in order to examine this impact.

Up to date, ADL are not included in the system of national accounts (SNA) as usually only pension liabilites which are financially funded are reported. However, in 2006 the Committee for Monetary, Financial and Balance of Payments statistics (CMFB) established a task force which was called the *Eurostat/ECB Task Force on the statistical measurement of the assets and liabilities of pension* (which will be referred to as the *Task Force* from now on). The Task Force was built in the course of the review of the SNA93[1] and was – among other issues – mandated to produce statistical estimates of the stocks and flows of accrued-to-date liabilities from pension schemes in general government.[2] These estimates were supposed to enter the national accounts via a supplementary table which was also to be developed by the Task Force. The members of the Task Force were pension and national accounting experts from the European Union (EU) member states as well as experts

---

[1] The System of National Accounts 1993 (SNA93) is a conceptual framework that sets the international statistical standard for the measurement of the market economy. It is published jointly by the United Nations, the Commission of the European Communities, the International Monetary Fund (IMF), the Organization for Economic Co-operation and Development (OECD) and the World Bank.

[2] See Eurostat/ECB Task Force (2008), p. 87 et sqq.

from the European Commission, the Organization of Economic Co-Operation and Development (OECD) and the International Monetary Fund (IMF). The Task Force was co-chaired by the European Central Bank (ECB) and Eurostat, the statistical office of the European Union. In 2007, the Research Center for Generational Contracts (RCG) at Freiburg University was asked to estimate the ADL for all EU member states represented in the Task Force. The aim of these calculations was to produce benchmark ADL figures for the national statistical bodies which eventually will be asked to fully take over this task. Subsequently, in 2008 the *Eurostat/ECB Contact Group on the statistical measurement of the assets and liabilities of pension schemes in general government* (which will be referred to as the *Contact Group* from now on) as the successor of the Task Force with an identical mandate instructed the RCG to carry out calculations for all countries represented in the Contact Group. The outcomes resulting from these mandates are the basis for the ADL presented in this study. Altogether, outcomes for 19 EU member states will be introduced.

The second issue regarding the future development of public pension schemes refers to the consequences of the demographic development for future retirees and contributors and examines the sustainability of the pension scheme by confronting the present value of future pension payments with the present value of future contributions (and possibly tax revenues). The corresponding balance can be regarded as the open-system net liabilities (OSNL) of a pension scheme. In case the OSNL amount to zero, the pension scheme can be characterized as fiscally sustainable.

The concept of fiscal sustainability has attracted increasing attention in the academic community since the 1980s. This applies especially to the fiscal consequences of demographic developments. In the beginning of the 1990s, Auerbach, Gokhale and Kotlikoff (1991, 1992, 1994) introduced the concept of generational accounting to examine the sustainability of a country's fiscal policy. Since that time, this concept has continuously been enhanced by the RCG in Freiburg and has been applied to a country's fiscal system as a whole and to various subsystems like public pension or public health systems.

In this study, the method of generational accounting is employed to assess the accrued-to-date liabilities (ADL) and the open-system net liabilities (OSNL) of public pension schemes of various EU member states. The survey is organized as follows: In chapter 2, first of all the different kinds of pension liabilities are classified (section 2.1). In section 2.2, we present the methodology of generational accounting including our modifications developed to calculate the OSNL and the ADL of a pension scheme (the so-called Freiburg model). Section 2.3 gives an overview of the general assumptions as well as a description of the applied data. This includes information regarding population data, age-specific pension benefits, growth and discount rates as well as a case study for calculating pension profiles. In section 2.4 we briefly describe the limitations and possible extensions of the Freiburg model. Finally, in section 2.5 we explain the rationale of the supplementary table developed by the Task Force, which is utilized in this study to present the outcomes of our ADL calculations.

Chapter 3 reports the findings of our ADL calculations for 19 EU member states, supplying one section per country. We proceed in alphabetical order of the EU country codes, starting with Austria (AT), followed by Bulgaria (BG), the Czech Republic (CZ), Germany (DE), Spain (ES), Finland (FI), France (FR), Greece (GR), Hungary (HU), Italy (IT), Lithuania (LT), Latvia (LV), Malta (MT), the Netherlands (NL), Poland (PL), Portugal (PT), Sweden (SE), Slovakia (SK) and finishing with the United Kingdom (UK). All sections are structured in the same manner. At first we give an overview of the country's demographic situation; secondly we describe the countries' public pension systems and recent pension reforms. Each of these country sections finishes with a presentation of our findings. Chapter 3 ends with a cross-country comparison of our results. Furthermore the main determining factors for the level of ADL are identified. We show that besides other factors the initial level of pension expenditures is the most important driver for ADL.

Referring to the issue of fiscal sustainability mentioned above, we provide an excursus from our ADL estimations and present calculations of the open-system net liabilities (OSNL) for four selected countries in chapter 4. These are – again in alphabetical order – Germany, Lithuania, the Netherlands and Sweden. The aim of our country selection is to include a wide range of possible pension scheme designs and varying demographic developments. The country sections are followed by a cross-country comparison of the OSNL in section 4.5; the chapter finishes with a comparison of the OSNL and the ADL of the according countries which we presented in section 4.6. We find that there is no correlation between the ADL and the sustainability of a pension scheme. The last chapter of this study summarizes and gives a rough outline for further research in the field of measuring pension liabilities.

2 Methodology and data basis

2.1 Concepts for measuring implicit pension debt

Before beginning any calculation of implicit pension debt (IPD) it should be made perfectly clear what kind of liability is referred to, or – more precisely – to which degree entitlements from private households are included.[3] In the relevant literature, three main definitions of pension liabilities are well-established:[4]

Accrued-to-date liabilities: These contain the actual pension payments and the present value of pensions to be paid in the future based on accrued rights; no rights can be accumulated after the base year, neither by present nor by future workers.

Current workers and pensioners' liabilities:[5] In this case allowance is made for the pension scheme to continue its existence until the last presently living contributor dies, while no new entrants are allowed. New entitlements can be accumulated only by existing members of the pension scheme.

Open-system gross liabilities:[6] These also include the present value of pensions of new workers under current rules; the range of options extends from including only children not yet in the labour force, to an infinite perspective.

Table 1 shows these definitions in an overview:

---

[3] It has to be pointed out that the pension payments taken into account in this study generally refer to old-age, disability and survivor pensions. These may be paid out of government employer pension schemes or social security pension schemes.In cases where only old-age pensions are referred to, this is denoted explicitly. Moreover, as far as feasible any kind of means-tested social assistance is excluded. All benefit payments are considered gross of taxation and social contributions.

[4] See Franco (1995), p. 2. As Holzmann (1998), p. 3 points out, Kane and Palacios (1997) have introduced another terminology describing the different scopes of pension liabilities: (a) accrued termination liability; (b) present value of anticipated benefit payments to current participants; and (c) "going concern" liability. These definitions are taken from the US private sector. However, in this study we opted for the terminology introduced by Franco (1995) as this is commonly used in the academic community.

[5] The concept of current workers and pensioners' liabilities is displayed here only for the sake of completeness. It will not be discussed in further detail in this survey.

[6] Note that Franco (1995) refers to open-system liabilities only. We extended this naming to open-system gross liabilities to ease the distinction between a concept including or excluding future contributions.

4

Table 1: Definitions of pension liabilities

Scope of liabilities	Definition of liabilities
1) Accrued-to-date liabilities	Present value of pensions in disbursement; present value of future pensions due to **past** contributions of **current** workers
2) Projected current workers' and retirees' liabilities	1) + present value of future pensions due to **future** contributions of **current** workers
3) Open-system gross liabilities	1) + 2) + present value of pensions due to contributions of **future** (worker's) **generations**

Source: Holzmann et al. (2004), p. 13.

Table 1 demonstrates that the difference between the three main definitions of pension liabilities reflects alternative views on how future pension benefits can be considered. For instance, looking at the concept of open-system gross liabilities, current pensioners and workers as well as future workers (and thus all future retirees) are taken into consideration. In contrast, accrued-to-date liabilities regard only rights accrued by existing and former workers until the base year.

In regard to accrued-to-date liabilies (ADL), the question might arise if these are actually entitlements of private households which the government can be sued for. If this was the case, one could view ADL on a level with public debt which in most cases represents entitlements of private households against the government, respectively the public sector. Kotlikoff (1986) suggests to regard social security contributions as loans given from individuals to the public sector. He shows that under certain conditions an old age security scheme financed on a pay-as-you-go (PAYG) basis is equivalent to explicit public debt and should thus be accounted likewise.[7] In contrast to that, Holzmann et al. (2004) argue that there are several differences between unfunded pension promises and government bonds;[8] members of a PAYG scheme are usually forced to participate while bonds are disbursed on voluntary basis. Consequently, bonds can be sold or borrowed against while pension promises cannot be traded at all. Furthermore, contrary to the return on government bonds the yield of a PAYG scheme is quite uncertain and depends

---

[7] See Kotlikoff (1986), p. 54 et sqq.

[8] See Holzmann et al. (2004), p. 5 et sqq.

on many variables including the possibility that the government may change the benefit formula. This means that the pension promises of the government (or in other words: accrued-to-date liabilities) can be reduced in the course of a political decision (i.e. a pension reform) which is not possible in the case of government bonds.[9] Summing up it can be stated that there are indeed a couple of differences between implicit (pension) debt and explicit debt. Nevertheless, for many cases it seems useful to classify accrued-to-date liabilities (ADL) as public debt.

There are several good reasons why appropriate estimates of ADL are needed. One of these reasons is given by the fact that the existence of a PAYG scheme has an impact on the saving behaviour of individuals. Feldstein (1974) emphasizes that social security pensions generally have two effects on personal savings: On the one hand, personal savings are reduced because they replace household assets. On the other hand, personal savings are increased because the longer period of retirement induced by the existence of social security pensions requires a higher amount of assets.[10] As the net effect of these two effects is not certain a priori, the measurement of ADL can help examining this question and explaining different saving behaviour between countries.[11,12] In section 3.20, a brief attempt will be made to establish a connection between the dimension of a country's ADL and the net private saving rate of that country.

In additon to that, ADL do co-determine the intertemporal budget constraint of the government. The higher the ADL turn out to be, the higher financial markets will estimate the risk of explicit public debt to be defaulted. In case the dimension of ADL is not known, financial markets will probably compensate this uncertainty with

---

[9] Holzmann et al. (2004) admit that governments can also default on explicit government debt, for instance by reducing of interest, inflation tax or changes in taxation of interest. However, according to Holzmann et al. (2004) most governments find it easier to reduce their pension liabilities than to default their explicit public debt.

[10] See Feldstein (1974), p. 908.

[11] Feldstein (1974) shows that for the US personal savings would be higher in the absence of social security (see p. 916 et sqq.). In an updated study, Feldstein (1996) reexamines the results of his 1974 paper by again applying a social security wealth (SSW) approach. His findings show that in the US the social security program reduces overall private saving by nearly 60 per cent (see Feldstein (1996), p. 162 et sqq.).

[12] In fact, the concept of ADL has already been used to explore the saving behavior of different countries. See for example Durant and Reinsdorf (2008).

a risk premium.[13] This link emphasizes the importance of appropriate estimations of ADL.

Estimates of ADL can also be quite helpful when it comes to the assessment of a pension reform which has either been planned or already enacted. The difference of ADL before and after a pension reform demonstrates the losses (or in rare cases: the gains) of private households. Furthermore, if a partial or full shift to a financially funded scheme is intended, the ADL illustrate the costs of terminating the PAYG scheme.[14] Imagine a case where a PAYG scheme is about to be terminated without any information about the ADL belonging to that scheme. This could result in a political rejection of that reform due to high increases of explicit debt necessary to meet the entitlements. Disney (2001) argues that if the ADL of a pension scheme are not presented in government balance sheets at all, there will be a clear bias against a reform which will imply a transition to a partially funded scheme (and in that way turn the implicit liabilities to explicit ones).[15] However, this problem could be avoided by estimating and accounting the ADL of that pension scheme prior to any decision regarding a termination of that scheme or a transition to to a funded scheme.

At this point it is worth mentioning that the level of ADL is by no means a sustainability indicator. Sustainability in a fiscal sense is defined as a fiscal sector on the whole or a fiscal sub-system like the social security pension scheme which shows a balanced account of all future deficits/surpluses discounted to present value. In other words, a fiscal system is sustainable if it can be continued in the future without being forced to adjust settings like transfer or tax rates.[16] There are two reasons why ADL should not be called on when it comes to sustainability. First of all and most importantly, ADL only take into account one side of the coin, the expenditure side. Without considering the other side of the coin, the revenue side (contributions), any statement about sustainability becomes arbitrary. Secondly, as pointed out before ADL include only those pension entitlements which have been earned up to the base year. Thus it does not take into account any information regarding possible increases of pension expenditures due to demographic

---

[13] See Holzmann et al. (2004), p. 7.

[14] See Mink and Rother (2006), p. 249.

[15] See Disney (2001), p. 96.

[16] In a more specified definition, sustainability is given if present and future generations are treated equally in a fiscal sense. This can be analyzed by means of generational accounts. However, in this study we focus on the broader definition of sustainability given above.

development.[17] However, despite its poor informative value regarding sustainability questions, ADL certainly have some explanatory power when it comes to various other issues as the ones aforementioned.

Taking a closer look on the concept of open-system gross liabilities, the limited explanatory power of this indicator becomes evident. Compared to the concept of accrued-to-date liabilities which for example specifies the costs of terminating a pension scheme at once, there is no obvious information provided by the extent of open-system gross liabilities. For this reason we will introduce an additional indicator which provides information regarding the sustainability of the pension scheme examined: In the concept of *open-system net liabilities* the future expenditures of a pension scheme are confronted with the future assets, namely future contributions and possibly some kind of capital stock. In this way it can be tested if under the current legal status quo the pension scheme can be continued indefinitely without accruing any deficits in terms of present value (in other words: if the system is sustainable) or if it has to be adjusted to future demographic and economic circumstances.

Various estimates of pension liabilities have been conducted in the past, both on an international and on a national level. Hagemann and Nicoletti (1989), van den Noord and Herd (1993) and Kuné et al. (1993) belonged to the first to present pension liabilities on an international level, followed by Chand and Jaeger (1996) and Fredriksen (2001). One of the latest international estimates was presented by Holzmann et al. (2004) who examined the public pension systems of 35 low and middle income countries by applying the Pension Reform Option Simulation Toolkit (PROST) developed by the World Bank. On a national level, several surveys have been published for the case of German pension liabilities. Werding (2006), Ehrentraut (2006), Braakmann et al. (2007) and Heidler (2009) show pension liabilities for

---

[17] Oksanen (2009) suggests to apply projections for accrued-to-date liabilities (ADL) as an indicator for sustainability. From our point of view the open-system net liabilities (OSNL, explained later in this section) represent a more suitable to assess sustainability. However, Oksanen (2009) points out that projected ADL contain the information when the pension rights are accrued and not only when the pensions are paid out.

the German statutory pension scheme,[18] Besendorfer et al. (2006) and Braakmann et al. (2008) calculate pension liabilities for the civil servants pension schemes.[19]

---

[18] Werding (2006) calculates both accrued-to-date and open-system net liabilities, while Ehrentraut (2006) and Heidler (2009) focus on open-system net liabilities (although they refer to the terms "intertemporal public liabilities" and "sustainability gap" (liabilities in relation to GDP) rather than OSNL.

[19] It has to be pointed out that Besendorfer et al. (2006) estimate liabilities only for the pensions of the civil servants of the federal states and the municipalities in Germany (ADL as well as OSGL), whereas Braakmann et al. (2008) present figures for the civil servants of the central government only (ADL). Therefore the findings of these two surveys should not be compared.

2.2 Assessing pension liabilities: The methodology of generational accounting

Generational accounting is a well-recognized tool to assess the sustainability of a country's fiscal sector as a whole as well as of one of its (para-) fiscal subsystems. The method was developed by Auerbach, Kotlikoff and Gokhale (1991, 1992 and 1994) and has since its introduction been applied to as much as 29 different countries.[20] In the following we will provide a short description of the framework of generational accounting in general.[21] Subsequently we will focus on the framework of generational accounting applied to public pension schemes (section 2.2.1) and the modifications of the methodology which are required to calculate accrued-to-date liabilities (section 2.2.2).

The basis of generational accounting is the intertemporal budget constraint of the public sector which states that public debt has to be balanced by the payments of either present or future generations.

(1) $$B_b = \sum_{k=b}^{b-D} N_{b,k} + \sum_{k=b+1}^{\infty} N_{b,k}$$

Equation one declares that B_b, the net debt in the base year b, shall be balanced by the aggregate net taxes $N_{b,k}$ of all generations born between $b-D$ (D denotes the maximum age of an individual) and b on the one hand and aggregate net taxes of future generations to be born between $b+1$ and infinity (∞) on the other hand. To calculate the lifecycle net tax payments of generations, the net payment term $N_{b,k}$ is divided as follows:

(2) $$N_{b,k} = \sum_{s=\max\{b,k\}}^{k+D} T_{s,k} C_{s,k} (1+r)^{b-s}$$

T_{sk} stands for the average net tax paid in year s by a representative member of the generation born in year k, while C_{sk} denotes the number of members of the respective generation born in k.

---

[20] For an overview of studies using generational accounting to assess a country's fiscal situation see Hagist (2008), p. 34 et sqq. See Raffelhüschen (1999) and Bonin (2001) for a detailed depiction of theory and application as well as limitations of the method of generational accounting.

[21] The general description of generational accounting is based on Raffelhüschen (1999) and Bonin (2001).

The main indicator for the fiscal burden of current fiscal policy is then built by showing the residual value in case the intertemporal budget constraint is violated. This indicator is defined as:

(3) $$IPL_b = B_b - \sum_{k=b-D}^{\infty} N_{b,k}$$

In equation (4) the net tax payments of present and future generations has been combined to one term. The equation states that the intertemporal public liabilities of the base year b IPL_b result from the net debt in the base year minus the present value of net tax payments of present and future generations. In other words, the IPL_b represent the present value of the sum of all future deficits, assuming that the the present fiscal policy will be held constant indefinitely. From the IPL_b it is straightforward to derive the so-called sustainability gap:

(4) $$SG_b = \frac{IPL_b}{GDP_b}$$

Equation (4) shows that the sustainability gap of the base year b, SG_b, can be expressed as the ratio of intertemporal public liabilities IPL_b to the gross domestic product GDP_b of the respective base year. The indicators introduced in equation (3) and (4) should be kept in mind, as they will play an important role when assessing the liabilities of public pension schemes.

2.2.1   Generational accounting of public pension schemes

When applying generational accounting to the assessment of public pension schemes, some peculiarities in terms of the methodology have to be considered. On the one hand, the number of possible types of taxes is quite limited. Transfers from individuals to the pension scheme will be either paid as social contributions or as subsidies taken from tax revenues, while payment flows from the pension scheme will be pension benefits. In other words, the maximum number of different types of payment flows is in general set to three: pension contributions, tax subsidies and pension benefits.

Furthermore, a special treatment regarding the age-sex-specific distribution of future pension benefits will be introduced. The core presumption is a projection of per capita future pension benefits based on today's existing retirees' benefits. We outline below the entire calculation procedure in three steps:[22]

Step 1: First of all, age-sex-specific projections of base year's population need to be calculated. The demographic model used to generate these projections is based on a discrete and deterministic formulation of the cohort component method.[23] The three major determinants of future population changes are in general fertility, mortality, and migration. The development of survival rates is established by adjusting the initial set of survival rates with an exponential adjustment procedure.[24]

Step 2: We start with the estimation of the average age-sex-specific existing retirees' benefits in the base year. As mentioned before, the projection of these pension benefits is the centre piece of the calculations since we develop the claims of future retirees by manipulation of the existing retiree's benefits. It is important to note that in our calculations we only look at average individuals within the respective age groups, i.e., we do not separate groups of retirees. We rather separate the calculation of age-sex-specific benefits for existing and future retirees assuming that an average individual is to some extent an existing and a future retiree in every age-year of his/her life-cycle.

Before going further into detail we briefly sketch out the projection approach for existing retirees' benefits. First of all, the benefits are calculated by distributing the aggregated amount of today's pension expenditures to the different cohorts in retirement age. By this procedure we create an age-sex-specific benefits' cross-section profile generated from the budget and micro data of the observed country. Secondly, these average existing retirees' benefits are projected into the future by assuming that they remain constant except for indexation of the benefits.

Formally, the estimation of the existing retirees' benefits is based on the following identity:

$$(5) \qquad P_b = \sum_{k=b-D}^{b} P_{b,k} C_{b,k}$$

---

[22] This treatment has first been deployed at Heidler and Raffelhüschen (2005). The following description is mainly based on Heidler et al. (2009), p. 3 et sqq. For a closer look on the application of generational accounting to public pension schemes see also Heidler (2009), p. 45 et sqq.

[23] For a detailed description of the demographic model applied see Bonin (2001).

[24] This procedure is suggested by Pflaumer (1988). See also Bonin (2001), p. 248.

This identity states that the sum of age-specific individual pension benefits $p_{b,k}$ (in the base year b of the cohort born in k) weighted with the cohort size $C_{b,k}$ must equal the corresponding macroeconomic pension, denoted by P_b.[25] However, equation (5) is only valid in theory. While macroeconomic data, typically taken from national accounting statistics, is relatively exact, micro data is in general difficult to gather and tends to be afflicted with inaccuracies. To resolve this problem generational accountants estimate re-scaled age-sex-specific benefit profiles.

This is done in two steps. First, age-sex-specific information regarding per capita pension benefits has to be collected in order to capture the relative fiscal position of different age groups as accurately as possible. The vector of relative pension benefits by age taken from the statistics, $(\tau_{t,t-D},..., \tau_{t,t})$, is then denoted by $\tau_{t,k}$.[26] This vector is only supposed to show the relative pension position in period t of an individual born in the year k and thus imposes less restriction on the accuracy and availability of micro data on the absolute level. Second, the estimated relative age distribution is tallied with the corresponding aggregate pension benefit P_b by application of a proportional, non-age-specific benchmarking factor, denoted by φ. The relative distribution of pension payments is re-evaluated according to

(6)
$$p_{b,k} = \varphi \tau_{b,k}$$

for all living generations $b-D \leq k \leq b$, where φ is defined by

(7)
$$\varphi = \frac{P_b}{\sum_{k=b-D}^{b} \tau_{b,k} C_{b,k}}.$$

Equation (7) assures that equation (5) is finally satisfied such that the expenditures to existing retirees are assigned with age-sex-specific profiles to the base year population.

Finally, the resulting rescaled average age-sex-specific existing retirees' benefits are projected according to the indexation rules of the respective country:

---

[25] Please note that D represents the maximum age of an individual, which is generally 100 years according to our assumption.

[26] For ease of notation we drop the sex-specific notation as from now on.

(8) $\qquad p_{t,k}^{exis} = p_{b,k}(1+g)^{t-b},$

for all cohorts $b\text{-}D \le k \le b$ living in the base year.

This equation states that an individual already retired in base year b receives the same pension in a specific year t as in the base year b, merely corrected by the indexation g of pension in payment. Furthermore, equation (8) implies a phasing out of the stock of existing pension benefits since it only applies to all living generations. Thus all existing retirees' pensions of the base year will have disappeared at the latest when the youngest existing retiree of the base year is dead.

Step 3: The age-sex-specific pension profile for future retirees is calculated by manipulating the base year existing retirees' benefits. This is done in three steps. First, the difference of the existing benefits for a consecutive age year (during the base year) provides the pension benefits for new retirees.[27] These are valorised for a specific year t. Second, if necessary, a deduction factor is used (defined by a reform or for instance inherent like in NDC[28] systems). Third, the (cumulated) average future retirees' benefits are calculated by summing up year-by-year the new retirees' benefits and thus accounting for the fact that an individual can receive on average for any future year t a new retiree benefit.

Formally, the new retirees benefit $p_{t,k}^{new}$ in a specific year t for a cohort k is developed first by calculating the absolute change in existing retirees benefit of the cohort $b\text{-}(t\text{-}k)$ (the cohort with the same age $(t\text{-}k)$ in the base year b) to the cohort one year younger in the base year, namely $b\text{-}(t\text{-}1\text{-}k)$.[29] After that this base year payment is valorised with $(1+v)^{t-b}$ where v is the valorisation rate according to the benefit formula. On top on that the new retirees' benefits are diminished according to a deduction factor $\theta_{t,k}$ of the benefit formula.[30] Equation (9) sums up:

---

[27] Note that new retirees' benefits represent those benefits that are paid for the first time upon retirement in a specific year $t>b$.

[28] See Palmer (2006) for a detailed description of the principles of a notional defined contribution (NDC) system.

[29] Changes at latest after the age of 67 years are set to zero since new retirees' old-age benefits after the age of 67 are negligible. However, this does not hold for widow's pensions.

[30] We developed this approach in the course of our calculations. In the meantime, it has already been applied to other examinations; see Benz et al. (2009).

(9)
$$p_{t,k}^{new} = \theta_{t,k}\left[p_{b,b-(t-k)}^{exis} - p_{b,b-(t-1-k)}^{exis} \right](1+v)^{t-b},$$

for all living cohorts $b-D \leq k \leq b$.

Finally, the future (existing) retirees' benefits need to be calculated. This is done by cumulating year-by-year the $p_{t,k}^{new}$ according to equation (9). Therefore, the age-sex-specific future retiree pension benefits for a specific year t of the cohort k is defined by:

(10)
$$p_{t,k}^{fut} = p_{t-1,k}^{fut}(1+g) + p_{t,k}^{new},$$

for all cohorts $b-D \leq k \leq b$.

From this equation it follows that the average individual born in the year k receives a future benefit in the year t ($t>b$) which is composed of the pension payment one period earlier ($t-1$) corrected by the growth rate g plus the pensions paid to new retirees in this year. Thus, the age-sex-specific benefit profile for future retirees builds up step by step.

After this procedure the open-system net liabilities of a pension scheme can be expressed in the following way:

(11)
$$OSNL_b = B_b + \sum_{k=b-D}^{\infty} N_{b,k}^{exp} - \sum_{k=b-D}^{\infty} N_{b,k}^{rev}$$

According to equation (11), the open-system net liabilities $OSNL_b$ of a pension scheme are composed of the net debt B_b (which will in most cases be zero or even negative due to capital assets like a buffer fund) plus the present value of future pension expenditures (respectively future pension benefits) minus the present value of future revenues of the pension scheme (respectively future contributions). In other words, if the $OSNL_b$ amount to zero, the pension scheme is in a sustainable situation which means that it can be continued with the current setup for all times. Liabilities can also be expressed in relation to the respective GDP:

(12)
$$SG_b^{pens} = \frac{OSNL_b}{GDP_b}$$

Analogous to equation (4), the sustainability gap of a pension scheme in a certain year b is given by the ratio of open system net liabilities $OSNL_b$ to the GDP of the corresponding country in that year.

2.2.2 Measuring accrued-to-date liabilities – the Freiburg model

The Freiburg model represents a modification of the methodology of generational accounting employed at the Research Center for Generational Contracts (RCG), Freiburg University. The standard method of generational accounting has been developed further in order to meet the concept of accrued-to-date liabilities; the methodology of this modified version of generational accounting – the Freiburg model – will be described in section 2.2.2.1. Thereupon, we will put the focus on an important issue arising when accrued-to-date liabilities are to be calculated – the question of how to deal with future wage growth when transforming present entitlements to future pension benefits (section 2.2.2.2).

2.2.2.1 The methodology of the Freiburg model

The starting point for the calculation of the accrued-to-date liabilities with the Freiburg model is the application of generational accounting to public pension schemes[31]. Consequently, the standard method presented in section 2.2.1 has been modified in order to account for the accrued-to-date amount of benefits instead of considering future pension benefits in total. In other words, as current contributors in the base year have earned only a part of the entitlements necessary to receive a full pension, their pension payments have to be reduced to meet the concept of accrued-to-date liabilities. The corresponding framework for the respective calculations will be described in the following section. We pick up the description of section 2.2.1 after step 3 and proceed with an adjusted step 3*:

Step 3*: In order to meet accrued-to-date liabilities, only the part of the future pension benefits (of current workers) has to be considered which is earned until the base year. This means in turn that $p_{t,k}^{new}$ must be cut by a factor $\lambda_{t,k}$ representing the cohort-specific amount of entitlements of current contributors in relation to the full entitlements.

---

[31] The terms "public pension scheme", "government pension scheme" and "pension scheme in general government" are used as synonyms. However, we differentiate between two different types of public schemes. The "government employer pension scheme" indicates the pension scheme for civil servants, whereas the "social security pension scheme" describes a general pension scheme. For a discussion of the definition of government pension schemes see Eurostat/ECB Task Force (2008), p. 20 et sqq.

Future pension benefits are thus finally defined by

(13) $$p_{t,k}^{fut} = p_{t-1,k}^{fut}(1+g) + \lambda_{t,k}p_{t,k}^{new},$$

for all cohorts $b-D \leq k \leq b$.

Note that the accrued-to-date concept requires a definition of the valorisation and accruing process for the entitlements. As a matter of principle there are several possibilities to account for. Section 2.2.2.2 defines the two approaches applied in this survey, accumulated benefit obligations (ABO) and projected benefit obligations (PBO).

Step 4: Finally, the accrued-to-date liabilities of the pension scheme are calculated by discounting and summing up the above projected pension benefits over the cohorts living in the base year.

Thus, the accrued-to-date liabilities ADL_b can be expressed like this:

(14) $$ADL_b = \sum_{t=b}^{b+D} \sum_{k=b-D}^{b} \frac{(p_{t,k}^{exis} + p_{t,k}^{fut})}{(1+r)^{t-b}} C_{t,k}$$

Equation (14) states that every period t the existing retirees pension benefits ($p_{t,k}^{exis}$) and the pension rights accrued until the base year ($p_{t,k}^{fut}$) – which are both discounted by the factor $(1+r)$ for every future year $(t-b)$ – are multiplied with the number of members of this age cohort $C_{t,k}$. This is done for every age-group, beginning with the ones born in $k=b-D$, which goes back 100 years prior to the base year.

2.2.2.2 Measurement concepts of accrued-to-date liabilities

When measuring the amount of a pension scheme's accrued-to-date liabilities, the decision has to be made to what extent future wage increases of existing contributors are taken into account. There are numerous possible paths to be taken, most authors, however, opt for the measurement of either accumulated benefit obligations (ABO) or projected benefit obligations (PBO). First of all, it has to be made perfectly clear that the difference between ABO and PBO only refers to the question of how to project entitlements of individuals not yet retired into the future. This means that entitlements of those individuals already receiving pensions in the base year – and therefore disposing of full pension rights – are not influenced by the choice between ABO and PBO at all.

When we speak of ABO, what we mean is ABO indexed for prices.[32,33] Suppose that somebody has worked 20 out of 40 years. Given the benefit formula is expressed in terms of final pay (wage or salary) and years worked, ABO is half of the present value of what the end-40 years' entitlement would be if no allowance was made for future pay increases, whether from promotions or general increases in real pay rates. The real value of the entitlement accrued to date is preserved at the time of maturity. It follows that I) either estimates of price-indexed ABO must project future price increases and in doing so, they discount projected final price-indexed pay of 20 years ahead to the present, using a nominal interest rate which includes the same expectation of inflation or, alternatively, II) one must use today's real pay as the projected real pay in 20 years' time, and discount back by a real interest rate.

PBO is defined in the following way: It represents the entitlement today based on a projection of eventual entitlements at retirement. Thus, after 20 out of 40 years' service, the pension amount induced by the projected final pay level after 40 years of service including the impact of likely promotions as well as general wage growth is calculated, halved (20 out of 40 years), and today's entitlement is expressed by discounting it. In addition to promotions, the projection of eventual entitlements takes into account projected real increases in pay at the current grade and other grades, up to the time of retirement. Increases to reflect inflation are taken out, if the discount rate is expressed in real terms, otherwise they are included in both projected final pay levels and the discount rate.

This means that when referring to PBO the only factor that reduces the employee's pension entitlement in comparison with the retiree's pension entitlement is the smaller amount of years into service – in our example 20 out of 40 years. When applying ABO, not only the smaller amount of working years is considered, but also the generally lower payment in that time period, regardless if it stems from personal or general wage increases. This leads to the assumption that PBO entitlements will

---

[32] This definition is adapted from John Walton (member of the Eurostat/ECB Task Force) who kindly took stand to the difference between ABO and PBO. He points out that "ABO indexed for prices" is often referred to as IBO (indexed benefit obligations). But due to the fact that IBO is also regarded as another form of PBO in some cases, we work with "ABO indexed for prices" which in the following shall be called "ABO" for simplification reasons.

[33] Please note that the explanations for both ABO and PBO are based on a benefit formula which depends on the final pay before retirement only. We are well aware of the fact that most of the European pension systems take into consideration a longer history of contributions when it comes to the calculation of first paid pensions. In this case, the difference between ABO and PBO also depends on how former contributions are considered in relation to present contributions, or in other words: How are former contributions valorised at the point of retirement.

in most cases be higher than ABO entitlements, simply because ABO does not allow for future personal or general wage increases.[34]

Implementation of ABO and PBO in the Freiburg model

As described previously in this chapter, we estimate pension entitlements by calculating future pension payments. In basic terms, this is done by projecting present age-sex-specific pension payments into the future, taking into account the indexation of the respective pension scheme as well as any pension reforms which have been decided already and will have an impact on future pensions. In order to receive the ADL of a pension scheme, it is crucial to divide the beneficiaries of future pension payments into two groups: The first group consists of persons who already receive pension payments. The members of this group dispose of full pension entitlements as they have already retired and are not able to increase their pensions by paying contributions.[35] It follows that in our model the pension payments of this group – the "existing retirees" (or more precisely: persons who are already in retirement in the base year) – are projected in line with the relevant indexation until the last retiree dies.

The second group consists of persons who do not receive pension payments yet. They have earned some kind of pension entitlements in the past – regardless if they just took up employment one year ago or if they are close to retirement – and will probably earn more pension entitlements in the future, up to that point of time when they will retire. It follows that this group does not dispose of full pension entitlements yet. The ADL approach includes entitlements earned up to the base year only, therefore the projected future pension payments of a "future retiree" (or more precisely: a person who will retire after the base year)[36] has to be reduced. Here the question of ABO versus PBO enters the scene:

---

[34] In an unlikely case of zero future wage increases – neither from promotions nor from increases of the general wage level – ABO and PBO entitlements would be the same. Moreover, there are situations imaginable where ABO entitlements could exceed PBO's. This would be the case if either the general future real wage growth is assumed to be negative or if personal wage developments will decrease due to smaller wages for senior employees.

[35] This counts only for pension schemes which do not allow their beneficiaries to increase their pension after retirement, i.e. by taking up employment, paying contributions and thus augmenting their pension entitlements.

[36] Please note that "future retirees" involve all individuals that retire after the base year. In contrast to this, "new retirees" indicate individuals who retire in a certain year x in the future. Those individuals who retire in the year x will in that year enter the group of "future retirees". In the year x +1 they will still be "future retirees" but not "new retirees" anymore.

In a first step, we will distance ourselves from the accrued-to-date idea, just as it is exercised in the model primarily. In every single year after the base year, new pensioners will enter the pension scheme. The question to be answered first is what the amount of the first paid benefit will be in relation to the new pensioners' benefits in the base year. Let the amount of first paid pension – sometimes referred to as the primary insurance amount (PIA) – in the year t be $x(t)$ and the constant per-capita wage growth in real terms be g. When applying the PBO approach, the first paid pension will be defined like the following:

(15) $$x_{t+1} = x_t(1+g)$$

Since g is assumed to be constant over time, the first paid pension can also be expressed subject to the base year b.

(16) $$x_{t+1} = x_b(1+g)^{t-b}$$

Changing to the ABO approach, one has to bear in mind that no allowance is made for future pay increases. In the current case, only the general wage growth is observed. It follows that the first paid pension of a future year t in the ABO approach changes to:

(17) $$x_t = x_b$$

The difference between equations (16) and (17) can be explained by the different approaches of ABO and PBO. PBO takes into account general future wage growth while ABO does not consider any future changes of wage; the wage level of the base year is held constant in real terms.[37]

The second difference between ABO and PBO can be observed when reducing the primarily calculated full benefits of "new pensioners" according to the concept of ADL. The full benefits are reduced by a vector – the "accrued-to-date vector" –, which expresses the share of entitlements earned until the base year to the amount of entitlements which qualifies for a full pension. This share is given for every projection year. It decreases from a value close to one for primary pensions paid out shortly after the base year up to a value of close to zero for primary pensions paid out in the far future. This vector is multiplied with the respective accounts of full

---

[37] It is crucial that this only counts for the calculation of the first paid pension or PIA. When projecting a benefit which has already been paid out before, i.e. the indexation of existing benefits, a constant real wage growth is assumed. In this regard the ABO approach displays a schizophrenic world where in one situation future wage growth is considered and in the other it is not.

pension entitlements and the outcome is the amount of pension entitlements earned up to the base year for every projection year, the accrued-to-date entitlements. The difference between ABO and PBO in this regard is given by the different consideration of personal wage increases during working life. Generally, the wage at the beginning of a career is less than the average wage and only surpasses average earnings closer to retirement – PBO takes this effect into account, ABO does not.

Regarding the accrued-to-date vector in the PBO approach, only the missing amount of contribution years has to be taken into account, as the full pension primarily calculated by the model includes assumptions for personal and general wage growth. Let the average age of entering the work force and collecting first pension entitlements be 20 years, and the average retirement age 60 years. It follows that for an individual aged 35 in the base year, the PBO accrued-to-date entitlements add up to 15/40 of the full pension. According to this, the PBO accrued-to-date vector should show a value of 15/40 for this age group.

Applying the same example to the ABO approach, one does not only need to consider the 25 missing years up to the point of retirement, but also the wage (which has not developed up to the point of retirement) has to be taken into account. This means that in most cases the entitlements of an individual aged 35 in the base year will be less than 15/40 of the full pension. The question of how large the difference between the ABO and PBO accrued-to-date vector will be is answered by age-specific wage profiles from the respective country which show the development of an average career's wage.

In summary, the difference between ABO and PBO consists of two parts. The first part is the general wage growth, in most cases connected to general economic growth. The second part is the development of wage during an average career.

2.3 Data and general assumptions

Looking at the definition of accrued-to-date liabilities it would be easy to conclude that except for projecting the population no assumptions regarding the future have to be made – due to the fact that no entitlements can be accrued in the future.

However, this view is certainly wrong. First of all, almost every pension scheme features some kind of indexation which adjusts the pensions to economic circumstances on a regular basis. This means that pensions either grow in line with price inflation, per capita wage growth, or a mixed index according to the corresponding benefit formula. Hence, this index has to be estimated. Apart from that, in certain pension systems the indexation does not depend on per capita wage growth but rather on general GDP growth. Thus, an assumption regarding the future development of GDP has to be made. Furthermore there are pension systems like the general pension scheme in Germany where the indexation depends on a factor which measures the relation between retirees and contributors (known as the sustainability factor). In this case, an assumption regarding the future labour market has to be taken. These examples show that even when applying the concept of accrued-to-date liabilities as a supposedly safe concept without too many uncertainties, a lot of assumptions regarding the demographic and economic developments have to be made. Since a considerable number of European countries will be examined, the choice has to be made if one should draw upon country-specific assumptions regarding the future economic and demographic development or if uniform assumptions should be applied for all countries.

As we will discover later in this chapter in detail, the answer to that is twofold: When it comes to demographic assumptions, we trust the official projections of Eurostat and the corresponding assumptions which are country-specific. Regarding the economic development, we deploy uniform assumptions for all countries. We treat demographic and economic assumptions unequally across countries due to two reasons: From our point of view demographic forecasts are more reliable since they stem from one central framework (Europop) whereas cross-country economic forecasts are often based on methodologies which have been adopted individually by the different countries and are therefore not applicable for a cross-country comparison.[38] Furthermore when estimating pension liabilities the focus lies on the impact of the demographic development on liabilities. Thus, we apply country-

---

[38] Disney (2001, p. 96-97) stresses the fact that whenever pension liabilities are to be measured on a cross-country level, one common framework is useful for projecting the future economic development of the various countries.

specific assumptions to take into account country-specific characteristics and treat economic development with less priority by opting for uniform growth and discount rates across countries.

The following sections aim to introduce both the data and the assumptions to deploy the Freiburg model (section 2.3.1 and 2.3.2). In addition, we show an example of how the pension profiles used in the Freiburg model are calculated (section 2.3.3). We conclude by presenting some limitations and possible extensions of the Freiburg model (section 2.4) and the supplementary table developed by the Task Force (section 2.5).[39]

2.3.1 Necessary data

The general data description is valid for all country studies presented subsequently.[40] Where country studies deviate from the outlined default procedure to cope with national peculiarities, this is stated in the respective country chapter. Unless indicated otherwise, all population data has been taken from Eurostat.[41] Unless indicated otherwise, data regarding age- and sex specific pension payments have been supplied by the members of the Contact Group, i.e. the national statistical bodies or national central banks of the participating countries. This also applies to data regarding aggregate pension payments.

2.3.1.1 Population

At the outset of any calculation of implicit debt, projections of the base year population by age and sex, which reach as much as a maximum of 100 years into the future, are the base of the results presented in this study.[42] Most EU member states publish population projections conducted by their national statistical bodies. However, these official estimates typically cover only a time span of 30 to 50 years and thus are not far-sighted enough to meet the requirements of accrued-to-date liabilities. Therefore, it is necessary to conduct our own projections which prolong official forecasts. The starting point of the population projections used in this study is the population structure by age and sex observed at the start of the respective

---

[39] The following description is based on Heidler et al. (2009), p. 12 et sqq.

[40] Unless indicated otherwise, this also applies to the calculations presented in chapter 4 of this study.

[41] See http://www.ec.europa.eu/eurostat.

[42] According to the assumption that the maximum age is $D=100$.

base year 2005, 2006 or 2007. As the standard case, all demographic projections are based on data from Eurostat. Descriptions of the future demographic developments of the various countries examined can be found in the particular country chapters.

2.3.1.2 Age-sex-specific pension benefits

This data can generally be taken from micro-data surveys such as the Survey on Household Income and Wealth (SHIW) in Italy or the Socio-Economic Panel Study (SOEP) in Germany. However, in many cases the administration body of the pension scheme provides age-sex-specific data regarding the recipience of pension payments. As this data encompasses the full category of persons in question instead of a (representative) sample, it is considered better than sample data. In the case of our calculations, age-sex-specific pension benefits have been supplied by national central banks or national statistical bodies. Table 76 in the appendix provides an overview of our data sources.

2.3.1.3 Budget data

As explained in section 2.2.2.1, the pension scheme's expenditures of the base year are necessary to re-scale the age-sex-specific pension profiles. These budget figures are generally taken from national accounts' statistics. In our particular case, figures have mostly been supplied by national central banks or national statistical bodies. For an overview of the budget data sources see Table 77 in the appendix.

2.3.1.4 Characteristics of the pension scheme

The design of a pension scheme represents a crucial point when calculating its ADL. This involves the following main issues:

- Classification of the pension scheme (DB, NDC, hybrid system)[43]
- Consideration of past contributions
- Indexation of existing pensions
- Necessary years of service to receive a full pension
- Regulations regarding early and late retirement

The sources of these pieces of information are manifold; both international pension surveys[44] and country-specific pension literature contain comprehensive descriptions of the constructions of the various pension schemes.

---

[43] See Börsch-Supan (2007), p. 3 et sqq. for an explanation of the differences between defined benefit (DB) and NDC pension systems. Hybrid pension systems are usually a combination of DB and NDC systems and feature elements of both.

2.3.2 General assumptions

As stated above, a whole set of assumptions has to be taken when computing pension liabilities. The possibly strongest assumption states that fiscal policy will not change over time. In other words, the design of the pension scheme to be examined will stay indefinitely constant at the status quo of the base year including all the settings which have been displayed in section 2.3.1.4. The remaining common assumptions used in the Freiburg model will be introduced in what follows in the proceeding chapter:

2.3.2.1 Growth and discount rate

The projection of future age-specific pension benefits demands an assumption regarding the annual rate of wage growth. Since any long-term forecast of future growth remains arbitrary, we do not make use of sophisticated forecasts. Instead, a supposedly constant rate of wage growth is applied in all future periods. The growth rate is set to approximate the average long-term rate of productivity growth observed in the past. Considered that the correct value of the growth parameter is uncertain, we have not attempted to design specific growth patterns for the individual EU member states. We employ a growth rate of 1.5 per cent per annum in real terms. However, this procedure is open for discussions, and by using varying wage growth paths for different countries one might be able to show the impacts of diverging economic developments on the pension liabilities of the different countries in a more adequate way.

Similar to the growth rate parameter, forecasts regarding the prospective interest rate development are uncertain. Therefore, irrespective of national peculiarities, we apply a single uniform discount rate to take all pensions back to the base year. A reasonable range of interest rate assumptions is determined by the fact that public expenditures are significantly more uncertain than non-risky long-term government bonds on the one hand, but not as volatile as the return on risky assets on the other hand.

We generally opt for the lower bounds of the discount rate. Therefore we normally choose a standard real discount rate of three per cent per annum, which reflects the ten-year average of Euro area ten-year government bond yields.

At this point it is worth mentioning that the use of a constant discount rate as well as a constant wage growth rate implies a serious simplification. In general, more

---

[44] See for example European Commission (2007), MISSOC (2009) or OECD (2007).

comprehensive sensitivity analyses could take account of possible variations of these parameters. This also applies to the other key economic parameters (unemployment rates and participation rates respectively), or changes in the behaviour of economic actors.[45]

2.3.2.2 Fertility, mortality and migration

Following the component method, the age composition of the population is updated in each year by first subjecting the initial population structure to age-sex-specific mortality. Subsequently, the respective age-specific birth rates are applied for every projection year. The implementation of the component method requires assumptions with respect to the future development of age-specific mortality. The country-specific mortality rates are parameterised according to the assumptions of the baseline variant of the Eurostat population projection (EUROPOP). [46] Fertility rates are assumed to be constant, and migration is disregarded due to reasons explained in section 2.2.2.1.

2.3.3 Case study for calculating age-sex-specific pension profiles

For the sake of clarity, in the following we show a case study for the calculation of age-sex-specific pension profiles by demonstrating step 2 to 5 of section 2.2.2.1 for the case of the social security pension scheme in Germany for average males (see Figure 1 to Figure 5).[47]

As outlined in section 2.2.2.1, the estimation of the base year average existing retirees' benefits by age is the centre piece of the projection. This is done by aggregating a benefit profile by age and sex over the base year population and then re-evaluating it in a way that the aggregates based on micro-profiles and

---

[45] We will discuss this issue in further detail in section 2.4.

[46] As Eurostat does not show life expectancy data for the year 2007, we had to draw on the assumptions of EUROPOP2004. As the up-to-date version EUROPOP2008 does not contain these assumptions, EUROPOP2004 is also employed for life expectancies in 2050, due to consistency reasons. We are aware of the fact that EUROPOP2008 assumptions feature higher life expectancies until 2050 than EUROPOP2004. It can be stated that the outcomes presented in chapter 3 of this survey would be higher when applying EUROPOP2008.

[47] Please note that in this example wage growth rates have been set to zero.

population data correspond to the respective government budget aggregates in the base year.[48]

Figure 1: Rescaled profile of average existing retirees' benefits in 2006
(here: Social security pension scheme Germany, male, in Euro)

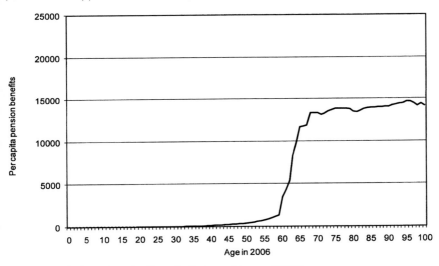

Source: Own calculations based on Deutsche Rentenversicherung (2007b)

Figure 1 shows an average rescaled profile of existing retirees' benefits for the living male cohorts in the year 2006. The increasing profile after the age of 50 years reflects an increasing share of pension cases. The decreasing profile for older cohorts results from past differences in working careers and indexation rules.[49]

To account for future cohort-specific development of existing retirees pension benefits, we phase out year-by-year the rescaled age-sex-specific existing retirees' profile and index the pension benefits according to the benefit formula (Figure 2).

---

[48] Since our projection method does not correct aggregates for business cycle effects, base year economic performance is perpetuated indefinitely. This may lead to a bias. Nonetheless this effect seems not as critical in case of considering pension expenditures only since they are for the most part dominated by demography.

[49] At this point it is worth mentioning that we employ age-sex-specific pension data which is broken down into one-year intervals. Most former surveys use five-year interval data which can lead to inaccuracies especially when looking at the cohorts retiring in.

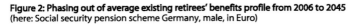

Figure 2: Phasing out of average existing retirees' benefits profile from 2006 to 2045
(here: Social security pension scheme Germany, male, in Euro)

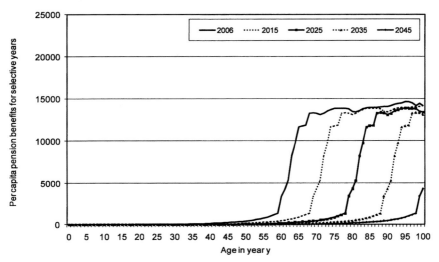

Source: Own calculations

As a result of our procedure, the profile of existing retirees is shifted to the right, due to the fact that no entrants after the base year conform to this profile. This is in line with the concept of our existing retirees' profile which illustrates the age-sex-specific distribution of pensions which have been received in the base year already. Figure 2 shows that in the year 2045 only very few retirees will receive pensions. Hence, in our example a couple of years after 2045 the profile for existing retirees will have been vanished as the last retiree from the base year will have been died.

As an intermediate step we develop the annual new retirees' benefits by taking the difference of the rescaled base year profile of the existing retirees pension benefit. We do this until the age of 67 because after this age-year, new retirees' benefits are negligible (see Figure 3).[50] This treatment allows designing maturation effects for future retirees' cohorts. It is necessary since the existing retirees' benefit profile after the age of 67 is not a good predictor for future retirees' benefits due to the fact that

---

[50] Please note that this does not count in case the age-sex-specific survivor pensions are available. In this case we consider the difference of the rescaled base year profile until the age of 90 in order to take into account widow's pensions in a more accurate way. After this age, the data usually is non-representative due to small numbers of cases in the age cohorts above 90.

both average benefits and the share of pension cases vary substantially across existing retirees cohorts reflecting past differences in working careers. This proceeding nonetheless maintains base year economic structures for new retirees indefinitely. In particular, the analysis thus abstracts from changes in labour force participation and unemployment rates for future new retirees' benefits.

Figure 3; Rescaled profile of average new retirees' benefits for 2006
(here: Social security pension scheme Germany, male, in Euro)

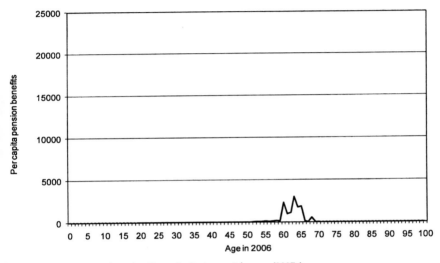

Source: Own calculations based on Deutsche Rentenversicherung (2007a)

These average new retirees' benefits are subsequently built up year-by-year to project future retirees' benefits. At the same time the payments need to be valorised at first and, in a second step upon retirement, indexed according to the benefit formula. Third, the level effects of legal amendments which had been passed into law in or prior to the base year but not yet come into full fiscal effect are taken into account. Figure 4 shows the development of future retirees' pension benefits for selected years. As can be seen after being built up almost completely (year 2055), in the case of Germany the profile is considerably lower as the existing retirees profile. This is due to reforms which are explained in the corresponding country chapter (section 3.4.2.2).

Figure 4: Build-up of average future (existing) retirees' pension benefits profile from 2006 to 2055
(here: Social security pension scheme Germany, male, in Euro)

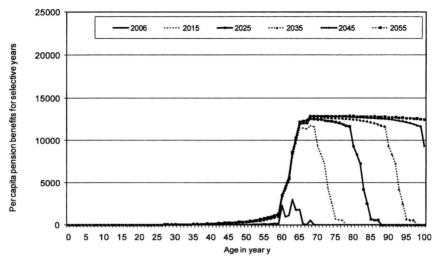

Source: Own calculations

In a final step Figure 5 reduces the future retirees' benefits to account for the accrued-to-date part only. Due to the fact that in this case the concept of PBO is applied to – which means that future wage growth of existing contributors is taken into account –, we cut the benefits linearly according to the ratio of (years in the job until base year) to (average years in the job).[51]

It can be seen that as a result of the reduction of future pension benefits, the pensions of the individuals aged 70 in the year 2015 are the highest of the whole profile. This is due to the fact that this age group was 61 in the base year 2006, hence they have accrued a large part of full pension entitlements. All age cohorts older than them receive less pensions according to this profile, as they predominantly have already been into retirement in the base year and thus are represented in the existing retirees profile. In contrast, all age cohorts younger than the observed one have accumulated less pension entitlements up to the base year, thus they receive less pension in the accrued-to-date concept.

---

[51] For a detailed explanation see section 2.2.2.2.

Figure 5: Accrued-to-date amount of average future retirees' pension benefits profile from 2006 to 2055
(here: Social security pension scheme Germany, male, in Euro)

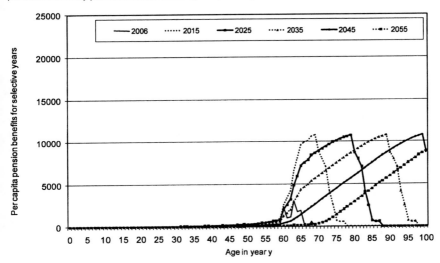

Source: Own calculations

2.4   Limitations and possible extensions of the Freiburg model

When setting up a model one is confronted with the classical trade-off between simplicity and accuracy. On the one hand the model should reflect reality as precise as possible. On the other hand models are by definition abstractions of reality; and therein lies one of their major strengths. They display a complex phenomenon in a simple and clear manner and therefore have to leave out irrelevant information. Hence, the crucial question when setting up models is: What are the relevant input factors to be chosen? We have answered this question with the description of assumptions and input data in section 2.3.1 and 2.3.2. In the following we will take a closer look on the resulting limitations of the Freiburg model. In this context, we give various examples taken from the results of our accrued-to-date liabilities in chapter 3. Furthermore, a divergent answer to the above raised question shall be given and possible extensions of the model – i.e. additional relevant input factors – shall be considered.

To understand the outcomes of the model it is essential to grasp the channels which lead to the respective results. In this context it is of interest how the outcomes change if one varies the assumptions taken. Sensitivity analyses which assess the robustness of a model are useful tools for this purpose. They give an indication to which extent the outcomes of the model are driven by the assumptions taken.

Table 2 illustrates the respective sensitivity analysis for the ADL of the German public pension system (base year 2006). Looking at these results a significant limitation of the Freiburg model becomes obvious. Given a small alteration of the assumed interest rate (r) from three to two percent the outcome changes considerably by 21.0 percent (using the PBO approach). Also the level of the growth rate (g) has a sensitive impact on the results of the Freiburg model – as shown in Table 2. Since the future is uncertain by nature, this constraint of the model cannot be overcome. Nevertheless, the sensitivity analysis demonstrates once again the importance of choosing appropriate assumptions.

Noting that the taken assumptions have a large influence on the results, the question arises which level of interest and growth rate shall be chosen when examining different countries – as done in chapter 3 of this survey. The choice lies in heterogeneous or homogeneous presumptions.

Table 2: Sensitivity analysis of the German social security pension scheme (ADL)

Parameters		Amount of ADL (relative deviation to scandard scenario)[52]
Discount rate (r)	Growth rate (g)	
2.0 %	1.0 %	9.6 %
2.0 %	1.5 %	21.0 %
2.0 %	2.0 %	34.2 %
3.0 %	1.0 %	- 8.5 %
3.0 %	1.5 %	0.0 %
3.0 %	2.0 %	9.8 %
4.0 %	1.0 %	- 22.1 %
4.0 %	1.5 %	- 15.6 %
4.0 %	2.0 %	- 8.2 %

Source: Own calculations

The former option is supported by the fact that countries widely differ in their development and therefore can be assumed to follow different growth and interest paths in the future. Nevertheless, we choose equal assumptions for all countries examined in our EU-comparison. Two main arguments play a role for this decision: *predictability* and *comparability*. Forecasting the demographic development for the coming decades is relatively straightforward since the future population can be assumed to be compounded to a large degree of the present population. However, *predicting* the development of economic growth and interest rates is rather demanding and connected with a great deal of uncertainty. Not only do economic indicators depend on numerous variables – and are therefore difficult to predict – but do they also feature large volatility.[53] Hence, the lack of ability to predict the future development of economic growth and interest rates is one important rationale for choosing identical assumptions in our cross-country comparison. Another reason in favour of homogeneous assumptions across countries is an enhanced comparability of results.[54] Heterogeneous assumptions which are often based on national forecasts – and which themselves are often based on dissimilar presumptions – would make the outcomes less comparable and therefore more vulnerable in the political discussion. Since the calculation of pension liabilities represents a

---

[52] For the base year 2006, a change of one percentage point is equal to around 65 bn. EUR of pension liabilities in the case of the German social security pension scheme. See section 3.4.2.3 for further details.

[53] For an overview on the main determinants of economic growth see Mankiw et al. (1992) or Barro and Sala-i-Martin (2003).

[54] See Franco et al. (2004), p. 16.

highly political issue – especially in the context of the Maastricht treaty and the current discussion of government insolvency – the political dimension of calculating pension liabilities should not be neglected. Nevertheless, homogeneous interest and growth rates limit the model to the extent that country-specific particularities cannot be accounted for.

Current research indicates and quantifies that the ageing process has a significant and heterogeneous impact on economic growth in EU countries.[55] As pointed out before, the future ageing development can be predicted relatively well. Therefore, the Freiburg model could be extended taking ageing-specific growth forecasts into account. However, in this context it is necessary to ensure that such growth-predictions are detached from policy considerations and that the agencies assigned to produce such forecasts represent independent bodies.

A further limitation to mention is straightforward and applies to every model: the model can only be as accurate as the given input data. This aspect represents a constraint especially for the calculation of pension reforms and of cohort-specific pension levels.

Particularly when modelling pension reforms commonly a lot of information is required. A short example shall illustrate this: Several pension systems in Europe implemented changes regarding the amount of the maximum pension. For example in Portugal a pension ceiling was introduced with the reform of 2006. Bulgaria on the contrary decided to let the maximum pension limit expire after the year 2009. In order to model such reforms comprehensive data about the distribution of reference earnings is necessary. Unfortunately, in many cases such detailed information is not available. As a consequence, various reforms cannot be accounted for accurately or at all in our calculations due to the limitation of input data.[56]

The same goes for possible side effects of pension reforms. Various countries enacted pension reforms in the recent years which significantly lower future pension levels. However, such reductions of pension levels can be significantly cushioned by the existence of minimum pensions. In other words, a pension reduction can be limited to the extent that pension levels in some countries cannot fall under a certain

---

[55] It can be assumed that economic growth per capita in the EU25 will be lowered by roughly one third due to the ageing process in the coming decades. However, this effect varies between each EU country. For an extensive view on the long term economic growth in the EU25 see Carone et al. (2006).

[56] Changes in the recognized insurance periods – such as crediting for child care or education periods – could not be considered in our calculations either due to a lack of data.

threshold, given by the amount of the minimum pension.[57] Since we normally do not have information about the distribution of pension levels we are not able to implement this side effect. A possible future extension of the Freiburg model could implement probabilities of receiving a minimum pension in the calculations. But it has to be stated once again that such an extension greatly depends on the quality of data supply.

Moreover, due to a lack of input data cohort effects cannot be considered in the Freiburg model either. Within our concept of measuring pension liabilities we take a look at the past, due to the fact that pension data reflects the insurance history of pensioners – such as past employment rates, business cycles and wages. However, we usually have no information about the insurance history of cohorts which are presently contributing into the system. In this sense the approach of the Freiburg model is comparable to an observation of planets located a long way off in the universe. While observing these planets we actually get a view of previous times – since the light takes a long time to reach the earth from these far away celestial bodies.[58]

Due to the limit of input data we have to assume that the pension level of future pensioners – or in other words of present contributors – will be the same as the pension level of new pensioners in the base year. As a result the pension level of future pensioners will only differ from the new pensioners' pension level in the base year due to pension reforms and indexation rules. Summarizing, the above outlined characteristic – one could call it the distant planet characteristic – of the Freiburg model confines the accuracy of the calculations by ignoring cohort effects. But this limitation can also be interpreted as its strength since it significantly limits the

---

[57] We assume that pension reductions of the latest pension reform particularly in France, Hungary and Portugal will be cushioned due to existing minimum pensions.

[58] Cohort effects should play a more significant role for the ADL the longer the reference contribution period in a pension system is – i.e. the further away the observed planet – and the more the present pension data reflects the further past. Another example shall illustrate this: German pensions are based and calculated on the entire career history. Therefore, for a present new pensioner his entire contributions over the last approximately 40 years are considered in the pension calculation. Of course, also periods of unemployment or self employment are reflected in the pension level. Due to increasing unemployment and self employment rates in recent decades the level of future pensioners can be expected to differ from the present values (see SVR (2007), p. 195). We assume that the more the pension system is based on the principle of equivalence – for example taking into account a long reference contribution period – the more the level of pensions for each age group will differ. In some countries such cohort effects however only play minor roles, for instance in the Netherlands. The calculation of Dutch pensions does not depend on the level of past income but only on the periods of residence in the Netherlands between the age of 15 and 65. For a description of the Dutch pension system see MISSOC (2009).

amount of information necessary for the calculation. Therefore, the model fits very well if only a limited amount of data can be provided – as it is mostly the case when undertaking large country comparisons.

There is also another significant limitation to be mentioned: The introduced model does not take into account future behavioural changes. So far we suppose that future pensioners will take retirement decisions similar to those of their present counterparts.[59] But what happens if future new pensioners will change their behaviour and retire significantly later (earlier) than today? The answer to this question depends on the respective pension scheme examined. If the pension increments (decrements) for late (early) retirement can be considered actuarial neutral the behavioural changes should have no impact on our results.[60] However, as Queisser and Whitehouse (2006) indicate numerous pension systems in the OECD cannot be considered actuarial neutral. A substantial number of countries does subsidize early retirement and penalizes late retirement since pension decrements as well as increments are lower than an actuarial neutral rate. As a consequence, we will overestimate (underestimate) pension liabilities if future pensioners decide to retire later (earlier) than today. In Table 3 we demonstrate the impact of a change in pension behaviour for the case of Germany. As illustrated, a postponement of the retirement by one (two) year(s) lowers the ADL for Germany by 2.7 (5.2) per cent.[61] Consequently, a possible extension of the Freiburg model could take into account predictions of future pension behaviour – similar to Berkel and Börsch-Supan (2004). However, due to our knowledge the data basis to forecast pension behaviour within a large cross-country comparison is presently not available.

---

[59] In addition, in case of pension reforms which lead to an increase of the statutory retirement age we assume that the pension behaviour is unaltered, effective retirement age stays constant and the respective retirees put up with resulting pension decrements. However, an exemption is made when the minimum retirement age is increased within the framework of a pension reform – for example in Austria (with the reforms of 2000 and 2003) or in the UK (with the reform of 2007). In such cases we increase in our calculations also the effective retirement age by the respective years.

[60] Actuarial neutrality in the context of pension systems means that the present value of accrued pension benefits does not change due to an earlier or later pension start date. For a detailed description of this concept see Queisser and Whitehouse (2006).

[61] For the calculation of these figures we assumed that from the year 2010 onwards all future new retirees aged 60 to 67 will postpone their retirement by one (two) year(s). The outcome greatly depends on the country-specific pension regulations – namely the pension increments and decrements – as well as the country-specific life expectancies.

Table 3: Impact of a change in retirement behaviour on ADL
(here: German social security pension scheme)

Behavioural change	Amount of ADL (relative deviation to scandard scenario)
Postponed retirement by one year	- 2.7 %
Postponed retirement by two years	- 5.2 %

Source: Own calculations

Another possible extension of the Freiburg model concerns the inclusion of employment rates. Applying the ABO approach we account for different age-specific gross wages over the life cycle as it has been outlined in section 2.2.2.2. However, pension entitlements depend not only on gross wages over the life cycle but also on the periods in which these wages have been earned – in other words periods of employment. Therefore, it would be consistent to include also employment rates – which can greatly differ over the life cycle and between countries – in the calculation of ABO pension liabilities.[62] We assume that this extension would slightly lower the (ABO) results of the Freiburg model. Two aspects play a role for this assumption: First of all, employment rates of the age groups 55 to 60 years old are relatively low in comparison to other cohorts. Secondly, pension benefits of these older age groups are relatively large since they are less discounted – being paid in the nearer future – than coming pension benefits of younger cohorts. In case of an extension of the model with respect to employment rates, the necessary input data could be taken from Eurostat.

In various countries the entitlement of a pension is dependent on a minimum period of membership or contribution in the pension system (MPC). For example, in Italy 20 years (for people insured before the year 1996) of contributions are necessary to receive a pension entitlement while in Belgium no minimum period of membership in the pension system is required.[63] Looking at these country-specific differences the question arises whether dissimilar MPC should be taken into account when calculating ADL. An argument in favour could be the following thought experiment: Imagine the pension system will be terminated and provisions will have to be made for all pension entitlements accrued-to-date. What does this imply for the calculation of ADL? Would Italy have to make fewer provisions since it has implemented a longer MPC than Belgium, given the ceteris paribus condition? In-

---

[62] See Eurostat (2009). Of course employment rates can also differ between cohorts. Since the data basis for an implementation of cohort specific employment rates is rather limited we would only recommend the consideration of country- and age-specific employment rates in the model.

[63] For an overview about the country-specific legal frameworks see MISSOC (2009).

tuition would say yes. But since we cannot be certain about such a political outcome we do not consider regulations regarding MPC in our model. It is nevertheless worth debating to extent the model by such MPC. But it also has to be noted that this would alter the results significantly – as shown in Table 4. In the case of Italy the ADL would be lowered by roughly eleven per cent when considering MPC, while in Belgium on the contrary such an extension of the model would have no impact on the results.

Table 4: Impact of a consideration of minimum contribution periods on ADL[64]

Country (MPC)	Amount of ADL (relative deviation to scandard scenario)
Italy (20 years)	–11.0 %
Lithuania (15 years)	–7.1 %
Germany (5 years)	–1.2 %
Belgium (0 years)	0.0 %

Source: Own calculations

Summarizing, the Freiburg model – like every model – clearly simplifies reality by using a limited set of input factors and assumptions. This feature leads to a number of limitations of the model discussed above. But it can also be considered as its strength since pension liabilities being a complex value can be estimated in a straightforward way. Therefore, the model fits very well when only a limited amount of data can be provided, as is mostly the case in extensive country comparisons. Nevertheless, various extensions of the model – such as a consideration of employment rates, ageing specific growth rates or minimum contribution periods – are worth discussing and could be implemented in the Freiburg model in further research efforts.

---

[64] Since we do not have information about the age-sex-specific contribution history we had to approximate the below given numbers. This estimation is based on the assumption that contributors which are younger than a certain threshold (= number of MPC in years + 1 + average age to enter the workforce in the respective country) have not accrued any entitlements. It is evident that the ADL turn out increasingly lower the higher the number of MPC considered. This is caused by the fact that with an increasing MPC not only more contributors fall under the above defined threshold but also are these contributors on average older and therefore increasingly higher entitlements remain out of consideration.

2.5   The rationale of the supplementary table

In the course of the update of SNA93, the dissatisfaction of many national accountants with the existing heterogeneous treatment of pension schemes depending on their funded or unfunded nature became evident. [65] It was argued that a different accounting of funded and unfunded schemes would lead to different effects on key variables like income, saving, financial assets or liabilities. After many discussions, a compromise on the treatment of pension schemes in the updated SNA was agreed to. According to this compromise, all pension schemes – regardless whether they were funded or not – were to be shown in a supplementary table.

One of the aims of the Task Force was to design this supplementary table on pensions. In this table, all flows and stocks of all possible pension schemes (autonomous pension funds, segregated non autonomous employer schemes, pension part of social security, etc.) are supposed to be displayed. It will thus include details of pension flows and stocks that are recorded in the core accounts plus those that are not included in the core accounts, that way giving a complete view of households' pension "assets", too. In this survey, liabilities are calculated only for general government pension schemes on the one hand and social security pension schemes on the other hand (both currently not being included in the core accounts). Therefore only the columns G and H of the supplementary table are relevant in chapter 3.[66] These are the columns shown in Table 5.

A brief description of the various rows of the supplementary table follows: The rows of the table relate to balance sheet positions, transactions and other economic flows associated with pension entitlements of the schemes included in the supplementary table. Row 1 and row 10 show the opening stock (which is equal to the closing stock of the previous year) and the closing stock of pension entitlements for the respective year. To allow meaningful comparisons across EU member states, pension entitlements at the end of the year (row 10) are related to countries' respective GDP in that year as well. This value is indicated underneath row 10. Representing the logic of the whole table, the receipt of contributions means an incurrence of liabilities while the payment of retirement benefits denotes a reduction of a liability. Row 2 sums up the different kinds of social contributions

---

[65] See Eurostat/ECB Task Force (2008), p. 14.

[66] Please note that in our supplementary table column G is not labeled entirely adequate due to space restrictions. It should read *general government employer pension scheme* instead of *general government* only. This counts in general for all supplementary tables displayed in this survey.

which can be divided into *Employer actual social contributions* (row 2.1), *Employer imputed social contributions* (row 2.2)[67], *Household actual social contributions* (row 2.3), and *Household social contribution supplements* (row 2.4). Row 2.4 can be regarded as the property income of the households and is equal to the unwinding of the nominal discount rate.[68]

Row 3 is solely associated with imputed transactions of social security pension schemes whereas row 4 represents the pension benefits paid during the year. Row 5 is intended to simply present the changes in pension entitlements due to contributions and benefits. Rows 6 to 9 show changes in volume due to transfers between pension schemes, changes of assumptions like discount rate, wage growth or life expectancy, and other economic flows. However, due to the fact that on the one hand constant discount and wage growth rates are assumed in this survey, while on the other hand no transfers between schemes or other changes in volume are taken into account; these rows will be zero in the following country-specific presentations. The exception of this rule is a pension reform which was passed in the year which the supplementary table represents. In that case the impact of this reform on the pension liabilities will be displayed in row 7.

Figures taken from national accounts are not specially marked. Figures calculated in the course of this study are encoded in italic numbers whereas cells which are not applicable in the respective pension scheme are shown in black (see Table 5).

Furthermore it is worth mentioning that in both cases – government employer pension schemes as well as social security pension schemes – there is a cell which accounts for the residual of the respective column. In case of government employer pension schemes (column G), this cell can be found in row 2.2 (*Employer imputed social contributions*); in social security pension schemes (column H), the residual is shown in row 3 (*Other (actuarial) increase of pension entitlements*). This residual can be either positive or negative, and there are various interpretations for a high or

---

[67] For defined benefit schemes, employer imputed social contributions are generally measured as the balancing item – any changes in entitlements over the year not included in other rows of the table are captured here. This row would capture any "experience effects" where the observed outcome of pension modelling assumptions (real wage growth rate, discount rate) differs from the levels assumed. For social security pension schemes, *employer imputed social contributions* as per definition do not exist, therefore this cell is blacked.

[68] For all calculations, we assume a constant discount rate of three per cent and an inflation rate of two per cent (where necessary). Thus the nominal discount rate applicable here is five per cent. The (fictitious) property income is then estimated by taking the average of the opening and closing stock of entitlements as a basis and in a second step discounting this by five per cent.

low (or even negative) value in these cells. One might argue that in case of a positive value the government (as the organizer of the pension schemes in both columns) is forced to compensate for that part of the difference between opening and closing stock of pension liabilities which is not levelled by the actual contributions less the pensions paid in that year. The Eurostat/ECB Task Force (2008) states that if the value in row 3 happens to be negative, this would indicate a social security scheme where the discount rate is higher than the scheme's internal rate of return. This would be feasible in a case where contributions have been raised above the actuarial required level – which is possible only in a defined benefit scheme, of course. Furthermore, in some countries government transfers to the pension scheme take place which are taken out of general tax revenues. These amounts should be included implicitly in row 3 as well.[69] Table 5 depicts a model of the supplementary table – the table will be used in this survey to demonstrate the results of our calculations in chapter 3.

---

[69] See Eurostat/ECB Task Force (2008), p. 27 et sqq.

Table 5: Model of the supplementary table

			Non-core national accounts	
			(figures in bn. EUR)	
			General Government	Social Security
			G	H
		Opening Balance Sheet		
	1	Pension entitlements		
		Changes in pension entitlements due to transactions		
Sum 2.1 to 2.4	2	**Increase in pension entitlements due to social contributions**		
	2.1	*Employer actual social contributions*		
	2.2	*Employer imputed social contributions*		
	2.3	*Household actual social contributions*		
	2.4	*Household social contribution supplements*		
	3	Other (actuarial) increase of pension entitlements		
	4	Reduction in pension entitlements due to payment of pension benefits		
2 + 3 - 4	5	**Change in pension entitlements due to social contributions and pension benefits**		
	6	Transfers of entitlements between schemes		
	7	Changes in pension entitlements due to other transactions		
		Changes in pension entitlements due to other economic flows		
	8	Changes in entitlements due to revaluations		
	9	Changes in entitlements due to other changes in volume		
		Closing Balance Sheet		
	10	Pension entitlements		
		Pension entitlements (% of GDP 2006)		
	11	Output		
	12	Assets held at the end of the period to meet pensions		

Source: Eurostat/ECB Task Force (2008), p. 21.

3   Accrued-to-date liabilities of 19 EU countries

In this chapter, the accrued-to-date liabilities of the public pension schemes from 19 EU member countries will be introduced. The chapter is to a great extent based on Müller et al. (2009). The countries will be presented in alphabetical order, following the official EU abbreviations. We will proceed in the following way: After a short introduction of the country in question, we give an overview of the demographic development in that country up to now as well as in the future. In this context, we put a special focus on the growth path of the cohorts aged 60 or more as these represent the potential future retirees. In a next step, we refer to the public pension system with a special regard to pension reforms recently enacted. Finally we present the results of our calculations in the form of a supplementary table which has been developed by the Task Force. All age-sex-specific profiles applied to our calculations can be found in the appendix of this study. The appendix also contains sensitivity analyses for our calculations. In these analyses we vary our main parameters per-capita growth and discount rate in order to identify the impact of these parameters on our outcomes. The chapter finishes with a cross-country comparison of ADL in section 3.20. In this section we also aim for identifying the main determining factors for the level of ADL.

3.1 AT – Austria

Austria is not only in terms of its geographic location in the "middle" of the EU but also in terms of its population size which amounts to 8.27 million inhabitants.[70] In 1995 it joined the newly established EU. A further EU-integration step was taken with the introduction of the Euro in 2002. The Austrian GDP in 2006 came up to 257.3 bn. EUR which corresponds to a per capita GDP of 31,000 EUR.[71]

3.1.1 The demographic development in Austria

Like most European countries the Austrian demography is characterized by a double ageing process. On the one hand total fertility rates have considerably declined in the period 1970 to 1985 ranging since this time around a low value of about 1.4. On the other hand life expectancy has significantly increased in past decades. While a female (male) born in 1980 could expect to live 76.1 (69.0) years, this number has risen to 82.8 (77.2) in 2006. This ageing development is reflected in age-specific population structure shown in Figure 6.

As demography usually mirrors past events one can clearly see the impact of the Second World War on the Austrian population. The population tree is partly cut at the age groups of 60 years corresponding to low fertility rates during that time. In the postwar period, fertility recovered quite rapidly which led to the so-called baby boom. Today this can be recognized in the numerically large cohorts aged 35-45. For our calculations the lower part of the tree is of minor importance since the methodology of ADL only takes into account contributions paid up to the base year. Cohorts aged 30 and younger can be expected to have collected only relatively little pension entitlements up to this date. Furthermore their pension payments – which they receive in the far future (in 30 years and more) – are significantly discounted to the present date. Therefore the pension entitlements of younger Austrians amount only to a little share of the Austrian ADL.

---

[70] Figure as at January 1st, 2006. We display country data for 2006 since this is a main base year for our calculations.

[71] All GDP figures in this study are expressed in nominal terms.

Figure 6: Population structure in Austria (2006)
age groups 0 to 100 years

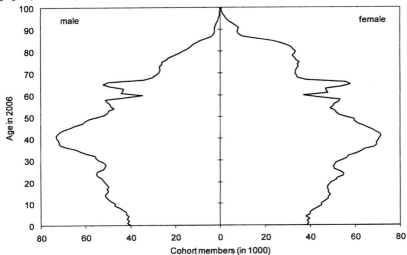

Source: Own calculations based on Eurostat (2009)

However, pensioners of today and of the closer future which have collected considerable pension entitlements play a decisive role for the level of the Austrian ADL. Therefore, it will be of importance that the pictured tree shows a maximum at the age group of around 40 in 2006. In other words, the amount of pensioners will significantly increase in the years to come. Figure 7 illustrates this expected development of elderly persons – aged 60 and older – in Austria between 2006 and 2045.

The figure shows that the number of elderly will increase significantly in Austria. However, the speed of this development is quite different in the coming decades. From 2006 to 2015 the rise in the number of elderly people is quite modest. As pointed out above this aspect is relevant for the ADL calculated in this survey. From 2015 to 2033 the slope becomes steeper with increasingly larger cohorts reaching the age of 60. Not only the population structure of 2006 can explain this rise in the number of elderly people but also the further increase in life expectancy.

Figure 7: Development of elderly persons (aged 60+) in Austria
indexed to 100 in 2006

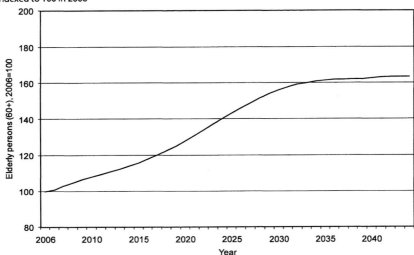

Source: Own calculations based on Eurostat (2009)

According to the assumptions of Eurostat, male (female) born in 2050 will live about five (six) years longer than their counterparts born in 2006. By 2033 there will be about 60 per cent more representatives of the age groups 60 and older. Only after 2033 this process will considerably slow down when all baby boomers have reached the age of 60. But – as has been pointed out above – this deceleration will have little impact on the ADL. Summing up, the number of future pensioners (people aged 60+) will considerably increase in Austria in the coming decades with a slow start (2006-2015) and a steep rise until 2033. In comparison to the other countries examined in this survey the Austrian ageing process represents the average.

3.1.2   The Austrian pension system

3.1.2.1   The principles of the Austrian pension system

As most Bismarckian Systems, the Austrian pension system is strongly dominated by the first pillar which is mandatory and based on a PAYG system. The second pillar (occupational pensions) and the third pillar (private pension plans) play a minor but increasing role for the Austrian old age provisions. Since the first pillar will be subject of our calculations, it shall be described in more detail. Up to 2005, the public PAYG scheme consisted of numerous different schemes for distinct occupational groups – reflecting the historical development of the Austrian pension system. With the harmonization law of 2004 a uniform pension system for all employed under 50 years has been introduced. This new pension system will gradually replace the many different pension schemes for self-employed, civil servants, farmers and for private sector workers.

In the uniform pension system entitlements are subject to individual life-time earnings. The maximum benefits of 80 per cent of average earnings are accrued at the statutory retirement age of 65 years if one has collected 45 years of insurance years. While past contributions are indexed by net wage growth, pension benefits are annually adjusted according to consumer price index (CPI).[72]

3.1.2.2 Recent reforms of the Austrian pension system

Triggered by present budgetary pressure and by future demographic challenges Austria passed substantial pension reforms in the last years. With the reform of 2000 early retirement ages were increased in the general schemes from 55 (60) to 56.5 (61.5) years for women (men). Furthermore early retirement induced by disability was abolished.

Key parameters of the Austrian pension system have considerably changed with the reform of 2003. One of its main elements was the gradual increase (until 2033) of the statutory retirement age for women to the present value of men: 65 years of age. According to our estimations this part of the 2003 reform will reduce the Austrian ADL by about two per cent of GDP in 2006.[73] Moreover, the base of average earnings for the pension calculation will be gradually extended from 15 to 40 years (until 2028) with the reform of 2003. We assume that this reform step will reduce pension benefits by about six per cent.[74] Furthermore the accrual rate will be lowered from two to 1.78 until 2009, which causes a reduction of pension benefits of eleven per cent. As a result the maximum replacement rate of 80 per cent will be reached after an insurance history of 45 instead of 40 years.

---

[72] At this point it is worth mentioning that in this survey we abstract away from pension taxation. In other words, all descriptions regarding pension schemes and per-capita pension amounts mentioned in this survey are expressed before-tax.

[73] This reform only has a minor impact on the Austrian pension liabilities since it only affects women born after 1963.

[74] Due to a lack of data the value of a six per cent reduction is derived by using German age-sex-specific earning profiles.

However, alongside a cap on pension losses was adopted. According to this legislation, a pension granted as of 2004 may only be ten per cent lower than a comparable pension granted at the end of 2003.[75] Finally, the reform of 2003 consisted of measures to further reduce early retirement in Austria including the abolishment of early retirement on account of unemployment, raising further minimum age for long-term insured men (women) to 65 (60) until 2017 as well as increasing pension deductions for earlier retirement.

Alongside the pension system of tenured civil servants has been reformed in 2003. This reform mirrors the steps taken in the private sector pension scheme. Thus, the period of the assessment base has been increased to 40 years (with a transition period until 2028) and the annual accrual rate has been reduced. Furthermore the statutory retirement age for civil servants has been increased to 65 and discount rates for early retirement at age 61.5 years have been introduced.

Cornerstones of the latest major reform of 2004, effective since 2005, were the introduction of a uniform pension system for all employed under 50 years and the introduction of a new system of individual transparent pension accounts with the guiding formula of 80/45/65 (i.e. the first pillar guarantees a pension benefit of 80 per cent of the assessment base after 45 years of insurance and at the statutory retirement age of 65 years). Alongside the cap on pension losses was reduced to five per cent and will only gradually be increased to ten per cent until 2024. This cap significantly offsets the cost savings achieved with the latest reforms. Thus, future pensions in our calculations are also only cut to a maximum limit of ten per cent (by 2028). Moreover, within the framework of the 2004 reform a sustainability factor has been introduced into the Austrian pension system. However, this factor has only little in common with its German or Portuguese counterparts. It only has an impact on future pension benefits if life expectancies deviate from the medium forecast of Statistics Austria. In our calculations we are not expecting such a deviation. Thus, the Austrian sustainability factor – in contrast to the German or Portuguese one - has no impact on our results. The reform of 2004 also changed the crediting of non-contributory periods such as child-care times or military service. Due to a lack of data we did not take into account this reform step in our calculations. Furthermore the possibility of early pension has been introduced through the establishment of a pension corridor. Retiring between 62 and 68 is either rewarded by pension credits in case of postponed retirement or discouraged by pension discounts when retiring early. Credits as well as discounts amount to 4.2 per cent of the assessment base per

---

[75] This cap does not apply to pension losses due to changes in the early retirement provision.

year.[76] However, individuals who pursue a profession regarded as extraordinarily straining are allowed to retire earliest at the age of 60 with a discount ratio of 2.1 per cent. Moreover, the reform of 2004 on the one hand replaced the inflation oriented revaluation of pension entitlements by a method based on the average increase of the respective contribution basis. On the other hand pensions will be indexed (from 2006 on) according to CPI.

3.1.3 Measuring the Austrian accrued-to-date pension liabilities

In contrast to all other countries examined in this survey except the UK, we did not receive any data supply from Austria – apart from the budget data shown below. The age- and sex-specific micro data for the pension system stems from the "Hauptverband der österreichischen Sozialversicherungsträger".[77] The respective profile figures can be found in the annex of this survey.[78]

ADL consist of all pension entitlements which have been accrued to the present by living generations. These entitlements result in respective present and future pension payments. As a starting point we want to take a look on the pension payments in the base years 2005 and 2006 which are illustrated in Table 6.[79]

In relation to GDP Austria has the highest aggregated pension payments of all countries examined in this survey. Overall, the Austrian pension expenditures in 2006 amounted to about 12.9 per cent of the GDP in 2006.

---

[76] However, this rule only applies if at least 450 insurance months have been acquired. Furthermore discounts (credits) cannot exceed 15 (12.6) per cent of pension benefits. Losses from actuarial deductions are excluded from the loss cap of ten per cent.

[77] Precisely the data on Austrian pension payments and beneficiaries by age and sex is taken from the "Pensionsversicherung – Jahresstatistik 2006" published by the Hauptverband der österreichischen Sozialversicherungsträger (2008).

[78] Due to a lack of data we first of all assumed that the age-sex-specific pension profiles of government employer pensions are relatively the same as in the social security pension system. The relative profiles thereafter have been scaled by the aggregated budget data of the government employer pensions.

[79] The so-called "Ausgleichszulage" is not included in the total expenditures of the social security pensions since it can be regarded as a social assistance. It amounted to 0.81 bn. EUR in 2005 and 0.85 bn. EUR in 2006.

Table 6: Social security and government employer pension payments Austria
(in bn. EUR)

Type of pension	Pension payments	
	2005	2006
Social security pensions (total)	23.04	24.05
Government employer pensions (total)	8.83	9.05

Source: Statistik Austria (2008)

Applying the methodology of calculating ADL for the Austrian pension system produces the following results, presented in the supplementary Table 7:

Table 7: Supplementary table Austria 2006 PBO
(in bn. EUR)

			Non-core national accounts (figures in bn. Euro)	
			General Government	Social Security
			G	H
		Opening Balance Sheet		
	1	Pension entitlements	246.99	644.58
		Changes in pension entitlements due to transactions		
Sum 2.1 to 2.4	2	Increase in pension entitlements due to social contributions	15.29	50.67
	2.1	Employer actual social contributions		9.75
	2.2	Employer imputed social contributions	0.46	
	2.3	Household actual social contributions	2.32	7.98
	2.4	Household social contribution supplements	12.51	32.94
	3	Other (actuanal) increase of pension entitlements		1.70
	4	Reduction in pension entitlements due to payment of pension benefits	9.05	24.05
2 + 3 - 4	5	Change in pension entitlements due to social contributions and pension benefits	6.24	28.32
	6	Transfers of entitlements between schemes	0.00	0.00
	7	Changes in pension entitlements due to other transactions	0.00	0.00
		Changes in pension entitlements due to other economic flows		
	8	Changes in entitlements due to revaluations	0.00	0.00
	9	Changes in entitlements due to other changes in volume	0.00	0.00
		Closing Balance Sheet		
	10	Pension entitlements	253.23	672.90
		Pension entitlements (% of GDP 2006)	98.42	261.53
	11	Output		
	12	Assets held at the end of the period to meet pensions		

Source: Own calculations

Column G – representing the liabilities for the civil servants – shows opening pension entitlements to the amount of 246.99 bn. EUR. This value is increased by household actual social contributions (2.32 bn. EUR), employer imputed social contributions (0.46 bn. EUR) as well as household social contributions supplements (12.51 bn. EUR). Pension benefits paid in 2006 add up to 9.05 bn. EUR, thus the change in pension entitlements amounts to 6.24 bn. EUR. The closing balance of pension entitlements comes up to 253.23 bn. EUR, equivalent to some 99 per cent of GDP in 2006.

The opening pension entitlements for the social security pension scheme accrue to a value of 644.58 bn. EUR. Employer actual social contributions are 9.75 bn. EUR, those from households add up to 7.98 bn. EUR. Household social contribution supplements come up to 32.94 bn. EUR. These figures lead to an increase in pension entitlements due to social contributions of 50.67 bn. EUR. Row 3 represents the residual figure which adds to 1.70 bn. EUR. Pension benefits paid out in 2006 reduce the entitlements by 24.05 bn. EUR. Finally the closing pension entitlements add up to a value of 672.90 bn. EUR which is equivalent to 261.53 per cent of the GDP. Adding up the pension entitlements of column G and H Austria shows pension entitlements to the amount of nearly 360 per cent of the GDP in 2006. When comparing the outcome of the various countries in section 3.20, we will discover that this is a relatively high result. However, results change if one holds today's salaries constant using the ABO approach. Table 8 illustrates the respective outcomes.

Table 8: Supplementary table Austria 2006 ABO
(in bn. EUR)

			Non-core national accounts (figures in bn. Euro)	
			General Government	Social Security
			G	H
		Opening Balance Sheet		
	1	Pension entitlements	216.75	565.66
		Changes in pension entitlements due to transactions		
Sum 2.1 to 2.4	2	Increase in pension entitlements due to social contributions	14.79	46.65
	2.1	Employer actual social contributions		9.75
	2.2	Employer imputed social contributions	1.48	
	2.3	Household actual social contributions	2 32	7.98
	2.4	Household social contribution supplements	10.98	28.92
	3	Other (actuarial) increase of pension entitlements		2.94
	4	Reduction in pension entitlements due to payment of pension benefits	9.05	24.05
2 + 3 - 4	5	Change in pension entitlements due to social contributions and pension benefits	5.74	25.54
	6	Transfers of entitlements between schemes		0.00
	7	Changes in pension entitlements due to other transactions		0.00
		Changes in pension entitlements due to other economic flows		
	8	Changes in entitlements due to revaluations	0.00	0.00
	9	Changes in entitlements due to other changes in volume		0.00
		Closing Balance Sheet		
	10	Pension entitlements	222.48	591.20
		Pension entitlements (% of GDP 2006)	86.47	229.78
	11	Output		
	12	Assets held at the end of the period to meet pensions		

Source: Own calculations

All numbers which have been taken from national accounts stay constant (values in row 2.1, 2.3 and 4). The other numbers are considerably lower in comparison to the method of PBO. Opening pension entitlements are lowered to 216.75 bn. EUR (column G) and 565.66 bn. EUR (column H). The closing pension entitlements likewise turn out to be smaller using the ABO approach. For the government employer pension scheme they accrue to 222.48 bn. EUR, corresponding to around 86 per cent of GDP in 2006. The respective figure for the social security pension scheme adds up to 591.20 bn. EUR or in other words 229.78 per cent of GDP. Comparing PBO and ABO results, the latter one turns out to be about twelve per cent lower (in terms of GDP) than the respective PBO outcomes.

3.2   BG – Bulgaria[80]

Bulgaria is populated by 7.72 million inhabitants.[81] It has made a transition from a centrally planned system to a market based economy. In the course of EU-accession in January 2007 Bulgaria experienced a boost in trade and high economic growth rates. The currency of Bulgaria is the Lev (BGN); [82] however, the Bulgarian government stated its will to join the Euro Currency Area by 2012. Bulgaria´s GDP in 2006 amounted to 49.4 bn. BGN, equal to 25.2 bn. EUR. GDP per capita added up to 3,300 EUR in 2006.

3.2.1   The demographic development in Bulgaria

As most post-communist countries Bulgaria experienced a considerable demographic decline in the last two decades. The main factors causing this development are decreasing fertility and high emigration rates. While total fertility amounted to about two in 1980, this value decreased to 1.37 until 2006. The result is reflected in the population structure – shown in Figure 8 – which resembles a tree cut down half way.

The tree gets thicker in the age groups 15 to 60 years old. This is important to mention since these cohorts represent the pensioners to come which are accounted for in the calculation of the ADL. Furthermore, it should be noticed that the tree at the upper end is still quite thick compared to other countries examined in this survey. Thus, present Bulgarian pensioners – cohorts aged 60 and older – are relatively numerous in 2006. As in the rest of Europe life expectancy in Bulgaria is expected to undergo considerable increases in the future. According to Eurostat, a Bulgarian male (female) born in 2006 can expect to live 69.2 (76.3) years. This value is assumed to rise to 78.2 (82.6) years for persons born in 2050.[83] Combining future life expectancy and the population structure in 2006 one can display the future development of people aged 60 and older – shown in Figure 9.

---

[80] We would like to thank Anatoli Hristov and his colleagues from the Bulgarian National Statistical Institute for valuable comments on this chapter.

[81] Figure as at January 1st, 2006. We display country data for 2006 since this is a main base year for our calculations.

[82] The exchange rate is 1.9558 BGN to the Euro as per December 29th, 2006. All exchange rates applied in this survey stem from official releases of the ECB (see *Euro foreign exchange reference rates*, http://www.ecb.int/stats/exchange/eurofxref/html/index.en.html)

[83] These figures are based on the assumptions of Eurostat given in Europop 2004.

Figure 8: Population structure in Bulgaria (2006)
age groups 0 to 100 years

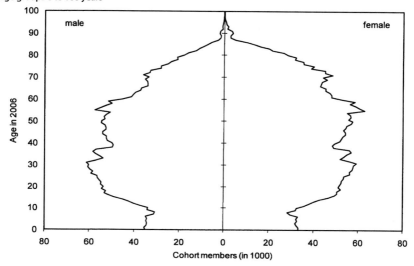

Source: Own calculations based on Eurostat (2009)

Figure 9 illustrates that the number of elderly people (60+) rises by about 20 per cent until 2040. It should be outlined that this is a relatively low increase in comparison to the other countries examined in this survey. This slow increase is mainly caused by the fact that the group aged 60 and older is already quite numerous in 2006. Applying the methodology of ADL one does not only take into account entitlements of present pensioners but also those of future retirees who have collected entitlements up to the base year (2006). Therefore, the development of elderly people in Bulgaria plays an important role for the calculations of this survey.

Figure 9: Development of elderly persons (aged 60+) in Bulgaria indexed to 100 in 2006

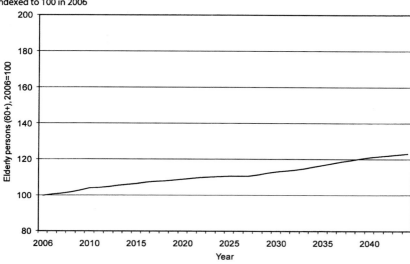

Source: Own calculations based on Eurostat (2009)

3.2.2 The Bulgarian pension system

3.2.2.1 The principles of the Bulgarian pension system

In common with other industrialized countries the Bulgarian pension system is based on a three pillar structure. The first pillar is represented by the public pension insurance functioning as a standard PAYG system. It is mandatory and covers all individuals hired by employers as well as self-employed, farmers, individuals working without a formal labour contract and others (nearly 30 insured types). The second pillar, the supplementary mandatory pension insurance, is based on a defined contributory fully funded principle. There are two types of funds within this second pillar. One is the so called universal pension fund and covers all persons born after December 31st, 1959. The second one is the professional pension fund which applies to persons working under special categories of labour (the so-called first and second labour category). The third pillar encompasses the private voluntary pension funds.

3.2.2.2 Recent reforms of the Bulgarian pension system

In recent years, Bulgaria has implemented profound pension reforms. With the reform of the year 2000 the Bulgarian government introduced a new benefit formula for the first pillar which strengthens the link between contributions and benefits. According to this new formula, the pension level depends on the length of participation, the individual insurable income as well as the average national insurable income. To be exact, the pension entitlement for each year of contribution depends on the personal contribution in relation to average national contributions. For the period of postponed retirement one calendar year of service yields three per cent increase of pension. Prior to the reform the three best consecutive years out of the last 15 years before retirement have been taken into account. The new formula results in an enhancement to the whole working life when calculating the pension benefits. With the extension of the reference period future pensions are expected to be lowered. According to our calculations the change in the reference period to the whole working life will lead to a reduction of the pension level of four per cent (eight per cent) for men (women).

Furthermore, the maximum pensions were increased from three to four minimum social old age pensions in the course of the reform in 2000. Since 2005 the maximum pension is 35 per cent of the maximum insurable income during the previous calendar year. From the year 2010 on there will be no such maximum limit to the amount of individual pension payments.[84] Until 2000, Bulgaria had relatively low pension age limits – 55 (60) years for women (men). Starting from 2000 a gradual increase of the pensionable age of six months per year has been introduced. From 2009 on the minimum retirement age will amount to 60 (63) for women (men).

The most recent reform was tackling the indexation of pensions. As of July 1st, 2007, pensions will be indexed under the so-called "golden Swiss rule". According to this regulation, pensions are adjusted to 50 per cent of the increase in the national consumer price index (CPI) and 50 per cent of the insurance income growth during the previous calendar year.

3.2.3 Measuring the Bulgarian accrued-to-date pension liabilities

In Bulgaria there is no special pension scheme for civil servants. Therefore only the social security pension scheme as the first pillar of the pension system is subject of our calculations. Table 9 displays the amount of pension payments paid out to the

---

[84] It can be assumed that the increase as well as the abolishment of the maximum pension will lead to a further rise in the Bulgarian pension liabilities. Since we have no information about the vertical distribution of insurable income in Bulgaria we are not taking into account these above mentioned legislation changes in our calculations.

different types of pensions for the period from 2005 to 2007. Non-contributory pension payments have been excluded from these figures.[85]

Table 9: Social security pension payments Bulgaria
(in million BGN)

Type of pension	Pension payments		
	2005	2006	2007
Old age pensions	3,061.68	3,313.49	3,980.47
Disability pensions	402.72	445.62	529.26
Survivor pensions	135.43	146.71	178.22
Total	3,599.83	3,905.82	4,687.95

Source: National Statistical Institute Bulgaria (2008)

As illustrated above, total pension expenditures in Bulgaria amounted to about four bn. BGN in 2006, which corresponds to 7.9 per cent of GDP in 2006.

Applying the methodology of calculating ADL described in chapter 2 of the survey, the estimations for the Bulgarian pension system produce the following results for the year 2006, shown in the supplementary table (PBO approach):[86]

---

[85] Since in Bulgaria non-contributory pension benefits have the character of a social assistance scheme they have been excluded from our calculations. For 2007 we have no data about the aggregated non-contributory pension payments. Therefore, we assumed that the proportion of non-contributory pension of the aggregated budget in 2007 is the average of the years 2005 and 2006.

[86] The supplementary tables for the year 2007 can be found in the appendix of this survey. They have not been included in the continuous text in order to ensure a certain convenience for the reader.

Table 10: Supplementary table Bulgaria 2006 PBO
(in bn. BGN)

| | | | Non-core national accounts (figures in bn. BGN) | |
| | | | General Government | Social Security |
			G	H
		Opening Balance Sheet		
	1	Pension entitlements		93.34
		Changes in pension entitlements due to transactions		
Sum 2.1 to 2.4	2	**Increase in pension entitlements due to social contributions**	*0.00*	*7.12*
	2 1	*Employer actual social contributions*		1.60
	2.2	*Employer imputed social contributions*	*0.00*	
	2.3	*Household actual social contributions*		0.70
	2.4	*Household social contribution supplements*	*0.00*	4.82
	3	Other (actuanal) increase of pension entitlements		3.07
	4	Reduction in pension entitlements due to payment of pension benefits		3.91
2 + 3 - 4	5	**Change in pension entitlements due to social contributions and pension benefits**	*0.00*	*6.28*
	6	Transfers of entitlements between schemes	*0.00*	*0.00*
	7	Changes in pension entitlements due to other transactions	*0.00*	*0.00*
		Changes in pension entitlements due to other economic flows		
	8	Changes in entitlements due to revaluations	*0.00*	*0.00*
	9	Changes in entitlements due to other changes in volume	*0.00*	*0.00*
		Closing Balance Sheet		
	10	Pension entitlements		99.62
		Pension entitlements (% of GDP 2006)		201.83
	11	Output		
	12	Assets held at the end of the period to meet pensions		

Source: Own calculations

The opening balance illustrates that the pension entitlements for the social security scheme add up to 96.91 bn. BGN in the beginning of the year 2006. On the one hand this amount is reduced by aggregated pension payments (3.91 bn. BGN) and other actuarial decreases of pension entitlements (0.44). On the other hand pension entitlements increase in 2006 due to household social contributions (0.7 bn. BGN), household social contributions supplements (4.82 bn. BGN) and employer social contributions (1.6 bn. BGN). Overall the pension entitlements increase by 6.28 bn. BGN which results in a closing balance of 99.62 bn. BGN. This accounts for nearly 202 per cent of GDP in 2006.

The same calculations have been conducted using the ABO approach. Since this method - in contrast to the PBO approach - does not take into account future wage growth, the results tend to be considerably smaller. Table 11 shows the respective outcomes.

Table 11: Supplementary table Bulgaria 2006 ABO
(in bn. BGN)

			Non-core national accounts (figures in bn. BGN)	
			General Government	Social Security
			G	H
		Opening Balance Sheet		
	1	Pension entitlements		83.02
		Changes in pension entitlements due to transactions		
Sum 2.1 to 2.4	2	Increase in pension entitlements due to social contributions	0.00	6.60
	2.1	*Employer actual social contributions*		1.60
	2.2	*Employer imputed social contributions*	0.00	▓▓▓▓
	2.3	*Household actual social contributions*		0.70
	2.4	*Household social contribution supplements*	0.00	4.30
	3	Other (actuarial) increase of pension entitlements	▓▓▓▓	3.16
	4	Reduction in pension entitlements due to payment of pension benefits		3.91
2 + 3 - 4	5	Change in pension entitlements due to social contributions and pension benefits	0.00	5.84
	6	Transfers of entitlements between schemes		0.00
	7	Changes in pension entitlements due to other transactions		0.00
		Changes in pension entitlements due to other economic flows		
	8	Changes in entitlements due to revaluations	0.00	0.00
	9	Changes in entitlements due to other changes in volume		0.00
		Closing Balance Sheet		
	10	Pension entitlements		88.87
		Pension entitlements (% of GDP 2006)		180.04
	11	Output		
	12	Assets held at the end of the period to meet pensions		

Source: Own calculations

Comparing Table 10 and Table 11 the differences in results using PBO or ABO approach can be seen very clearly. The actual contributions paid by employers and households stay the same – these are official figures and do not depend on the choice between ABO and PBO. However, quite significant changes appear when looking at the pension entitlements in the opening and the closing balance sheet. At the beginning of 2006, pension entitlements add up to 83.02 bn. BGN (whereas under PBO approach they were 93.34 bn. BGN), the entitlements at the end of the year show 88.87 bn. BGN (whilst under PBO they amount to 99.62). In terms of GDP the ABO result is about eleven percentage points lower than under the PBO approach.

3.3 CZ – Czech Republic

The Czech Republic has a population of 10.25 million inhabitants.[87] The national currency is the Czech Crown (CZK), the exchange rate is 27.485 CZK to the Euro.[88] The GDP in 2006 amounted to 3,215.6 bn. CZK which corresponds to 113.5 bn. EUR.

In the economy of the Czech Republic the service sector plays an important role. It accounts for about 58 per cent of GDP while the industrial sector makes up 39 per cent. Real estate and trade services each account for about one third of the service sector while the industrial sector is almost totally made up by the manufacturing business. The Czech Republic is one of the 2004 accession countries to the European Union. Therefore it is contractually bound to adopt the Euro in due course. However, convergence criteria are not yet met.

3.3.1 The demographic development in the Czech Republic

The demographic situation in the Czech Republic is characterized by a fertility rate which lies well below a sustainable level[89] since the beginning of the 1990s and a life expectancy of 73.5 (79.9) years for males (females) born in 2006. Until the beginning of the 1990s, the total fertiliy rate in the Czech Republic (Czechoslovakia at that time) showed a fertility rate of 1.9 children. However, in the course of the "velvet revolution" and the peacefully separation of the Czech Republic and Slovakia in 1993, fertility in the Czech Republic decreased considerably down to a value of around 1.3 children in 2006. Life expectancy is expected to rise by approximately six years for men and four years for women until it reaches 79.7 (84.1) years for men (women) born in 2050. Figure 10 shows the age-specific population structure for the Czech Republic in 2006.

It can be observed that the cohort indicating the largest number of individuals is the cohort aged 32 in the year 2006. This can be explained by the respective fertility rate which adds up to 2.43 children per woman in the year of 1974. After 1974, births have declined until the birth rate reached a level of 1.33 in the year 2006.

---

[87] Figure as at January 1st, 2006. We display country data for 2006 since this is a main base year for our calculations.

[88] Exchange rate as at December 29th, 2006.

[89] A sustainable level in fertility in terms of a constant population development over time is reached at a total fertility rate of approximately 2.1 children per woman not taking into account migration and changes in life expectancy. This level is also referred to as the replacement rate.

Figure 10: Population structure in the Czech Republic (2006)
age groups 0 to 100 years

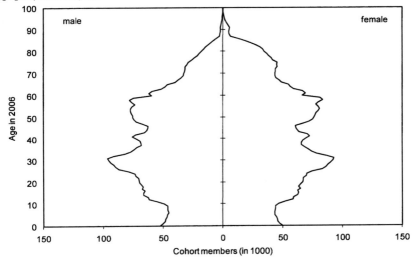

Source: Own calculations based on Eurostat (2009)

As this survey examines the liabilities due to future pension payments, the development of elderly persons represents an important aspect. This development is mainly determined by the population structure in the base year and the future life expectancy.[90]

As Figure 11 shows, the number of elderly persons in the Czech Republic will increase by more than 50 per cent until the year 2040. One reason for this is the large generation of 30 to 35 year old persons in 2006 who will enter the group of elderly persons in the years 2036 to 2041. The other reason is the life expectancy which is expected to rise considerably until 2050, as described above. This numerical increase will obviously have a major impact of the future pension payments, as will be indicated later in this chapter.

---

[90] As in all other country chapters of this survey, future migration is assumed to be zero.

Figure 11: Development of elderly persons (aged 60+) in the Czech Republic
indexed to 100 in 2006

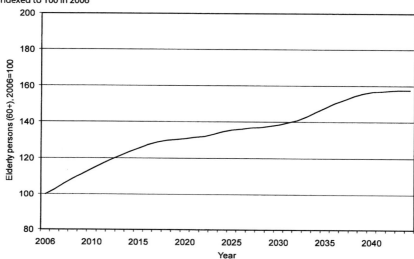

Source: Own calculations based on Eurostat (2009)

3.3.2 The Czech pension system

3.3.2.1 The principles of the Czech pension system

The Czech pension only marginally distinguishes between public and private employees since only members of the armed forces receive their pensions directly out of the state budget. All others are covered by the same mandatory defined benefit scheme. Furthermore, there is only one large fund for old-age, disability, and survivor pensions. To this fund every worker has to contribute 28 per cent of gross income split into 6.5 percentage points to be paid by employees and 21.5 percentage points by employers. Self-employed pay the same contribution rate, but their calculation base represents 50 per cent of the difference between incomes and expenses, at least half of the average gross monthly wage. Furthermore, there is an additional voluntary private fully funded scheme to which workers can contribute with tax-preferred contributions.

The pension is a combination of a basic flat rate pension of currently 1,400 CZK per month paid to everyone who is eligible to a pension and an earnings related part. The replacement rate is 1.5 percentage points per year of contribution on the average earnings of the years since 1985. The period over which earnings will be averaged will increase until 2015 from when on it will remain constant for 30 years. The minimum earnings-related pension is 770 CZK per month. Pension values are currently indexed to CPI growth incremented by one third of average real wage growth.

Eligibility to a full pension is achieved at a legally defined age after at least 25 years of contribution, with a generous regulation for periods of education and child-raising. The age is currently raised by two months per year for men and four months per year for women to reach a common 63 years in 2013. Women with children may retire earlier. With at least 15 years of contribution full pension can be claimed from the age of 65. Early retirement is only possible incurring lifetime pension deductions.

3.3.2.2   Recent reforms of the Czech pension system

Since 1989 there have been a number of small reforms. The fully funded voluntary scheme was introduced in 1994 and the tax-preferred status was introduced after 1995. In 1995, measures were taken to gradually increase the pension age from formerly 53-57/ 60 years (women/men) to 59-63/ 63 years until 2013, together with an age requirement harmonization between men and women. In 2003, the possibility to retire early with reduced payments only until the regular pension age is reached was abolished along with the possibility to receive working income without pension income being cut.

There has been an active discussion of reform measures in the Czech Republic for the last few years which, so far, has only resulted in a "National Strategy Report on Adequate and Sustainable Pensions". Thus, since the current pension system is increasingly perceived to be inadequate in facing the demographic change further reforms seem very likely. One good reason for that is the case of Poland which made severe adjustments to its pension system in a similar situation.

3.3.3   Measuring the Czech accrued-to-date pension liabilities

There is no separate pension employer scheme for civil servants in the Czech Republic, therefore only the social security pension scheme is subject to our calculations. However, pension benefits are administered by different institutions. The following table gives an overview of these institutions and their pension budgets in 2005 and 2006:[91]

---

[91] No data was supplied for the year 2007.

Table 12: Social security pension payments Czech Republic
(in bn. CZK)

Institution	Pension payments (2005)	Pension payments (2006)
Czech Social Security Administration (CSSA)	**241.17**	**266.22**
Old age pensions	174.11	193.93
Disability pensions	44.99	48.89
Survivor pensions	22.07	23.40
Ministry of Interior	**2.74**	**2.99**
Old age pensions	2.42	2.64
Disability pensions	0.17	0.17
Survivor pensions	0.15	0.18
Ministry of Defence	**3.14**	**3.29**
Old age pensions	2.84	2.98
Disability pensions	0.14	0.15
Survivor pensions	0.16	0.16
Ministry of Justice	**0.36**	**0.39**
Old age pensions	0.30	0.33
Disability pensions	0.04	0.04
Survivor pensions	0.02	0.02
Total	**247.41**	**272.91**

Source: Czech Statistical Office (2007)

Applying the methodology of calculating ADL described in chapter 2 of this survey, the estimations for the Czech social security pension system produce the following results, shown in the supplementary table (PBO approach).

As Table 13 shows, the balance starts with pension entitlements of 5,895.11 bn. CZK. Entitlements are increased by social contributions equal to 586.12 bn. CZK which can be divided into employer actual social contributions (200.56 bn. CZK), household actual social contributions (76.32 bn. CZK) and household social contribution supplements (309.24 bn. CZK). The last-mentioned entry is sometimes referred to as the capital cost. It can also be regarded as a fictitious rate of return of the pension liabilities in case they were funded.

Paid pension benefits in 2006 reduce the entitlements by 272.91 bn. CZK. The so-called other increase of pension entitlements adds up to 266.03 bn. CZK. Hence the balance of 2006 closes with pension entitlements of 6,474.35 bn. CZK, equal to about 200 per cent of GDP 2006. The rows 6 to 9 do not contribute to the entitlements as there has not been a pension reform in the Czech Republic in 2006 affecting future pension payments, likewise the assumptions regarding discount rate, wage growth and demographic development have not been changed either.

Table 13: Supplementary table Czech Republic 2006 PBO
(in bn. CZK)

				Non-core national accounts	
				(figures in bn. CZK)	
				General Government	Social Security
				G	H
			Opening Balance Sheet		
		1	Pension entitlements		**5,895.11**
			Changes in pension entitlements due to transactions		
Sum 2.1 to 2.4		2	Increase in pension entitlements due to social contributions		**586.12**
		2.1	*Employer actual social contributions*		200.56
		2.2	*Employer imputed social contributions*		▬▬▬
		2.3	*Household actual social contributions*		76.32
		2.4	*Household social contribution supplements*		309.24
		3	Other (actuarial) increase of pension entitlements	▬▬▬	266.03
		4	Reduction in pension entitlements due to payment of pension benefits		272.91
2 + 3 - 4		5	Change in pension entitlements due to social contributions and pension benefits		**579.24**
		6	Transfers of entitlements between schemes		**0.00**
		7	Changes in pension entitlements due to other transactions		**0.00**
			Changes in pension entitlements due to other economic flows		
		8	Changes in entitlements due to revaluations		**0.00**
		9	Changes in entitlements due to other changes in volume		**0.00**
			Closing Balance Sheet		
		10	Pension entitlements		**6,474.35**
			Pension entitlements (% of GDP 2006)		**200.35**
		11	Output		
		12	Assets held at the end of the period to meet pensions		

Source: Own calculations

Results quite different to those under PBO approach can be observed when applying the ABO approach. Again, comparing Table 13 and Table 14 the differences in results using PBO or ABO approach can be seen very clearly. The actual contributions paid by employers and households stay the same – these are statistical figures and do not depend of the choice between ABO and PBO. However, quite significant changes must be stated when looking at the pension entitlements in the opening and the closing balance sheet. At the beginning of 2006, pension entitlements add up to 4,856.53 bn. CZK (whereas under PBO approach they were 5,895.11 bn CZK), the entitlements at the end of the year show 5,338.48 bn. CZK (whilst under PBO they amount to 6,474.35). In terms of fraction of GDP the ABO result shows nearly 35 percentage points less than under PBO approach.

Table 14: Supplementary table Czech Republic 2006 ABO
(in bn. CZK)

				Non-core national accounts (figures in bn. CZK)	
				General Government	Social Security
				G	H
			Opening Balance Sheet		
		1	Pension entitlements		**4,856.53**
			Changes in pension entitlements due to transactions		
Sum 2.1 to 2.4		2	Increase in pension entitlements due to social contributions		**531.76**
	2 1		*Employer actual social contributions*		200.56
	2 2		*Employer imputed social contributions*		▉
	2 3		*Household actual social contributions*		76.32
	2 4		*Household social contribution supplements*		254.88
		3	Other (actuarial) increase of pension entitlements		223.10
		4	Reduction in pension entitlements due to payment of pension benefits		272.91
2 + 3 - 4		5	Change in pension entitlements due to social contributions and pension benefits		**481.95**
		6	Transfers of entitlements between schemes		*0.00*
		7	Changes in pension entitlements due to other transactions		*0.00*
			Changes in pension entitlements due to other economic flows		
		8	Changes in entitlements due to revaluations		*0.00*
		9	Changes in entitlements due to other changes in volume		*0.00*
			Closing Balance Sheet		
		10	Pension entitlements		**5,338.48**
			Pension entitlements (% of GDP 2006)		*166.02*
		11	Output		
		12	Assets held at the end of the period to meet pensions		

Source: Own calculations

It should be mentioned that the PBO/ABO choice also has an impact of the household social contribution supplements as well as the other (actuarial) increase of pension entitlements; the contribution supplements are affected because the average of opening and closing pension liabilities is the basis for estimating this figure. Changing pension liabilities will therefore always change contribution supplements at the same time.

3.4   DE – Germany

Germany's population amounted to 82.44 million persons as at January 1st, 2006.[92] Thus, it represents the largest country of the European Union in terms of population. Since 2002, Germany's currency is the Euro. The GDP in 2006 came up to an amount of 2,321.5 bn. EUR which corresponds to a per capita GDP of 28,200 EUR. The German economy is dominated by the service sector which accounts for about 69 per cent of GDP compared to about 29 per cent in the industrial sector. The largest single categories within the two sectors are trade related (25 per cent) and financial services (50 per cent) in the service sector as well as the manufacturing business (80 per cent) in the industrial sector.

3.4.1   The demographic development in Germany

As with most of the European countries, the demographic situation in Germany can be described by two main aspects: Fertility rates have decreased since the beginning of the 1970's and currently are at a level just below 1.4 children per woman; life expectancy has increased in the last decades and is assumed to rise further. Figure 12 shows the demographic structure in Germany for the year of 2006.

Looking at the age-specific distribution of persons, some historic events and turning points can be monitored. The first one can be identified at the cohort of persons aged around 60 years in 2006. The relatively low numbers can be attributed to World War II and corresponding low fertility rates during that time. In the postwar period, fertility recovered quite rapidly which led to the so-called baby boom. These are the age groups between 35 and 55 years old in 2006. The baby boom was followed by the baby bust – analogous to many other industrialized countries at the end of the 1960's a birth rate slump began which can be ascribed to the introduction of the birth control pill as well as other social changes (e.g. different role perception for women). Numerically, the total fertility rate reached its maximum of 2.53 in 1964. After that, it dropped to a value of 1.50 in the 1970's and amounted to 1.32 children per woman in 2006.[93]

---

[92] Figure as at January 1st, 2006. We display country data for 2006 since this is a main base year for our calculations.

[93] Please note that until 1991, these figures only apply to the western part of Germany. This is one reason for the further decline in birth rates during the 1990's when the combined total fertility rate dropped to a value of 1.24 children per woman (1994), due to a tremendous decrease of birth rates in the eastern part of Germany after reunification.

Figure 12: Population structure in Germany (2006)
age groups 0 to 100 years

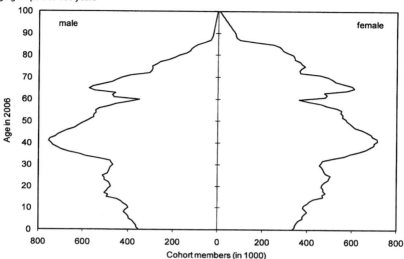

Source: Own calculations based on Eurostat (2009)

The German population experienced considerable increases in average life expectancy in the past decades. Males (females) born in 1960 faced a life expectancy of 66.5 (71.7) years. This value grew up to 77.2 (82.4) years in 2006, and is assumed to rise further to 82.0 respectively 86.9 years by 2050. Figure 13 demonstrates the assumed development of persons aged 60 or more in Germany between 2006 and 2045.

The increase in elderly persons in Germany can be classified as quite moderate, compared to other countries observed in this survey. The maximum of this development is reached in the year 2032, after this point figures begin to decline. This is due to the fact that after 2030 the so-called baby bust generation born after 1970 will enter the observed age-group. As these cohorts are relatively small in numbers (see Figure 12), it is straightforward that the number of elderly persons will decrease after 2030. In 2045, the group of persons aged 60 or older will still be nearly 35 per cent larger than in 2006.

Figure 13: Development of elderly persons (aged 60+) in Germany
indexed to 100 in 2006

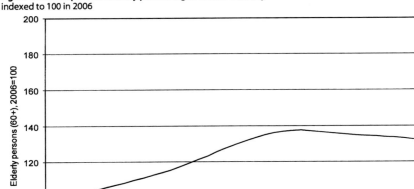

Source: Own calculations based on Eurostat (2009)

As described later in this chapter, there is a special pension system for civil servants in Germany. There are two reasons for the use of separate population data for civil servants. First, the data supply for this group is excellent. Secondly, the age-specific structure of this group diverges considerably from the general population which might lead to other results calculating the pension liabilities. The age-specific structure of this group in 2006 is demonstrated in Figure 14.[94]

---

[94] The group of persons shown in Figure 16 include current civil servants in 2006 as well as the former civil servants who retired in 2006. Please note that there are two groups of persons employed in the public sector in Germany. One is treated as general employees when it comes to issues of social insurance (including public pensions); this group receives benefits from the social security pension scheme as well as supplementary benefits from a special scheme called VBL. The other group – referred to as civil servants in this survey – receives pension benefits from a special general government employer pension scheme.

Figure 14: Structure of civil servants' population in Germany (2006)
age groups 0 to 100 years

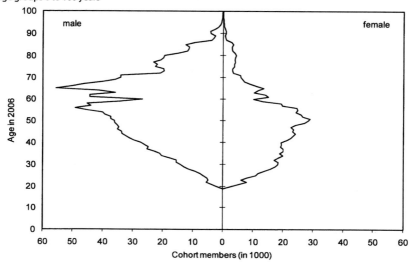

Source: Own calculations based on Statistisches Bundesamt (2007a, 2007b, 2006a, 2006b, 2005a, 2005b)

It is apparent when analyzing the age-structure of this group that there are major differences to the structure of the general population. The first big discrepancy is the majority of males in relation to females. This is because especially before the 1970s mainly males were engaged as civil servants. Another noticeable feature is the decline of persons in the age cohorts 30 to 50 years old in 2006. This can be traced back to unsteady behaviour in employment over time. Due to lack of special data, life expectancies for civil servants are assumed to be the same as for the general population. Figure 15 shows the development of persons aged 60 or older from 2006 until 2045.

It can be observed that the increase of elderly persons stops at the year 2025; afterwards, this age group diminishes again. In 2045, it even falls below the level of 2006 – admittedly, part of this effect must be ascribed to the fact that no new employment is allowed in this projection. However, it must be stressed that until 2025 the number of persons aged 60 or older rises by more than 35 per cent.

Figure 15: Development of elderly civil servants (60+) in Germany
indexed to 100 in 2006

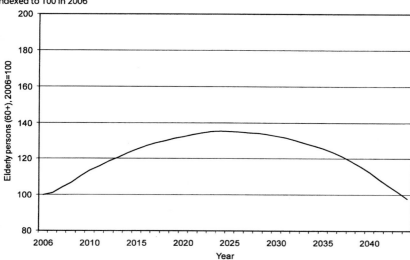

Source: Own calculations based on Statistisches Bundesamt (2007a, 2007b, 2006a, 2006b, 2005a, 2005b)

3.4.2 The German pension system

3.4.2.1 The principles of the German pension system

In the German old age pension system there is a structural separation between privately employed people, farmers, self-employed persons and civil servants. Only the pensions of privately employed people civil servants and farmers are financed by state systems, self-employed persons are in schemes which are not state controlled.[95] While there is a point system based on contributions for private employees and farmers, civil servants do not pay contributions; their post-retirement payments are seen as a compensation for their life-time duty to serve the country and are in a way part of their salary.

For private sector employees there is a mandatory PAYG scheme to which they have to contribute 19.9 per cent of their income, where payments are made by the employer and the employee to equal parts. In 2001, a publicly subsidied private

---

[95] In fact, the *old age insurance for farmers* (AdL) is regarded as part of the German social security pension scheme in this survey.

pension – the so-called "Riester-Rente" – was introduced to which workers can contribute up to four per cent of their income. This scheme is fully funded. Contributions or premiums respectively are tax-preferred as taxes only need to be paid on benefits. At the same time an upper bound was set to contributions for the first pillar (20 per cent until 2020, 22 per cent until 2030).

By contributing to the mandatory scheme people earn pension points with one point corresponding to one year of average earnings. Earnings above an annually adjusted threshold are not taken into account. The benefits are then calculated as the product of accumulated points and the point values (different in East and West) after retirement. The pension point value is annually adjusted by the growth of gross wages net of pension contributions and notional contributions to the "Riester-Rente". Furthermore, a sustainability factor was introduced which anchors the point value to the ratio of contributors to retirees.

The regular retirement age is still 65 (to be incremented between 2011 and 2029 to 67) with a possibility for early retirement after the age of 60 which was raised to 63 from 2006. There is a penalty of 0.3 percentage points per month of early retirement and a bonus of 0.5 percentage points per month of late retirement.

The pension for civil servants is calculated as a ratio of the final salary they have earned for at least three years before retirement. The regular retirement age is 65.[96] The replacement rate is about 1.79 percentage points per year of service, with a maximum of 71.75 per cent.[97] Per year of retirement before the age of 63 there is a deduction of 3.6 percentage points. Retirement is not possible before the age of 60.

3.4.2.2   Recent reforms of the German pension system

In 1992, benefit indexation was moved from gross wage indexation to net wage indexation. Furthermore, the deductions for early retirement were only legislated in 1992. In 2001, the net wage indexation was in part taken back to anchor benefits to the development of gross wages net of pension contributions. A severe system change was achieved in that reform by the introduction of the financially funded "Riester-Rente", its preferred tax position and the fact that contribution rates were given an upper bound. Three years later in 2004 the sustainability factor was

---

[96] However, there are exceptions for certain professional groups like policemen or firemen who have a regular retirement age of 60.

[97] In 2001, the government decided to reduce the replacement rate from 75 per cent in 2003 to 71.75 in 2010. In 2007, the replacement rate amounted 72.97.

introduced which connected pension point values to the development of the ratio of contributors to retirees. A gradual increment in the retirement age was postponed and finally legislated in 2007. Regular retirement age will be raised from 65 to 67 years between 2011 and 2029. Furthermore, a catch-up factor was introduced to the pension formula in 2007 which takes into account non-implemented deductions from the past between 2011 and 2013.

3.4.2.3 Measuring the German accrued-to-date pension liabilities

For calculating the pension liabilities, four pension schemes had to be taken into account. The first two were the general pension insurance (DRV) and the old age insurance for farmers (AdL) which were classified as social security (column H in the supplementary table). Table 15 shows the pension benefits for these schemes in 2005, 2006 and 2007 as a starting point:

Table 15: Social security pension payments Germany
(in bn. EUR)

Institution	Pension payments		
	2005	2006	2007
General pension insurance (DRV)	229.03	230.76	231.99
Old age insurance for farmers (AdL)	2.97	2.93	2.88
Total	232.00	233.69	234.87

Source: Statistisches Bundesamt (2008)

These payments include old age benefits, disability benefits and survivor benefits. To account for the recent pension reforms of the DRV, certain assumptions had to be made. To estimate the so-called sustainability factor (the future ratio of contributors to retirees) we took the future ratio of persons aged 20 to 60 to persons aged 60 or older as an approximation. Concerning the future contribution rate, we estimated it to rise to 22 per cent in 2030 and stay constant thereafter. The increase of the retirement age enacted in 2007 has been taken into account for the pension liabilities of 2007 only, because for the base year 2006 we took the legal status quo of 2006 as a basis.[98]

Providing the government employer pension scheme in column G of the supplementary table, the general civil servants' scheme and the supplementary

---

[98] The supplementary tables for 2007 can be found in the appendix of this survey. They have not been included in the continuous text in order to ensure a certain convenience for the reader.

pension scheme for employees in the public sector not being civil servants come up to the following pension payments in 2005, 2006 and 2007, shown in Table 16:

Table 16: Government employer pension payments Germany
(in bn. EUR)

Institution	Pension payments		
	2005	2006	2007
General civil servants' scheme	41.40	41.57	42.27
Supplementary pension scheme (VBL)	4.04	4.08	4.24
Total	45.44	45.65	46.51

Source: Statistisches Bundesamt (2008), Versorgungsanstalt des Bundes und der Länder (2008, 2007, 2006)

Analogous to Table 15, these payments consist of benefits regarding old age, disability and survivors. For calculation of liabilities of the general civil servants' scheme, the population shown in Figure 14 was used. The pension reform for civil servants from 2001 has been implemented by cutting the future pensions accordingly. For the supplementary pension system, the whole population was included.

Table 17 displays the respective results of our calculations, beginning with the PBO approach. Starting with the general government employer pension scheme (column G), pension entitlements in the beginning of 2006 accrue to 1,008.44 bn. EUR. There are no actual contributions in this scheme; the imputed social contributions amount to 112.95 bn. EUR. Household social contributions supplements account for 53.44 bn. EUR. Pension benefits paid out in 2006 reduce the entitlements by 45.65 bn. EUR which leads to a change in benefits of 120.74 bn. EUR (row 5). Pension entitlements at the end of 2006 amount to 1,129.18 bn. EUR, which is equal to 48.7 per cent of GDP in 2006.

With respect to column H, the opening stock of pension entitlements shows a value of 6,689.53 bn. EUR. Actual contributions account for 73.27 bn. EUR (employer) and 83.68 bn. EUR (households). The household contribution supplement comes up to 335.51 bn. EUR, the residual value indicates -217.32 bn. EUR. Pension benefits in 2006 amount to 233.69 bn. EUR which leads to a change in pension entitlements of 41.46 bn. EUR. Thus, the closing stock of pension entitlements shows 6,730.99 bn. EUR, corresponding to nearly 290 per cent of GDP in 2006.

Table 17: Supplementary table Germany 2006 PBO
(in bn. EUR)

			General Government	Social Security
			Non-core national accounts (figures in bn. EUR)	
			General Government	Social Security
			G	H
		Opening Balance Sheet		
	1	Pension entitlements	*1008.44*	*6,689.53*
		Changes in pension entitlements due to transactions		
Sum 2.1 to 2.4	2	**Increase in pension entitlements due to social contributions**	*166.39*	*492.46*
	2.1	*Employer actual social contributions*	0.00	73.27
	2 2	*Employer imputed social contributions*	112.95	
	2 3	*Household actual social contributions*	0.00	83.68
	2 4	*Household social contribution supplements*	53.44	335.51
	3	Other (actuarial) increase of pension entitlements		-217.32
	4	Reduction in pension entitlements due to payment of pension benefits	45.65	233.69
2 + 3 - 4	5	**Change in pension entitlements due to social contributions and pension benefits**	*120.74*	*41.46*
	6	Transfers of entitlements between schemes	*0.00*	*0.00*
	7	Changes in pension entitlements due to other transactions	*0.00*	*0.00*
		Changes in pension entitlements due to other economic flows		
	8	Changes in entitlements due to revaluations	*0.00*	*0.00*
	9	Changes in entitlements due to other changes in volume	*0.00*	*0.00*
		Closing Balance Sheet		
	10	Pension entitlements	*1129.18*	*6,730.99*
		Pension entitlements (% of GDP 2006)	*48.70*	*289.91*
	11	Output		
	12	Assets held at the end of the period to meet pensions		

Source: Own calculations

The same calculations were conducted using the ABO approach. Table 18 shows the respective results. Representing statistical figures from national accounts, numbers in row 2.1, row 2.3 and row 4 stay constant. Opening pension entitlements change to 916.58 bn. EUR (column G), respectively 6,044.37 bn. EUR (column H). Due to the fact that they depend on opening and closing pension entitlements, residual figures (row 2.2 in column G and row 3 in column H) as well as household social contribution supplements change as well. The closing pension entitlements of the general government employer pension scheme accrue to 1,012.54 bn. EUR, equal to almost 44 per cent of GDP; the respective figure for the social security pension scheme adds up to 6,093.13 bn. EUR or roughly 262 per cent of GDP. This means that the outcome lies nearly ten per cent below the result using the PBO approach.[99]

---

[99] Braakmann et al. (2007) estimate ADL for the German social security pension scheme which are roughly 20 per cent below the ADL shown in this study. This can be traced back to different methodology as well as different parameter choices regarding growth and discount rate.

Accrued-to-date liabilities of 19 EU countries

Table 18: Supplementary table Germany 2006 ABO
(in bn. EUR)

			Non-core national accounts (figures in bn. EUR)	
			General Government	Social Security
			G	H
		Opening Balance Sheet		
	1	Pension entitlements	**916.58**	**6,044.37**
		Changes in pension entitlements due to transactions		
Sum 2.1 to 2.4	2	Increase in pension entitlements due to social contributions	**141.61**	**460.39**
	2.1	*Employer actual social contributions*	0.00	73.27
	2.2	*Employer imputed social contributions*	93.38	■
	2.3	*Household actual social contributions*	0.00	83.68
	2.4	*Household social contribution supplements*	48.23	303.44
	3	Other (actuarial) increase of pension entitlements	■	-177.94
	4	Reduction in pension entitlements due to payment of pension benefits	45.65	233.69
2 + 3 - 4	5	Change in pension entitlements due to social contributions and pension benefits	**95.96**	**48.76**
	6	Transfers of entitlements between schemes	*0.00*	*0.00*
	7	Changes in pension entitlements due to other transactions	*0.00*	*0.00*
		Changes in pension entitlements due to other economic flows		
	8	Changes in entitlements due to revaluations	*0.00*	*0.00*
	9	Changes in entitlements due to other changes in volume	*0.00*	*0.00*
		Closing Balance Sheet		
	10	Pension entitlements	*1012.54*	*6,093.13*
		Pension entitlements (% of GDP 2006)	*43.60*	*262.47*
	11	Output		
	12	Assets held at the end of the period to meet pensions		

Source: Own calculations

3.5   ES – Spain

Spain is the second largest country of the European Union in geographical terms. It has a population of 43.75 million inhabitants as at January 1st, 2006.[100] The Spanish economy has been growing steadily since the transition towards democracy started in 1975. The accession to the European Community in 1986 furthered the Spanish economic expansion accompanied by a falling unemployment rate and a reduced inflation rate. It is one of the twelve countries which introduced the Euro currency on January 1st, 2002. Its GDP is estimated to be 982.3 bn. EUR in 2006, the corresponding per capita GDP amounts to 22,300 EUR. The Spanish labour force is estimated to be about 21.6 million.

3.5.1   The demographic development in Spain

From a demographical point of view, Spain represents a special case among the countries examined in this survey. To investigate this issue a little further, one has to go back to the 30s and 40s of the previous century. From 1936 to 1939 the Spanish Civil War took place resulting in a victory of the Nationalist forces under General Franco. However, in World War II Spain was neutral, and no acts of war took place on Spanish territory. These two historic facts can still be recognized in the age-specific population structure of 2006 which is illustrated in Figure 16.

At the cohorts aged 65 to 70 years in 2006 a numerical decline can be observed. This can be traced back to the uncertain times of the Spanish Civil War – we know from the countries previously examined that in times of war or country-wide riots, fertility rates rapidly decrease. For the same reason, low fertility rates during World War II cannot be observed, simply because the population in Spain was not involved.

However, the second main feature of the Spanish population structure can very well be monitored in other industrialized countries. It is the decline of fertility rates starting in the beginning of the 1970s – often referred to as the baby bust (which followed the so-called baby boom generation), accompanied by the introduction of birth control pill (although this was not the only reason for the sudden drop of birth rates). It is indeed worth mentioning that the baby bust in Spain started a little later than in the other countries. Numerically, the total fertility rate sank from a level of nearly 3.0 children per woman in 1970 to 2.2 children in 1980 and reached its minimum late in 1996 with a value of 1.16 children per woman on average.

---

[100] We display country data for 2006 since this is a main base year for our calculations.

Figure 16: Population structure in Spain (2006)
age groups 0 to 100 years

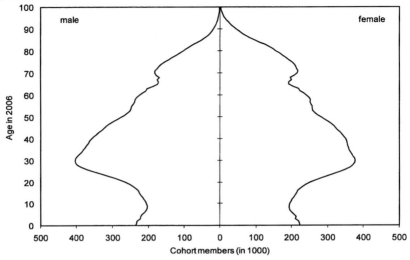

Source: Own calculations based on Eurostat (2009)

Average life expectancy in Spain amounts to a relative high value compared to other European countries. A male (female) born in 2006 can expect to live 77.7 (84.4) years. According to the assumptions of Eurostat this value is going to rise to 81.4 respectively 87.9 years for males/ females born in 2050. Figure 17 gives an overview of the quantitative development of persons aged 60 or older.

From the perspective of 2006, the number of elderly persons is expected to grow considerably. In 2030 there will be nearly 50 per cent more representatives of this age group, and until 2045 this figure will have increased by 75 per cent in relation to 2006. However, it has to be noted that in the years between 2006 and 2020 the rise in numbers is quite modest – this is an important aspect as this period turns out to be more relevant for the ADL calculated in this survey.

Figure 17: Development of elderly persons (aged 60+) in Spain
indexed to 100 in 2006

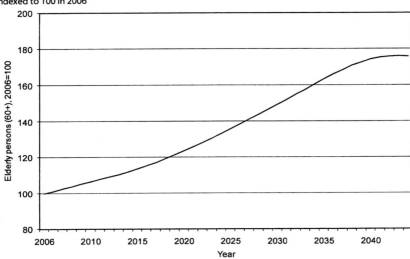

Source: Own calculations based on Eurostat (2009)

3.5.2 The Spanish pension system

3.5.2.1 The principles of the Spanish pension system

The Spanish public pension system consists of two schemes: A non contributory basic scheme provides assistance for the low-income earners and a labour-market contributory system provides social security for the rest.

The basic scheme grants means-tested assistance for individuals who earn less than a certain threshold (4,043 EUR as of 2005). No previous contributions are required in order to obtain the benefits. The labour market-based social security is financed by contributions from employers and employees. Contributions are excluded from the income tax base while pension benefits are taxed as labour income. Hence, the public pension system is administered and managed by the Seguridad Social (SS) as a defined benefit PAYG system.

Eligibility for the benefits requires an entry age of 65 years and at least 15 years of contribution. The pension benefit is related to the number of contribution years and the contributions paid. The earnings base is pay over the last 15 years. Benefits start at 50 per cent of the earnings base if an individual retires at 65 with the minimum required years of contribution. Each additional year until 25 increases the benefits by three per cent and afterwards by two per cent each additional contribution year until 35. Early retirement is penalized with benefit reductions of eight per cent for every year of premature retirement; by six per cent in the case of individuals who have contributed for at least 40 years. Pensions are adjusted in line with inflation.[101]

The reform of 2002 has further abolished the mandatory retirement age in the private sector (65 years of age) and incentivized labour after that age by increasing pension benefits by two per cent for each additional year of work. Moreover, pensions have been made compatible with part-time work, adjusting the pension benefits to the length of the working day.

3.5.2.2 Recent reforms of the Spanish pension system

The *New Law on Social Security Measures* which came into force on January 1st, 2008 changed some parameters regarding early retirement pensions and old age pensions. The goal of this pension reform was to increase labour participation and improve the balance of the pension system in terms of long-term sustainability. The following adjustments have been conducted: Preconditions to partial retirement have been incremented; incentives for postponing old-age retirement have been improved and certain aspects of invalidity pensions have been altered.[102]

3.5.3 Measuring the Spanish accrued-to-date pension liabilities

Analogous to the previous chapters, we use the pension benefits paid in 2005, 2006 and 2007 as a starting point. These are shown in Table 19.[103]

---

[101] For a closer look on the Spanish pension system, see OECD (2007), p. 181-182.

[102] For a closer look on the pension reform 2007 in Spain see Ministry of Labour and Social Affairs (2008).

[103] For the year 2007, no breakdown of total pension payments was available.

Table 19: Social security pension payments Spain
(in bn. EUR)[104]

Type of pension	Pension payments		
	2005	2006	2007
Old age pensions	45.47	48.85	
Disability pensions	8.34	8.93	
Survivor pensions	15.14	15.94	
Total	68.95	73.72	79.81

Source: INE (2008)

Aggregate pension benefits in 2006 add up to an amount equal to 7.5 per cent of GDP. Applying the Freiburg model to calculate the ADL using the PBO approach first, the following outcomes are generated, indicated in Table 20:[105]

Table 20: Supplementary table Spain 2006 PBO
(in bn. EUR)

			Non-core national accounts (figures in bn. EUR)	
			General Government	Social Security
			G	H
		Opening Balance Sheet		
	1	Pension entitlements		*1,871.03*
		Changes in pension entitlements due to transactions		
Sum 2.1 to 2.4	2	Increase in pension entitlements due to social contributions		*179.69*
	2.1	*Employer actual social contributions*		61.39
	2.2	*Employer imputed social contributions*		
	2.3	*Household actual social contributions*		21.37
	2.4	*Household social contribution supplements*		96.93
	3	Other (actuarial) increase of pension entitlements		29.02
	4	Reduction in pension entitlements due to payment of pension benefits		73.72
2 + 3 - 4	5	Change in pension entitlements due to social contributions and pension benefits		134.98
	6	Transfers of entitlements between schemes		*0.00*
	7	Changes in pension entitlements due to other transactions		*0.00*
		Changes in pension entitlements due to other economic flows		
	8	Changes in entitlements due to revaluations		*0.00*
	9	Changes in entitlements due to other changes in volume		*0.00*
		Closing Balance Sheet		
	10	Pension entitlements		*2,006.01*
		Pension entitlements (% of GDP 2006)		*204.21*
	11	Output		
	12	Assets held at the end of the period to meet pensions		

Source: Own calculations

---

[104] Unfortunately no further breakdown was given for the year 2007.

[105] The supplementary tables for the year 2007 can be found in the appendix.

Pension entitlements in the beginning of 2006 come up to 1,871.03 bn. EUR. Actual contributions from employers (61.39 bn. EUR) and households (21.37 bn. EUR) as well as household social contribution supplements to the amount of 96.93 bn. EUR increase the pension entitlements by 179.69 bn. EUR (see row 2). Entitlements are reduced by pension payments amounting to 73.72 bn. EUR, the residual value in row 3 accounts for 29.02 bn. EUR. Thus pension entitlements of the social security pension scheme constitute 2,006.01 bn. EUR in the end of 2006. This corresponds to around 204 per cent of the Spanish GDP in 2006. Obviously, results change when switching over to the ABO approach. Table 21 displays the respective results:

Table 21: Supplementary table Spain 2006 ABO
(in bn. EUR)

			Non-core national accounts (figures in bn. EUR)	
			General Government	Social Security
			G	H
		Opening Balance Sheet		
	1	Pension entitlements		*1,623.20*
		Changes in pension entitlements due to transactions		
Sum 2.1 to 2.4	2	**Increase in pension entitlements due to social contributions**		*166.83*
	2.1	*Employer actual social contributions*		61.39
	2.2	*Employer imputed social contributions*		
	2.3	*Household actual social contributions*		21.37
	2.4	*Household social contribution supplements*		84.06
	3	Other (actuarial) increase of pension entitlements		23.09
	4	Reduction in pension entitlements due to payment of pension benefits		73.72
2 + 3 - 4	5	**Change in pension entitlements due to social contributions and pension benefits**		*116.20*
	6	Transfers of entitlements between schemes		*0.00*
	7	Changes in pension entitlements due to other transactions		*0.00*
		Changes in pension entitlements due to other economic flows		
	8	Changes in entitlements due to revaluations		*0.00*
	9	Changes in entitlements due to other changes in volume		*0.00*
		Closing Balance Sheet		
	10	Pension entitlements		*1,739.40*
		Pension entitlements (% of GDP 2006)		*177.07*
	11	Output		
	12	Assets held at the end of the period to meet pensions		

Source: Own calculations

Statistical figures from national accounts shown in row 2.1, row 2.3 and row 4 are of course not affected by the switch to ABO. But this does not hold for pension entitlements itself and those figures which depend on opening and closing entitlements (household social contribution supplements and the residual figure in row 3). Opening pension entitlements accrue to 1,623.20 bn. EUR; household social contribution supplements come up to 84.06 bn. EUR. The other (actuarial) increase of pension entitlements as the balance figure amounts to 23.09 bn. EUR while closing pension entitlements add up to a value 1,739.40 bn. EUR. This corresponds to roughly 177 per cent of GDP in 2006.

3.6   FI – Finland

Finland has a population of 5.26 million inhabitants as at January 1st, 2006.[106] The national currency is the Euro since Finland is one of the twelve countries which introduced the Euro currency on January 1st, 2002. Finland has a highly industrialized free-market economy with a per capita output even higher than other western economies such as France, Germany or Sweden. The largest sector of the economy is services at 65.7 per cent, followed by manufacturing and refining at 31.4 per cent. The GDP in 2006 added up to 167.0 bn. EUR; this corresponds to a per capita GDP of 31,700 EUR.

3.6.1   The demographic development in Finland

Finland is, after Norway and Iceland, the most sparsely populated country in Europe. Nevertheless, it features a rather interesting demographic history in terms of fertility. The fertility rate after World War II showed an unusual high figure of 3.5 births per woman – most other European countries faced fertility rates well below replacement level of 2.1 –, it dropped to a minimum of 1.5 in 1973 as in most other European countries at that time, finally stabilized at a value of around 1.8 and stayed at that level until 2006. The current fertility rate can be regarded as the upper end in a European context, comparable to countries like Denmark, Sweden or the UK. Figure 18 shows the age-specific population structure of Finland in 2006.

The baby-boom shortly after World War II can clearly be observed at the age cohort of 60 year old males and females. Looking at the cohorts aged 30 to 35 in 2006, the minimum of births in 1973 can be seen. Since then, the number of births stabilized and the demographic change does not seem to be as severe as it is in many other European countries. Nevertheless, Figure 18 shows very clearly that the numerically strongest cohort is the one at the age of around 60 – people who just retired or will retire soon. Figure 19 shows the numerical development of elderly persons, starting from 2006 until 2045.

---

[106] Figure as at January 1st, 2006. We display country data for 2006 since this is a main base year for our calculations.

Figure 18: Population structure in Finland (2006)
age groups 0 to 100 years

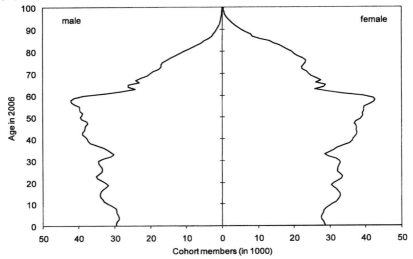

Source: Own calculations based on Eurostat (2009)

As shown in the following figure, the number of elderly persons in Finland will increase quite rapidly. The first reason for that can be found when looking at the cohort size of 60 year old persons in the age pyramid in Figure 18. Another important reason is the rising life expectancy; a male (female) person born in 2006 can expect to reach an age of 75.9 (83.1) on average. This figure is assumed to rise up to 81.9 (86.5) in 2050. Nevertheless, one has to point out that the number of elderly persons will reach its peak between 2025 and 2030. After that, this figure will decrease slowly which can be ascribed to the development of birth rates in the second half of the 20th century.

Figure 19: Development of elderly persons (aged 60+) in Finland
indexed to 100 in 2006

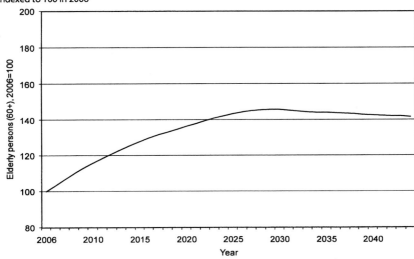

Source: Own calculations based on Eurostat (2009)

3.6.2 The Finnish pension system

3.6.2.1 The principles of the Finnish pension system

In Finland, almost all gainful employment is covered by pension provision. Self-employed persons, farmers, seamen and public-sector employees have their own pension acts. The public pension system (the first pillar) is made up of two statutory pension schemes: one is the national pension scheme guaranteeing a minimum pension to all residents whereas the other is an employment-based, earnings-related pension scheme. The schemes for private-sector employees are partially pre-funded while the public-sector schemes are PAYG financed.

Voluntary pension schemes are not very common in Finland compared to many other European countries. The reason for this is, among other things, that the statutory earnings-related pension scheme has no upper limit for the pensionable earnings or for the pension. In 2000, pensions for voluntary schemes represented only 4.4 per cent of all pension benefits while contributions were 5.6 per cent of total contribution. While the second pillar occupational schemes are decreasing, individual savings are increasing their importance.

The statutory schemes are closely linked together, with the amount of national pension depending on the size of the earnings-related pension benefits. Increases in the earnings-related pension reduce the national pension by 50 per cent of the increase in the earnings-related pension. If the earnings-related pension is above a defined level, the national pension is not paid at all. Therefore only about half of pensioners who receive an earnings-related pension also receive a national pension. At the same time there are 100,000 pensioners getting only national pension. Taking all pension types into account the total number of pensioners in 2004 was roughly 1.3 million.

National pensions are intended to provide a basic retirement income for those whose earnings-related pensions are small or non-existent. All residents of Finland are eligible for the national pension. It is a flat-rate benefit, financed through taxes and contributions, and is based on residence for people over 65 without a sufficient earnings related entitlement. It is means-tested, which means that only those who do not receive an income pension can receive the national pension at its maximum level.[107]

The financing of earnings-related pensions is a combination of a fully funded and a PAYG system based on pension contributions from both employers and employees. The pre-funded scheme covers approximately one quarter of earnings-related pension outlays, the rest is financed through the PAYG system. Despite the partially funded system in pensions, Finland's earnings-related pension scheme is entirely of the defined-benefit type. The pre-funding is collective in the sense that it actually has no effect on the size of the pension. The main purpose of the pre-funding is to smooth pension contributions in the coming years. The financial position of the earnings-related pension scheme is fairly good as the system is running on surpluses. The annual surplus amounts to some 2.5 per cent in relation to GDP. The market value of the pension fund's assets was 58.7 per cent of GDP in 2004.

The earnings-related pension scheme consists of several pension acts, which together cover the different sectors of the economy. In practice, all work between 18 and 67 years of age, as employee or as an entrepreneur, is insured through the

---

[107] According to the final report of the European Central Bank/ Eurostat Task Force (2008), social assistance benefits shall not be considered in the supplementary table (see p. 20). The national pension scheme in Finland can be regarded as a social assistance scheme, thus, it will not be included in our calculations.

earnings-related pension acts.[108] The individual pension is accumulated according to the following rules:

Pensions accrue from all earnings between the age of 18 to 52 at the rate of 1.5 per cent of wages a year, from 53 to 62 at 1.9 per cent and from 63 to 68 at 1.5 (if he or she draws an old-age pension) or 4.5 per cent a year without any cap. For a full-career worker working from age 20 until retirement at age 65, the total lifetime accrual will be 77.5 per cent of pensionable earnings.[109]

3.6.2.2 Recent reforms of the Finnish pension system

The Finnish pension system has been relatively stable over the last two decades as no major structural changes have been made. However, the severe recession in the 1990s forced cuts in labour costs and outlined the underlying problems of long-term sustainability of the pension system. A number of parametric changes have been implemented in the 1990s; these include, amongst others, an increase of the retirement age and a reduction of the target replacement rate both in the public sector.

These modifications have been commonly perceived as a flexibility of the system showing the ability of the system to adapt to the changing circumstances. From the other side, these parametric reforms have had quite substantial cost containing effects. Without these reforms, the contribution rate would have had to increase by eight percentage points over the next 30 years.

Since 1999, buffer funds have been developed in the earnings-related pension system in order to control sudden disturbances caused by recessions. This measure is linked to Finland's participation in the European Economic and Monetary Union (EMU), as during a recession the EMU requirements would otherwise be difficult to meet. The development of buffer funds entails that in the period of strong economic growth the contribution rate can be raised, and lowered during recession.

---

[108] The private sector pension acts are the employees pensions act (TyEL), the seamen's pensions act (MEL), the self-employed persons' pensions act (YEL), the farmers' pensions act (MYEL) and the farm closure allowance act (LUTUL); the public sector pension acts are the state employees' pensions act (VaEL) the local government pensions act (KuEL), the Evangelical-Lutheran church pensions act (KiEL) and the pension regulation for employees of the social insurance institution (KELA).

[109] For a detailed description of the pension scheme in Finland, see European commission (2007), p. 331 et sqq.

A major reform of the Finnish private sector earnings-related pension system was agreed on in 2001-2002. The agreement was justified by the need to mitigate rising pension costs due to population ageing, similar to arguments spurring many other recent reforms in Europe. The large reform package consisted of an interesting combination of measures that were expected to improve both the economic and social sustainability of the pension system. The main aims were to base the pensionable pay on average earnings of the whole career, to change the indexation of pension rights to 80:20 before retirement are and 20:80 after retirement (wage growth: CPI), to introduce a life expectancy coefficient which adjusts pension expenditure according to the changes in life expectancy, and to implement a flexible retirement age for the old age pension between ages 63 and 68.[110]

3.6.3 Measuring the Finnish accrued-to-date pension liabilities

The following tables show the total pension expenditures of the various pension schemes, beginning with the private sector in Table 22:

Table 22: Social security pension payments Finland
(in bn. EUR, private sector)

Type of pension	Pension payments		
	2005	2006	2007
Old age pensions	5.49	5.91	6.38
Disability pensions	1.93	1.82	1.85
Survivor pensions	0.86	0.91	0.96
Total	8.28	8.64	9.19

Source: Statistics Finland (2008)

Expressed as a fraction of the GDP in the respective year, the pension expenditures changed from 5.3 per cent in 2005 to 5.2 per cent in 2006 and 5.1 per cent which means that expenditures for private sector pension developed rather constantly with a small downward trend.

Table 23 shows the respective pension payments for the public sector pensions, divided into the general state employees' pension act (VaEL) on the one hand and all other public employees' pension acts on the other hand:

---

[110] For a detailed description of if the 2005 pension reform in Finland see Lassila and Valkonen (2006).

Table 23: Social security pension payments Finland
(in bn. EUR, public sector)

Institution	Pension payments		
	2005	2006	2007
VaEL	2.98	2.98	3.11
Old age pensions	2.37	2.38	2.49
Disability pensions	0.29	0.29	0.30
Survivor pensions	0.32	0.31	0.32
Other public employees pensions	2.55	2.63	2.81
Old Age pensions	1.95	1.98	2.10
Disability pensions	0.45	0.50	0.55
Survivor pensions	0.15	0.15	0.16
Total	5.53	5.61	5.92

Source: Statistics Finland (2008)

Expressed as a share of the GDP in the respective year, pension expenditures in the public sector in 2005 added up to 3.5 per cent. In 2006, this figure amounted to 3.4 per cent, and in 2007 it showed a value of 3.3 per cent. Similar to the expenditures in the private sector, the development has a minor downward trend. Applying the methodology of the Freiburg model, the respective outcomes for the year 2006 are shown in Table 24 and Table 25 (PBO and ABO):[111]

The social security open balance accounts for 497.85 bn. EUR. These liabilities can be split into liabilities of the public sector adding up to 199.85 bn. EUR and those of the private sector amounting to 298.00 bn. EUR. Social contributions add up to 39.75 bn. EUR; total pension benefits in that year amount to 14.25 bn. EUR (5.62 bn. EUR paid out in the public sector, 8.63 bn. EUR in the private sector). The closing balance of 2006 shows pension entitlements adding up to 503.52 bn. EUR or some 301 per cent of GDP. The public sector accounts for 200.21 bn. EUR (119.86 per cent of GDP) of the closing balance, liabilities of the private sector accrue to 303.32 bn. EUR (nearly 182 per cent of GDP in 2006).

---

[111] According to P. Koistinen-Jokiniemi (Statistics Finland), the pension schemes of the public sector are to be recorded in Column H of the supplementary table. The supplementary tables for the year 2007 can be found in the appendix of this survey.

Table 24: Supplementary table Finland 2006 PBO
(in bn. EUR)

			Non-core national accounts (figures in bn. EUR)	
			General Government	Social Security
			G	H
		Opening Balance Sheet		
	1	Pension entitlements		497.85
		Changes in pension entitlements due to transactions		
Sum 2.1 to 2.4	2	**Increase in pension entitlements due to social contributions**		39.75
	2 1	*Employer actual social contributions*		11.14
	2 2	*Employer imputed social contributions*		▉
	2 3	*Household actual social contributions*		3.58
	2 4	*Household social contribution supplements*		25.03
	3	Other (actuanal) increase of pension entitlements	▉	-19.84
	4	Reduction in pension entitlements due to payment of pension benefits		14.25
2 + 3 - 4	5	**Change in pension entitlements due to social contributions and pension benefits**		5.67
	6	Transfers of entitlements between schemes		0.00
	7	Changes in pension entitlements due to other transactions		0.00
		Changes in pension entitlements due to other economic flows		
	8	Changes in entitlements due to revaluations		0.00
	9	Changes in entitlements due to other changes in volume		0.00
		Closing Balance Sheet		
	10	Pension entitlements		503.52
		Pension entitlements (% of GDP 2006)		301.44
	11	Output		
	12	Assets held at the end of the period to meet pensions		

Source: Own calculations

Not surprisingly, the outcomes using the ABO approach turn out to be considerably lower. The opening balance shows entitlements accrued from the social security pension scheme adding up to 396.52 bn. EUR. 159.81 bn. EUR can be assigned to pensions of the public sector; the private sector accounts for liabilities amounting to 236.71 bn. EUR. The closing pension entitlements account for 401.89 bn. EUR, equal to 240.60 per cent of GDP. These consist of entitlements of the public sector accruing to 160.23 bn. EUR (almost 96 per cent of GDP) and entitlements of the private sector adding up to 241.66 bn. EUR (nearly 145 per cent of GDP). In relation to the outcomes of the PBO approach in Table 24, the reduction adds up to nearly 20 per cent (60 percentage points of GDP).

Table 25: Supplementary table Finland 2006 ABO
(in bn. EUR)

			Non-core national accounts (figures in bn. EUR)	
			General Government	Social Security
			G	H
		Opening Balance Sheet		
	1	Pension entitlements		396.52
		Changes in pension entitlements due to transactions		
Sum 2.1 to 2.4	2	Increase in pension entitlements due to social contributions		34.68
	2.1	*Employer actual social contributions*		11.14
	2.2	*Employer imputed social contributions*		
	2.3	*Household actual social contributions*		3.58
	2.4	*Household social contribution supplements*		19.96
	3	Other (actuarial) increase of pension entitlements		-15.06
	4	Reduction in pension entitlements due to payment of pension benefits		14.25
2 + 3 - 4	5	Change in pension entitlements due to social contributions and pension benefits		5.37
	6	Transfers of entitlements between schemes		0.00
	7	Changes in pension entitlements due to other transactions		0.00
		Changes in pension entitlements due to other economic flows		
	8	Changes in entitlements due to revaluations		0.00
	9	Changes in entitlements due to other changes in volume		0.00
		Closing Balance Sheet		
	10	Pension entitlements		401.89
		Pension entitlements (% of GDP 2006)		240.60
	11	Output		
	12	Assets held at the end of the period to meet pensions		

Source: Own calculations

3.7   FR – France

The population of the French Republic amounted to 63 million inhabitants.[112] The national currency in France is the Euro. The GDP amounted to 1,807.5 bn. EUR in 2006 which is in accordance with a per capita GDP of 28,600 EUR.

The French economy is largely dominated by the service sector which accounts for about 77 per cent of GDP (excluding state sector) compared to about 20 per cent in the industrial sector. The largest single contributions within the service sector stem from enterprise and financial services including estate services (each accounting for about one third) and trade services (about 20 per cent). Intermediates are the largest single category in the industrial sector accounting for about one third of value added.

3.7.1   The demographic development in France

Compared to most other EU members, France has had a relatively high fertility rate. On average, a French woman gives birth to almost two children. This corresponds to a total fertility rate of 2.0 in 2006. As with most industrialized countries, life expectancy in France rose in the past and is expected to rise further in the future. Life expectancy for a male person born in 2006 was 77.4 years, respectively 84.4 years for a female person. Until 2050, life expectancy is assumed to rise to 82.7 and 89.1 accordingly (male/female).[113] Figure 20 shows the age-specific population structure in France for the year of 2006.

The structure of the population holds almost no major surprises. Looking at the age cohort of 30, a reduction can be observed. This may be explained by the introduction of the birth control pill in the beginning of the 1970s which caused lower fertility rates. However, unlike other countries like (West-) Germany, fertility rates recovered quite fast and climbed up to a level at nearly the replacement rate.

Another special feature can be found at the cohorts aged 60 to 70 years in 2006. The lower numbers, compared to younger age cohorts, can be explained by World War II and the times when parts of France were occupied. Evidence shows that under such circumstances fertility rates normally decrease due to an insecure future and the absence of males.

---

[112] Figure as at January 1st, 2006. We display country data for 2006 since this is a main base year for our calculations.

[113] These figures apply to Metropolitan France only.

Figure 20: Population structure in France (2006)
age groups 0 to 100 years

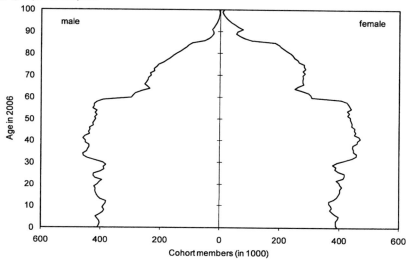

Source: Own calculations based on Eurostat (2009)

The relative number of elderly persons – persons who are 60 years and older – is determined by the age-specific population structure and the assumed life expectancy. Figure 21 illustrates this development until the year 2045. Starting from the year 2006, a constant rise in elderly persons until 2032 can be observed. At that time, the number of elderly persons will have increased by 60 per cent compared to 2006. From that year on, the increase slows down due to the age-specific population structure in 2006 which shows a decline in the age group of around 30 (see Figure 20).

Figure 21: Development of elderly persons (aged 60+) in France
indexed to 100 in 2006

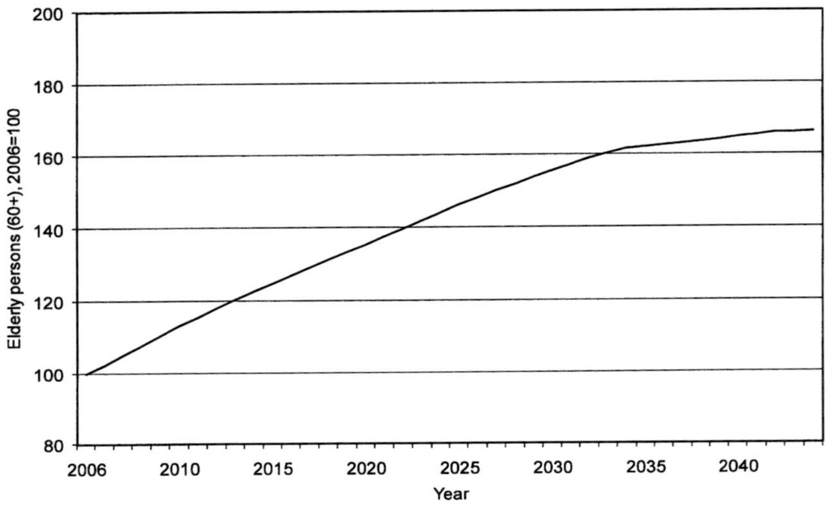

Source: Own calculations based on Eurostat (2009)

3.7.2 The French pension system

3.7.2.1 The principles of the French pension system

In the French pension system there is a strict separation between publicly and privately employed workers. In the public sector there are 2.5 million active members and 1.5 million former public employees receiving old-age pensions. In the sector covered by the social security pension scheme 22 million active members face 8.8 million old-age pensioners.[114] Public employees are in a one-pillar defined benefit scheme whereas all others are in a two pillar scheme with a mixture of a basic defined benefit and a mandatory complementary point-value system. There are about seven slightly different basic schemes for privately employed and self-employed workers and another eight for public sector employees.

The basic pension for non-public employees is a defined benefit scheme intended to achieve a replacement rate of 50 per cent of average earnings of the N years with highest earnings. N is currently incremented from ten years for those born 1933 or

---

[114] Figures are taken from European Central Bank/ Eurostat Task Force (2008).

earlier by one year per cohort to 25 years for those born 1948 and after. Eligibility for full pension requires at least one out of two conditions: a minimum age of 65 combined with a demanded contribution time T (160 quarters) or a minimum contribution time C currently being raised linearly from 150 quarters for the cohorts of 1943 and earlier to 160 for to the 1948 cohort. Between the 1948 and 1952 cohorts T and C are increased by one quarter per year up to 164 quarters. Thereafter these two parameters are meant to rise in line with life expectancy, assigning two thirds of additional lifetime to working and the remainder to retirement.

The pension is prorated by the ratio of actual contribution A to C with a maximum of 1. Per year of retirement before contribution time T or 65 years of age (earliest age is 60) there is an additional deduction of ten per cent to be reduced to five per cent soon. For every year above minimum full pension requirements there is a bonus of three per cent. Benefits are price-indexed.

The mandatory complementary scheme is a defined contribution point scheme. Employers pay 60 per cent of the contributions, employees pay 40 per cent. Only 80 per cent of actual contributions are transferred into points. The number of points is the annual contribution over reference salary; the pension claim equals the number of points times the point value. The reference salary is indexed to wage growth whereas the point value is indexed to the CPI. There is a reduction of one percentage point per quarter when pension is claimed before age 65.

The public sector pension scheme has, as yet, only one pillar which is defined benefit. The target replacement rate of a full pension is 75 per cent of the final wage earned for at least six months. The minimum required contribution time T for a full pension has been raised by two quarters per year since 2003 and will fall in line with the one in the private sector scheme at 160 quarters in 2008. Thereafter the same rules will be applied for both schemes. To calculate the pension the 75 per cent are prorated by the ratio of actual contribution to T, at most by one. Targeted pension age is 65. Since 2006 there is a deduction per year that retirement is chosen before a certain age R or before T quarters of contribution. R will be incremented gradually from 61 years in 2006 to 65 in the end; the deduction will finally reach five per cent per year for privately employed people.

3.7.2.2 Recent reforms of the French pension system

There have been two major pension reforms in France in the last years. The first one, the so-called Balladur reform goes back to 1993, the other one – the Fillon reform – was enacted in 2003. The Balladur reform in 1993 affected only the pensions in the private sector. The detailed components were the following:

- Gradual increase of the duration condition by one quarter each year from 37.5 years in 1993 to 40 years in 2003

- Shift of number of years on which past wages are averaged for calculating the replacement rate; from ten years in pre-1993 conditions one year increase each year until reaching the value of 25 years in 2008

- Change of formula used for re-evaluating past wages; re-evaluation from 1993 according to prices instead of general productivity growth

- Indexation of pensions after entry according to prices instead of wages.

The Fillon reform in 2003 affected mainly the pensions paid in the public sector, but there were also some amendments in the private sector. All changes of the reform enacted in 2003 are described here:

- Increase of the duration condition in the public sector from 37.5 years in 2003 to 40 years in 2008 (which meant a convergence of conditions for private and public sector)

- Further increase of the duration condition in the public sector as well as the private sector to 41.75 years in 2020.

All of these reform steps were taken into account when calculating the accrued-to-date liabilities. According to our estimations, the over-all effect of both of the above mentioned reforms until the year 2020 is a decrease of new pensions by more than 25 per cent in the public sector and nearly 22 per cent in the private sector in comparison with a fictitious situation without any reforms.

3.7.3 Measuring the French accrued-to-date pension liabilities

The French pension system possesses a government employer pension scheme for the public sector and a social security pension scheme for the private sector. Table 26 and Table 27 show the pension expenditures of these schemes for the years 2005 to 2007.[115]

---

[115] A further breakdown of pension payments was not available. Data source: Banque de France, Dominique Durant (email dated January 14th, 2009). Please note that since 2006 pensions of the "La Poste" employees are deemed to be financed through a separate scheme which does not belong to the general government scheme. Nevertheless, in our calculations the "La Poste" pensions have been added to the general government scheme (see Source: Banque de France (2008)

Table 26: Social security pension payments France
(in bn. EUR)

Type of pension	Pension payments		
	2005	2006	2007
Total	171.00	180.76	188.83

Source: Banque de France (2008)

Table 27: Government employer pension payments France
(in bn. EUR)

Type of pensions	Pension payments		
	2005	2006	2007
Total	35.90	37.90	39.80

Source: Banque de France (2008)

The mandatory complementary scheme for non-public employees which has been described earlier in this chapter has not been considered in our calculations as it is classified as a core account. Thus, it is not applicable in this survey. Table 28 presents the results of our calculations for the year 2006 in the supplementary table introduced earlier, based on the PBO approach: [116]

Not surprisingly, the liabilities of the social security scheme are considerably higher than those of the government employer pension scheme. This is due to the fact that the pure amount of beneficiaries represented in column H exceeds the ones represented in column G by almost six times. Pension entitlements at the beginning of the year amount to 1,011.12 bn. EUR. Social contributions increase this figure by 128.46 EUR, pensions paid in 2006 decrease it by 37.90 bn. EUR. This results in a closing stock of liabilities accounting for 1,101.69 bn. EUR which is equal to some 61 per cent of GDP in 2006.

Table 27). The total pension payments for "La Poste" pensions accounted for 2.9 bn. EUR in 2005 and 2006 and 2.8 bn. EUR in 2007.

[116] The supplementary tables for the year 2007 can be found in the appendix of this study.

Table 28: Supplementary table France 2006 PBO
(in bn. EUR)

				Non-core national accounts (figures in bn. EUR)	
				General Government	Social Security
				G	H
			Opening Balance Sheet		
		1	Pension entitlements	*1011.12*	*5,158.50*
			Changes in pension entitlements due to transactions		
Sum 2.1 to 2.4		2	**Increase in pension entitlements due to social contributions**	*128.46*	*405.07*
	2.1		*Employer actual social contributions*	16.00	140.00
	2 2		*Employer imputed social contributions*	55.64	
	2 3		*Household actual social contributions*	4.00	0.00
	2.4		*Household social contribution supplements*	52.82	265.07
		3	Other (actuarial) increase of pension entitlements		*61.35*
		4	Reduction in pension entitlements due to payment of pension benefits	37.90	180.76
2 + 3 - 4		5	**Change in pension entitlements due to social contributions and pension benefits**	*90.56*	*285.66*
		6	Transfers of entitlements between schemes	*0.00*	*0.00*
		7	Changes in pension entitlements due to other transactions	*0.00*	*0.00*
			Changes in pension entitlements due to other economic flows		
		8	Changes in entitlements due to revaluations	*0.00*	*0.00*
		9	Changes in entitlements due to other changes in volume	*0.00*	*0.00*
			Closing Balance Sheet		
		10	Pension entitlements	*1101.69*	*5,444.16*
			Pension entitlements (% of GDP 2006)	*61.48*	*303.81*
		11	Output		
		12	Assets held at the end of the period to meet pensions		

Source: Own calculations

The social security pension liabilities (column H) add up to 5,158.50 bn. EUR at the beginning of 2006. These liabilities are increased by social contributions (405.07 bn. EUR) and decreased by paid pensions (180.76 bn. EUR). The other (actuarial) increase of pension entitlements as the residual amounts to 61.35 bn. EUR. This yields in a closing stock of entitlements adding up to 5,444.16 bn. EUR or almost 304 per cent of GDP in 2006.[117]

As described before, there is not one single approach to estimate the ADP for a certain pension scheme. Therefore all calculations have also been conducted using the ABO approach. Table 29 exhibits the respective findings:

---

[117] Durant and Frey (2007) applied the PROST model developed by the World Bank to the social security pension scheme of France. For 2005, their findings show ADL turning out to be 24 per cent higher than our results. This can mainly be traced back to a lower discount rate of two per cent used in Durant and Frey (2007).

Table 29: Supplementary table France 2006 ABO
(in bn. EUR)

				Non-core national accounts (figures in bn. EUR)	
				General Government	Social Security
				G	H
			Opening Balance Sheet		
		1	Pension entitlements	838.63	4,350.43
			Changes in pension entitlements due to transactions		
Sum 2.1 to 2.4		2	Increase in pension entitlements due to social contributions	108.56	363.64
	2.1		*Employer actual social contributions*	16.00	140.00
	2.2		*Employer imputed social contributions*	44.87	
	2.3		*Household actual social contributions*	4.00	0.00
	2.4		*Household social contribution supplements*	43.70	223.64
		3	Other (actuarial) increase of pension entitlements		61.76
		4	Reduction in pension entitlements due to payment of pension benefits	37.90	180.76
2 + 3 - 4		5	Change in pension entitlements due to social contributions and pension benefits	70.66	244.63
		6	Transfers of entitlements between schemes	0.00	0.00
		7	Changes in pension entitlements due to other transactions	0.00	0.00
			Changes in pension entitlements due to other economic flows		
		8	Changes in entitlements due to revaluations	0.00	0.00
		9	Changes in entitlements due to other changes in volume	0.00	0.00
			Closing Balance Sheet		
		10	Pension entitlements	909.30	4,595.06
			Pension entitlements (% of GDP 2006)	50.74	256.43
		11	Output		
		12	Assets held at the end of the period to meet pensions		

Source: Own calculations

As expected, the results from these calculations are considerably lower than under the PBO approach. In figures, the closing balance sheet of the government employer pension scheme (column G) lies nearly 18 per cent below the results in Table 28. In the case of the social security pension scheme the result is almost 16 per cent lower than before. All other figures stay either the same (taken from national accounts) or are slightly modified depending on the opening and closing balance of entitlements.[118]

---

[118] For a detailed description of the differences between ABO and PBO approach see section 2.2.2.2.

3.8 GR – Greece

Greece has a population of 11.13 million inhabitants.[119] It belongs to the twelve countries which introduced the Euro currency on January 1st, 2002. Today, the service industry makes up the largest, most vital and fast-growing sector of the Greek economy, followed by industry and agriculture. The GDP of Greece in 2006 amounted to 213.2 bn. EUR, the per capita GDP added up to 19,100 EUR.

3.8.1 The demographic development in Greece

The demographic history in Greece is characterized by relatively high fertility rates between 2.0 and 2.5 children per woman until the beginning of the 1980s. Since then, a strong decline of birth rates can be observed which bottomed out to a minimum of only 1.24 children per mother in 1999. After that, the birth rate recovered very slowly, in 2006 the fertility rate showed a value of close to 1.40. Figure 22 illustrates the age-specific population structure in 2006.

Figure 22: Population structure in Greece (2006)
age groups 0 to 100 years

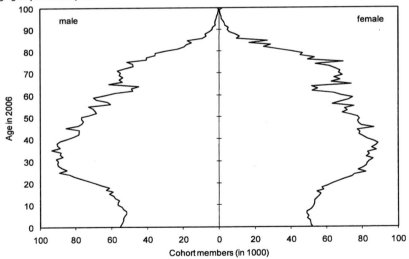

Source: Own calculations based on Eurostat (2009)

---

[119] Figure as at January 1st, 2006. We display country data for 2006 since this is a main base year for our calculations.

The Greek population structure from the age cohorts of 20 up to the 100 year old persons generally does not show any big surprises. A slump of births can be seen around the age of 65 years; this can probably be traced back to World War II. However, a big change can be observed when it comes to the amount of persons between the age of zero and 20 years. These age groups show the falling fertility rate since the beginning of the 1980s. Thus, the so-called baby-bust which began at the end of 1960s in many European countries was postponed in Greece and began around 15 years later.

In terms of life expectancy, Greece experienced large increases in the past. Males (females) born in 1970 faced a life expectancy of 71.6 (76.0) years. Until 2006, this value grew up to 77.2 (81.9 years). In other words, life expectancy at birth has been grown by more than five years for both men and women during the last 36 years. It is assumed to rise further to a value of 80.3 years for men and 85.1 years for women in 2050. Thus life expectancy in Greece will probably continue to rise in the future, but the growth is expected to decelerate (3.1 years for men and 3.2 years for women in 44 years). Figure 23 shows the assumed development of the number of elderly persons (persons aged 60 or older) in Greece between 2006 and 2045.

Figure 23: Development of elderly persons (aged 60+) in Greece
indexed to100 in 2006

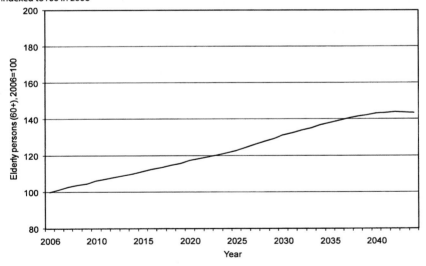

Source: Own calculations based on Eurostat (2009)

It can be seen that the number of elderly persons – who represent the number of potential future pensioners in Greece – develops on a constant growth path. Around 2040, there will be around 40 per cent more potential pensioners than in 2006. This development has a considerable impact on the Greek public pension liabilities which will be shown later in this chapter.

3.8.2 The Greek pension system

3.8.2.1 The principles of the Greek pension system

The Greek pension system is very fragmented. It is the result of a long series of partial legislative initiatives over the last fifty years. Notwithstanding the institutional fragmentation in hundreds of pension funds and schemes, it is basically related to the public pillar. While no major reforms were introduced in the last decade on old age pensions, some measures have been adopted to reduce the institutional complexity and to improve the effectiveness of pension programmes especially to protect the elderly against the risk of poverty. In terms of financing, the Greek pension system is in principle a PAYG system while in terms of structure it is a defined-benefit scheme. As to its legal status, it is mandatory and run by the wider public sector. The share of population covered by this system is nearly 100 per cent. The normal pension age is 65 for men and 60 for women, equalized at 65 for all people entering the labour force from 1993. The primary pension depends upon the question whether labour-market entry has been taken place before or after 1993. The following description applies to the latter:

The primary pension is two per cent of earnings for each year of contributions up to 35 years. There is a maximum replacement rate of 70 per cent for people retiring at the normal age or earlier. The earnings measure is the average over the last five years, earlier earnings are valorized in line with increases defined in national incomes policy.[120] The indexation of pensions is discretionary, but it usually follows the inflation rate.

3.8.2.2 Recent reforms of the Greek pension system

In the beginning of the 1990s, the Souflias reform and the Sioufas reform were passed. These reforms reduced replacement rates, raised eligibility standards especially for public sector employees and tightened the criteria for the payment of an invalidity pension. For the cohorts of workers entering the labour market from 1993 onwards, common eligibility rules were introduced. Especially the indexation

---

[120] For further details see OECD (2007), p. 130 et sqq.

rule was cut down to price indexation. The last major reform – the Reppas reform – was passed in 2002. The most important changes were the introduction of a uniform retirement age for the members of all funds and the gradual reduction of replacement rates for public sector employees to 70 per cent starting from January 2008.[121]

3.8.3 Measuring the Greek accrued-to-date pension liabilities

The following results apply only to the social security pension system in Greece. Due to lack of data, it was not possible to calculate pension liabilities for government employer pension schemes. The pension expenditures on which our calculations are based are shown in Table 30:[122]

Table 30: Social security pension payments Greece
(in bn. EUR)

	Pension payments		
	2005	2006	2007
Total	16.87	18.37	20.26

Source: Statistics Greece (2008)

Unfortunately, no further breakdown into the different types of pensions has been given. It can be seen that the total pension payments in 2005 added up to 16.871 bn. EUR and grew up to 18.371 bn. EUR in 2006 and 20.255 bn. EUR in 2007. Thus, the payments grew by 20 per cent between 2005 and 2007. Nevertheless, the share in the GDP added up to 8.5 per cent in 2005, 8.6 per cent in 2006 and 8.8 per cent in 2007 which is a rather constant development.

Applying the methodology described in chapter 2 of this survey, Table 31 shows the respective results for the year 2006, starting with the outcomes of the PBO approach:[123]

---

[121] For detailed information about the pension reforms in Greece, see Triantafillou (2005), p. 8 et sqq.

[122] The figures in this table are taken from the questionnaire which was filled out by the National Statistical Service of Greece (NSSG) and sent to the ECB.

[123] The supplementary tables for the year 2007 can be found in the appendix of this survey.

Table 31: Supplementary table Greece 2006 PBO
(in bn. EUR)

				Non-core national accounts (figures in bn. EUR)	
				General Government	Social Security
				G	H
			Opening Balance Sheet		
		1	Pension entitlements		458.29
			Changes in pension entitlements due to transactions		
Sum 2.1 to 2.4		2	Increase in pension entitlements due to social contributions		40.93
	2.1		*Employer actual social contributions*		8.28
	2.2		*Employer imputed social contributions*		
	2 3		*Household actual social contributions*		8.90
	2 4		*Household social contribution supplements*		23.76
	3		Other (actuarial) increase of pension entitlements		11.10
	4		Reduction in pension entitlements due to payment of pension benefits		18.37
2 + 3 - 4		5	Change in pension entitlements due to social contributions and pension benefits		33.66
	6		Transfers of entitlements between schemes		0.00
	7		Changes in pension entitlements due to other transactions		0.00
			Changes in pension entitlements due to other economic flows		
	8		Changes in entitlements due to revaluations		0.00
	9		Changes in entitlements due to other changes in volume		0.00
			Closing Balance Sheet		
		10	Pension entitlements		491.95
			Pension entitlements (% of GDP 2006)		230.74
		11	Output		
		12	Assets held at the end of the period to meet pensions		

Source: Own calculations

The opening balance of the social security scheme shows pension entitlements of 458.29 bn. EUR. These are increased by social contributions to the amount of 40.93 bn. EUR and decreased by the payment of pension benefits in 2006 adding up to 18.37 bn. EUR. Row 3 as the residual shows an increase of 11.10 bn. EUR of entitlements. In total the change in pension entitlements (row 5) accounts for 33.66 bn. EUR which leads to a closing balance of 491.95 bn. EUR, corresponding to nearly 231 per cent of the Greek GDP in 2006.

The following Table 32 demonstrates the outcomes of our calculations using the ABO approach. As expected, pension liabilities turn out to be considerably lower. The opening balance shows entitlements adding up to 430.31 bn. EUR. Social contributions increase these entitlements by 39.51 bn. EUR; pension benefits paid out in 2006 reduce them to 18.37 bn. EUR. The residual in row 3 shows an increase of 11.79 bn. EUR, the total change of pension entitlements amounts to 18.37 bn. EUR. This leads to a closing balance of 463.24 bn. EUR of pension entitlements which corresponds to around 217 per cent of GDP in 2006. Compared to the closing balance of 2006 using the PBO approach, the pension entitlements are around 13 per cent of GDP less using ABO

Table 32: Supplementary table Greece 2006 ABO
(in bn. EUR)

			Non-core national accounts (figures in bn. EUR)	
			General Government	Social Security
			G	H
		Opening Balance Sheet		
	1	Pension entitlements		*430.31*
		Changes in pension entitlements due to transactions		
Sum 2.1 to 2.4	2	**Increase in pension entitlements due to social contributions**		*39.51*
	2.1	*Employer actual social contributions*		8.28
	2.2	*Employer imputed social contributions*		▓▓▓▓▓
	2.3	*Household actual social contributions*		8.90
	2.4	*Household social contribution supplements*		22.34
	3	Other (actuarial) increase of pension entitlements		*11.79*
	4	Reduction in pension entitlements due to payment of pension benefits		18.37
2 + 3 - 4	5	**Change in pension entitlements due to social contributions and pension benefits**		*32.93*
	6	Transfers of entitlements between schemes		*0.00*
	7	Changes in pension entitlements due to other transactions		*0.00*
		Changes in pension entitlements due to other economic flows		
	8	Changes in entitlements due to revaluations		*0.00*
	9	Changes in entitlements due to other changes in volume		*0.00*
		Closing Balance Sheet		
	10	Pension entitlements		*463.24*
		Pension entitlements (% of GDP 2006)		*217.27*
	11	Output		
	12	Assets held at the end of the period to meet pensions		

Source: Own calculations

3.9   HU – Hungary

Hungary has a population of 10.07 million inhabitants.[124] The Hungarian economy has made a positive transition from a centrally planned system to a market based economy. The private sector accounts for over 80 per cent of GDP. The accession to the European Union in May 2004 further boosted trade in particular and the economy altogether. The Hungarian Forint (HUF)[125] is the currency of Hungary – however, the Hungarian government has expressed its will to join the Euro Currency Area. This is not expected to happen before 2012 since Hungary currently fails to meet the Maastricht criteria. Hungary's GDP in 2006 amounted to 23,785.2 bn. HUF which corresponds to 90.0 bn. EUR; the per capita GDP added up to 8,900 EUR. The Hungarian labour force boasts only 4.21 million people due to one of the lowest labour force participation rates of the OECD. With just 57 per cent of the employable population participating in the economy this figure is well below the EU 25 average (63.8 per cent) as well as below the EU 15 average (65.2 per cent). The unemployment rate shows that 7.4 per cent of the workforce is unemployed.

3.9.1   The demographic development in Hungary

Hungarian's demographic history can be characterized by relatively high fertility rates which have decreased considerably since the mid-1990s, and special developments after the Hungarian Revolution of 1956. Figure 24 shows the age-specific population structure in 2006.

The first focus is on the relatively small sized cohorts around the age of 40 to 45 years in 2006. This phenomenon can be explained by looking at the political situation in Hungary 50 years ago. After the Hungarian Revolution which was defeated by Soviet troops, many young Hungarians fled. This migration pattern resulted in smaller cohort sizes and lowered the number of births at that time. Furthermore, the ones who stayed most probably faced an uncertain future; thus the relatively small cohort size can be explained by migration and declining fertility rates around the year of 1956.

---

[124] Figure as at January 1st, 2006. We display country data for 2006 since this is a main base year for our calculations.

[125] The exchange rate of the Hungarian forint to the Euro is 251.77 as per December 29th, 2006.

Figure 24: Population structure in Hungary (2006)
age groups 0 to 100 years

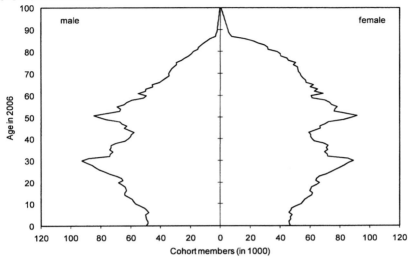

Source: Own calculations based on Eurostat (2009)

As can be seen in Figure 24 numbers of births recovered quite rapidly which can be ascribed to big cohort sizes of potential mothers (cohorts aged 50 to 55 in 2006) and increasing fertility rates. After increases in cohort size up to the age of around 30, cohorts start to decrease once more which can again be traced back to smaller numbers of potential mothers (cohorts aged around 40 to 45). The exiguous fertility rate observed since the mid-1990s which goes down to 1.3 children per woman can be identified at the age groups of zero to 15 years.

As with all other countries examined in this survey, life expectancy in Hungary is expected to undergo a considerable increase in the future. According to official statistics, a Hungarian male (female) born 2006 can expect to live 69.2 (77.8) years. This expectation is assumed to rise to 78.1 (83.4) years for persons born in 2050. Figure 25 illustrates the consequences of this development:

107

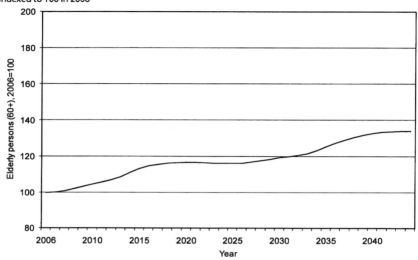

Figure 25: Development of elderly persons (aged 60+) in Hungary
indexed to 100 in 2006

Source: Own calculations based on Eurostat (2009)

It should be noted that the numerical rise of elderly persons turns out not as extreme as seen in other countries examined in this survey. After an increase of elderly persons between the years of 2006 and 2015, this number stays more or less constant until 2030. This is due to the fact that between 2015 and 2030 less persons than before enter the age group of "60+" (compare age groups 30 to 50 in Figure 24). After 2030 their number begins to rise slowly again – however, in comparison to other countries, the increase in life expectancy does not seem to have a huge impact on the number of elderly persons.

3.9.2 The Hungarian pension system

3.9.2.1 The principles of the Hungarian pension system

The Hungarian pension system has a three pillar structure. The first pillar is the public pension provision, the second pillar the mandatory private pension and the third pillar is the voluntary private provision. This current pension system was created during the pension reform of 1998. The old pension system, entirely designed as a PAYG scheme is still available for workers who joined the labour market prior to the reform, new entrants are automatically enrolled into the new scheme. The new scheme diverts some eight per cent of pensionable earnings to private pension funds while 18 per cent are used to finance the PAYG element of the public pension system.

The statutory retirement age for men has been raised from 60 to 62 and will reach the same level for women by 2009. Furthermore, a minimum of 20 years of service is required for both the minimum pension and the earnings-based pension. Compared with the old scheme, the new mixed pension system has a lower accrual rate of earnings. The rate has fallen from 1.65 per cent to 1.22 per cent of earnings each year of service. The earnings base is being expanded to cover the whole work life – however, currently income only since 1988 is being accounted for. In addition, a maximum has been set to pensionable earnings, and pension payments are indexed half to the development of nominal wages and half to that of prices.

Early retirement regulations will also be tightened. Currently, early retirement is possible for men at age 60 and for women at age 57. This age limit will be equalised to 59 years for both men and women in 2009. The early retirement age will then gradually increase to 60 until 2013. Also, from that year on, the pension base will be shifted from net to gross earnings while pensions will be made subject to taxation.

3.9.2.2 Recent reforms of the Hungarian pension system

In November 2006 the Hungarian government decided a pension reform which reduces all pensions paid out first after July 1st, 2008 (primary pensions) by nine per cent compared to the legal status before.

3.9.3 Measuring the Hungarian accrued-to-date pension liabilities

As with the pension system in the Czech Republic, there is no special pension scheme for civil servants in Hungary. Therefore only the social security pension scheme as the first pillar of the pension system in Hungary is subject to our calculations.

Table 33 displays the amounts of different types of pension benefits paid in 2005, 2006 and 2007.[126]

---

[126] Unfortunately no further breakdown was given for the year 2007.

Table 33: Social security pension payments Hungary
(in bn. HUF)

Type of pension	Pension payments		
	2005	2006	2007
Old age pensions	1,407.71	1,555.69	
Disability pensions	572.48	617.64	
Survivor pensions	131.70	141.17	
Total	2,111.89	2,314.50	2,520.00

Source: Magyar Nemzeti Bank (2008)

Applying the pension payments mentioned above to the Freiburg model, the following results are generated for the year 2006, starting with the PBO approach in Table 34: [127]

Table 34: Supplementary table Hungary 2006 PBO
(in bn. HUF)

				Non-core national accounts (figures in bn. HUF)	
				General Government	Social Security
				G	H
			Opening Balance Sheet		
		1	Pension entitlements		58,815.52
			Changes in pension entitlements due to transactions		
Sum 2.1 to 2.4		2	Increase in pension entitlements due to social contributions		4,514.29
		2.1	Employer actual social contributions		1,186.00
		2.2	Employer imputed social contributions		■
		2.3	Household actual social contributions		327.00
		2.4	Household social contribution supplements		3,001.29
		3	Other (actuarial) increase of pension entitlements	■	3,464.85
		4	Reduction in pension entitlements due to payment of pension benefits		2,314.50
2 + 3 - 4		5	Change in pension entitlements due to social contributions and pension benefits		5,664.65
		6	Transfers of entitlements between schemes		0.00
		7	Changes in pension entitlements due to other transactions		-3,243.94
			Changes in pension entitlements due to other economic flows		
		8	Changes in entitlements due to revaluations		0.00
		9	Changes in entitlements due to other changes in volume		0.00
			Closing Balance Sheet		
		10	Pension entitlements		61,236.23
			Pension entitlements (% of GDP 2006)		257.46
		11	Output		
		12	Assets held at the end of the period to meet pensions		

Source: Own calculations

---

[127] The supplementary tables for the year 2007 can be found in the appendix of this survey.

Pension entitlements in the beginning of 2006 add up to 58,815.52 bn. HUF. They are increased by social contributions (4,514.29 bn. HUF), and decreased by pensions paid in 2006 (2,314.50 bn. HUF). Row 7 presents the effect of the pension reform for new pensions described above; this reform causes a decrease in entitlements of 3,243.94 bn. HUF.[128] The final pension entitlements then amount to 61,236.23 bn. HUF, equal to roughly 257 per cent of GDP in 2006. The same calculations have been conducted using the ABO approach. The respective results are shown in Table 35:

Table 35: Supplementary table Hungary 2006 ABO
(in bn. HUF)

			Non-core national accounts (figures in bn. HUF)	
			General Government	Social Security
			G	H
		Opening Balance Sheet		
	1	Pension entitlements		50,604.97
		Changes in pension entitlements due to transactions		
Sum 2.1 to 2.4	2	Increase in pension entitlements due to social contributions		4,104.80
	2.1	Employer actual social contributions		1,186.00
	2.2	Employer imputed social contributions		
	2.3	Household actual social contributions		327.00
	2.4	Household social contribution supplements		2,591.80
	3	Other (actuarial) increase of pension entitlements		3,108.34
	4	Reduction in pension entitlements due to payment of pension benefits		2,314.50
2 + 3 - 4	5	Change in pension entitlements due to social contributions and pension benefits		4,898.64
	6	Transfers of entitlements between schemes		0.00
	7	Changes in pension entitlements due to other transactions		-2,436.77
		Changes in pension entitlements due to other economic flows		
	8	Changes in entitlements due to revaluations		0.00
	9	Changes in entitlements due to other changes in volume		0.00
		Closing Balance Sheet		
	10	Pension entitlements		53,066.85
		Pension entitlements (% of GDP 2006)		223.11
	11	Output		
	12	Assets held at the end of the period to meet pensions		

Source: Own calculations

Similar to the calculations of other pension schemes before, results using the ABO approach are considerably lower. This holds for the opening pension entitlements adding up to 50,604.97 bn. HUF, the social contributions amounting 4,104.80 bn. HUF, and the other (actuarial) increase of pension entitlements showing 3,108.34 bn. HUF. Especially the changes due to other transactions in row 7

---

[128] It is worth mentioning that this effect would also have taken place if the pension reform had been decided earlier than 2006. In that case, the impact would have been integrated in the opening balance, and no extra entry would have been made.

show a big difference to the ones under PBO approach (almost 25 per cent less). This is due to the fact that the pension reform only influences new pensions – these can vary quite heavily under the different approaches accounting for benefit obligations.

The closing balance of pension entitlements adds up to 53,066.85 bn. HUF, equal to some 223 per cent of GDP in 2006. This represents a decrease of nearly 14 per cent compared to the PBO approach.

3.10 IT – Italy

Italy currently has the fourth largest population in the European Union. It adds up to 58.75 million inhabitants as of January 1st, 2006.[129] The economy of Italy remains divided into a developed industrial North, dominated by private companies, and a less developed agricultural South. Unemployment has been steadily decreasing (6.7 per cent in 2007, its lowest level since 1992) but is severe in the South, where the unemployment rate partly exceeds 20 per cent. Women and youth show significantly higher rates of unemployment than men. The GDP in 2006 accounted for 1,480.0 bn. EUR, corresponding to a per capita GDP of 25,100 EUR.

3.10.1 The demographic development in Italy

Similar to many other Western European countries, Italy has experienced considerable changes in terms of fertility in the last 40 years. In 1965, the fertility rate amounted to more than 2.5 births per woman. The sudden drop in birth rates in most industrialized countries at the end of the 1960s (also referred to as the baby bust) took place only in a weakened form. Until 1977 the fertility rate stayed close to replacement level. Since that date the birth rates decreased more rapidly until they reached a minimum of only 1.19 births per woman in 1996. Today an average woman in Italy gives birth to 1.32 children, which represents one of the lowest fertility rates in Europe. Figure 26 demonstrates the population structure in Italy as at January 1st, 2006.

The figure shows a numerical peak around the age cohort of 40 years. These cohorts are often referred to as the baby boom generation being born in the mid of the 1960s. Not surprisingly, the younger age cohorts are numerically smaller due to decreasing birth rates. The age cohorts from zero to ten years seem to recover from that decline. However, this can be explained by the size of the baby boom generation who represent the fertile cohorts in question.

---

[129] We display country data for 2006 since this is a main base year for our calculations.

Figure 26: Population structure in Italy (2006)
age groups 0 to 100 years

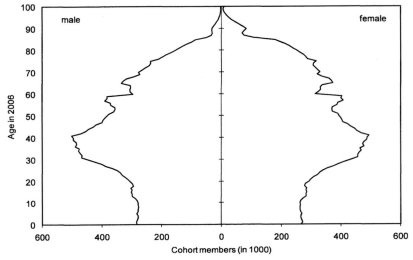

Source: Own calculations based on Eurostat (2009)

Following the general development in Western civilization, Italy has undergone considerable increases in life expectancy in the last 50 years. A male (female) person born in 2004 can expect to reach an age of 77.9 (83.8) years on average. This life expectancy is even assumed to rise further to 83.6 for men and 88.8 for women born in the year 2050. Figure 27 illustrates the numerical development of elderly persons in Italy between 2006 and 2045. This development has a strong influence on the magnitude of Italian pension liabilities.

From the perspective of 2006, the number of elderly persons is expected to grow continuously but on a rather modest path, compared to other members of the EU. In 2020, there will be around 20 per cent more representatives of this age group; in 2040 this number will have increased by close to 40 per cent in relation to 2006.

Figure 27: Development of elderly persons (aged 60+) in Italy
indexed to 100 in 2006

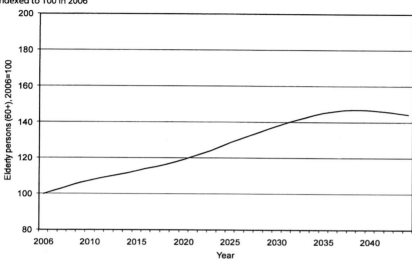

Source: Own calculations based on Eurostat (2009)

3.10.2 The Italian pension system

3.10.2.1 The principles of the Italian pension system

As a result of the reform enacted in 1995, the Italian pension system is moving gradually to a new regime applied to all labour market entrants after December 31st, 1995. The new regime will be fully phased in after 2030-2035. Meanwhile, there will be a transition period which only affects workers already employed at the end of 1995. In particular, two different calculation methods will be used depending on the years of contribution at the cut-off date. Workers with at least 18 years of contribution at the end of 1995 will maintain the earnings-related method. A so-called pro-rata, mixed regime will be applied to workers with less than 18 years of contribution at the end of 1995. Accordingly, the pension is obtained as a sum of two components: the first one, related to the contribution years before 1995, is calculated following the earnings-related method with reference wages, for the contribution years between 1993 and 1995, gradually extended to the entire career; the second one is calculated according to the contribution-based method. The 1995 reform led to a shift of the method of benefit calculation from a PAYG and defined-benefit system, to a notional defined contribution (NDC) system.

A national agreement between the Italian government and trade unions, signed in March 1997, has established harmonised rules for almost all employment in the public and private sector. Under the earnings-related and mixed regimes (workers already insured as of 1995) the age requirement to an old age pension is 65 for men and 60 for women jointly with a minimum contribution period of 20 years for males and females. Before 1992, the minimum retirement ages were, respectively, 60 and 55 for the private sector employees and the minimum contribution period was 15 years.

Under the contribution-based regime (new entrants into the system after 1995) for males, the possibility to receive a pension at an age lower than 65 is allowed to those with 40 or more years of contributions, or to those with no less than 35 years of contributions and of 60 years of age, for the employed, and 61 years for the self-employed. The age limit is to rise by a year from 2010 and another year from 2014, thus reaching 62 and 63 respectively. For females, the possibility to receive a pension is allowed at 60 with five years of contribution or, alternatively, with 40 or more years of contributions regardless of the age.

The indexation rules for pensions after retirement are the following: The indexation is 100 per cent of the inflation rate for the part of pension up to three times the minimum pension, 90 per cent for the part between three and five times the minimum, and 75 per cent for the part above five times the minimum.[130, 131]

3.10.2.2 Recent reforms of the Italian pension system

To ensure fiscal consolidation and long-term fiscal sustainability, a pension reform process was started in Italy at the beginning of the 1990s. After cutting down a quarter of the prospective public sector pension liabilities with the pension reform in 1992, a major reform was passed in 1995 introducing NDC in the PAYG pension pillar. This reform was in many ways similar to the one in Sweden which was undertaken in 1994. The Italian NDC pension reform has been described in the previous chapter.[132]

---

[130] Due to lack of more detailed information we assume an indexation of 100 per cent of inflation for all pensions.

[131] A short summary on the public pension system in Italy can be found in OECD (2007), p. 142 et sqq. For an extensive description of the pension system see European Commission (2007), p. 161 et sqq.

[132] For further details of the Italian NDC pension reform, see Franco and Sartor (2006).

116

In 2004, the Law 243/2004 envisaged two main interventions to the public pension system: one with short-term effects and one with structural effects noticeable in the medium-long term. The main short-term effects were incentives to put off retiring. In the medium-long term alterations to the requirements for pension entitlements have been made, e.g. the increase of the age limit by a year from 2010 and another year from 2014.

3.10.3 Measuring the Italian accrued-to-date pension liabilities

Unlike most other countries, additional data sources had to be used in the case of the micro pension profiles for the Italian pension system. We calculated a pension profile which is based on the survey on household income and wealth (SHIW) 2006.[133] This pension profile can be found in the appendix of this survey.

For our calculations we used budget data from three different social security pension schemes. These are the employees social security pensions, the professional workers social security pensions, and the other self-employed than professional workers social security pensions. These three schemes have been combined in Table 36, showing the social security pension payments for 2005 and 2006 in Italy.[134]

Table 36: Social security pension payments Italy
(in bn. EUR)

Type of pension	Pension payments	
	2005	2006
Old age pensions	166.07	174.78
Disability pensions	2.92	3.02
Survivor pensions	5.72	5.74
Total	174.71	183.54

Source: Statistics Italy (2008)

In 2005, social security pension payments come up to 12.2 per cent of GDP in Italy; in 2006 they aggregate to 12.4 per cent of the respective GDP. This share belongs to the highest in Europe. The government employer pension payments of 2005 and 2006 are summed up in Table 37:

---

[133] See Bank of Italy (2006).

[134] No data was given for the year 2007.

Table 37: Government employer pension payments Italy
(in bn. EUR)

Type of pension	Pension payments	
	2005	2006
Old age pensions	0.52	0.57
Disability pensions	0.01	0.01
Survivor pensions	0.01	0.01
Total	**0.54**	**0.59**

Source: Statistics Italy (2008)

It is worth mentioning that government employer pension payments seem to be considerably low. They amount to only 0.4 per cent of GDP in 2005 and 2006. Obviously, the pension scheme in question applies to a special, rather small group of civil servants in Italy only.

Employing the above listed pension expenditures on the methodology of the Freiburg model, the following outcomes are generated which are displayed in Table 38. Similar to the previous chapters, we start by applying the PBO approach.

Table 38: Supplementary table Italy 2006 PBO
(in bn. EUR)

			Non-core national accounts (figures in bn. EUR)	
			General Government	Social Security
			G	H
		Opening Balance Sheet		
	1	Pension entitlements	13.92	4,503.52
		Changes in pension entitlements due to transactions		
Sum 2.1 to 2.4	2	Increase in pension entitlements due to social contributions	2.04	367.48
	2 1	*Employer actual social contributions*		102.87
	2 2	*Employer imputed social contributions*	1.19	
	2.3	*Household actual social contributions*	0.12	32.87
	2 4	*Household social contribution supplements*	0.73	231.74
	3	Other (actuarial) increase of pension entitlements		78.49
	4	Reduction in pension entitlements due to payment of pension benefits	0.59	183.54
2 + 3 - 4	5	Change in pension entitlements due to social contributions and pension benefits	1.45	262.43
	6	Transfers of entitlements between schemes	0.00	0.00
	7	Changes in pension entitlements due to other transactions	0.00	0.00
		Changes in pension entitlements due to other economic flows		
	8	Changes in entitlements due to revaluations	0.00	0.00
	9	Changes in entitlements due to other changes in volume	0.00	0.00
		Closing Balance Sheet		
	10	Pension entitlements	15.37	4,765.95
		Pension entitlements (% of GDP 2006)	1.04	322.03
	11	Output		
	12	Assets held at the end of the period to meet pensions		

Source: Own calculations

As expected the pension entitlements of the government employer scheme turn out to be relatively small. The opening balance shows entitlements of 13.92 bn. EUR. These are increased by social contributions accounting for 2.04 bn. EUR and decreased by pension benefits amounting 0.59 bn. EUR. The closing balance presents entitlements adding up to 15.37 bn. EUR, which is equivalent to only one per cent of the GDP in 2006. These minor entitlements can be ascribed to the low pension benefits paid out in the base year (see Table 37).

The outcomes of the social security pension scheme are of much bigger dimensions. Opening pension entitlements in column H display 4,503.52 bn. EUR, which are increased by social contributions adding up to 367.48 bn. EUR and decreased by pension benefits amounting to 183.54 bn. EUR. The final pension entitlements of 2006 add up to 4,765.95 bn. EUR which corresponds to around 322 per cent of Italy's GDP in 2006. The analogical figures for the ABO approach are shown in Table 39:

Table 39: Supplementary table Italy 2006 ABO
(in bn. EUR)

			Non-core national accounts (figures in bn. EUR)	
			General Government	Social Security
			G	H
		Opening Balance Sheet		
	1	Pension entitlements	**12.90**	**4,175.50**
		Changes in pension entitlements due to transactions		
Sum 2.1 to 2.4	2	Increase in pension entitlements due to social contributions	**1.94**	**350.63**
	2 1	*Employer actual social contributions*	0.00	102.87
	2 2	*Employer imputed social contributions*	1.14	
	2 3	*Household actual social contributions*	0.12	32.87
	2 4	*Household social contribution supplements*	0.68	214.89
	3	Other (actuarial) increase of pension entitlements		77.48
	4	Reduction in pension entitlements due to payment of pension benefits	0.59	183.54
2 + 3 - 4	5	Change in pension entitlements due to social contributions and pension benefits	1.35	244.58
	6	Transfers of entitlements between schemes		0.00
	7	Changes in pension entitlements due to other transactions		0.00
		Changes in pension entitlements due to other economic flows		
	8	Changes in entitlements due to revaluations	0.00	0.00
	9	Changes in entitlements due to other changes in volume	0.00	0.00
		Closing Balance Sheet		
	10	Pension entitlements	14.25	4,420.08
		Pension entitlements (% of GDP 2006)	0.96	298.66
	11	Output		
	12	Assets held at the end of the period to meet pensions		

Source: Own calculations

Placing emphasis on the social security pension scheme in column H the opening balance amounts to 4,175.50 bn. EUR. The total social contributions account for 350.63 bn. EUR in the ABO case, as a matter of course pension benefits remain at

183.54 bn. EUR. The closing balance of 2006 displays pension entitlements adding up to 4,420.08 bn. EUR, corresponding to nearly 299 per cent of GDP in 2006. In relation to the PBO outcome, the ABO result turns out to be around seven per cent lower (23 percentage points of GDP).

3.11 LT – Lithuania[135]

Lithuania – the biggest Baltic country – has 3.40 million inhabitants.[136] After the fall of the iron curtain it has made a positive transition from a centrally planned system to a market based economy. In the course of EU-accession in January 2004 Lithuania experienced a boost in the trade and tourism sector and considerably high economic growth rates. The currency of Lithuania is the Litas (LTL).[137] After Lithuania only narrowly missed qualifying for membership in the Euro zone in 2006, it is expected to join the Euro currency area in the coming years. Lithuania's GDP in 2006 amounted to 82.8 bn. LTL, corresponding to 24.0 bn. EUR. The respective per capita GDP added up to 7,050 EUR.

3.11.1 The demographic development in Lithuania

With declining fertility rates and rises in life expectancy the Lithuanian demography follows the same trend as the rest of Europe. However, comparing the absolute numbers of fertility and life expectancy with the rest of the EU, Lithuania is not representing the European average. Not only is the total fertility rate of 1.31 beyond the EU-average, but life expectancy is much lower than in the majority of the EU countries. According to Eurostat a male (female) Lithuanian born in 2006 can expect to live for 65.3 (77) years. This value is expected to increase further until 2050 to 75.5 (83.7) for men (women).[138] Both factors – life expectancy and fertility – have a significant effect on the age specific population structure shown in Figure 28.

As can be observed in most former Soviet republics, the population structure is characterized by a large gap between male and female mortality as well as life expectancy rates resulting in the asymmetric form at older ages in Figure 28. Sharply decreased fertility rates in the last 15 years are also reflected in the population structure which as a result resembles a tree cut down half way. It is worth mentioning that this demographic decline, which occurred in post-communist countries in the late 1980s and early 1990s, started in Lithuania slightly

---

[135] We would like to thank Tomas Paulauskas from Statistics Lithuania for valuable comments on this chapter.

[136] Figure as at January 1st, 2006. We display country data for 2006 since this is a main base year for our calculations.

[137] The exchange rate is 3.4528 LTL to the Euro as per December 29th, 2006.

[138] These figures are based on the estimation of Eurostat given in Europop 2004.

121

later in the middle of the 1990s. The tree gets thicker in the age groups 20 to 50 years old.

Figure 28: Population structure in Lithuania (2006)
age groups 0 to 100 years

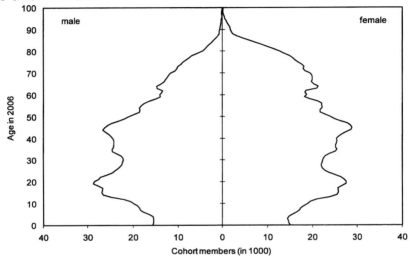

Source: Own calculations based on Eurostat (2009)

The large cohort sizes of these age groups can also be explained by looking back in the history of Lithuania. During the birth years of these cohorts, starting in the end of the 1950s and ending in the 1980s, Lithuania experienced a swift industrialization and urbanization accompanied with lower mortality rates and high fertility rates of a value above two. These well represented cohorts aged 30-50 years will not reach the retirement age in the coming decade. Therefore the number of elderly people aged 60 years and older does not change significantly in the next ten years – as illustrated in Figure 29. This development is of major importance for the calculation of the ADL, since pension payments in the closer future – which are mainly paid to people aged 60 and older – have the biggest impact on our calculations.

From 2015 until 2045 the number of elderly people will increase by about 35 per cent. This enhancement is on the one hand caused by the rise in life expectancy and on the other hand by the above mentioned large cohorts entering the retirement age. This augmentation of elderly people in Lithuania turns out to be not as substantial as observed in most other EU countries.

Figure 29: Development of elderly persons (aged 60+) in Lithuania
indexed to 100 in 2006

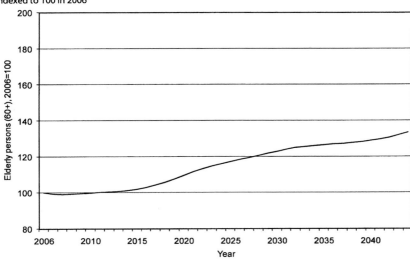

Source: Own calculations based on Eurostat (2009)

3.11.2 The Lithuanian pension system

3.11.2.1 The principles of the Lithuanian pension system

As in most industrialized countries the Lithuanian pension system pursues a mixed strategy between PAYG and funded pension schemes. It is based on a three pillar system. The dominating first pillar is mandatory and designed as a PAYG pension system. In 2006, the legal basis for the second pillar, the occupational pension schemes, has been introduced. The third pillar consists of voluntary supplementary pension savings and life insurances. Within the mandatory publicly run first pillar, private sector workers and employees of the public sector dispose of different pension schemes. While the social insurance system is universal and covers both public and private employment, some groups of public employees have their own distinct pension arrangements as a supplement. Due to its broad coverage of the Lithuanian population we first take a closer look on the social insurance pension system. It is composed of old age, disability as well as survivor pensions. Old age and disability pensions consist of two parts: the basic and the supplementary pension. While the basic pension only depends on the length of the social insurance period the supplementary pension is determined by additional factors. These include the accrual rate, the length of the social insurance period, the individual wage coefficient (a ratio between person's monthly earnings and the state insured income) as well as the state insured income of the respective period. Benefits of the supplementary pension in Lithuania are therefore to a greater extent linked to past contributions. The present legal retirement age is 60 (62.5) years for women (men) – having been gradually increased in recent years. After reaching the retirement age, a person can continue to work and receive his/her earnings from work together with the old age pension. If one chooses to retire after (before) the legal retirement age, the pension will be increased (reduced) by 0.67 (0.4) per cent for every month. Looking at the indexation of pensions, the basic pension is increased upon decision of the government. The supplementary part of a pension is adjusted according to current year's average insured income.[139]

The state pension scheme works independently from the social insurance pension system. It is financed by the state budget and awarded to officials and military personnel, judges, scientists, persons for distinguished achievements for the state (1st and 2nd degree) as well as for victims and deprived persons. Furthermore, the state pensions consist of the so-called social assistance state pensions which are paid to persons who do not have a sufficient social insurance record.

3.11.2.2 Recent reforms of the Lithuanian pension system

As most European countries Lithuania is challenged by an ageing society; therefore it underwent major pension reforms in recent years. With the pension reform starting in 1995, statutory retirement ages have been considerably increased in Lithuania. More precisely, women's (men's) legal retirement age gradually rose from 55 (60) in 1995 to 60 (62.5) in 2006.

Another major reform was initiated in 2004. Its cornerstone was the establishment of the funded tier of the public pension system. Accordingly, a person insured for the full pension insurance (including basic and supplementary pensions) may choose to switch to the funded tier. This implies that he/she directs a part of social insurance contributions, dedicated for the supplementary part of the old age pension, to a personal account in a chosen privately managed pension fund. The part of the contributions directed to private pension funds was the following: 2.5 (2004), 3.5 (2005), 4.5 (2006) and 5.5 percentage points of total 26 per cent paid for the pension insurance in 2007. For our calculations it is important to notice that the

---

[139] Since we have no information about the future indexation of basic pensions – because it is indexed ad hoc by the government – we have to make the following assumption: For our calculations we presume that full pensions (basic and supplementary pensions) are indexed to 70 per cent by the growth of the insured income and to 30 per cent according to the CPI.

supplementary part of the social insurance old age pension is reduced respectively. In the long run this reform will have a substantial impact on the pension system. However, taking the year 2006 as the base year of our calculations, this reform plays only a minor role since most of pension entitlements have been accrued under the pre-reform system.

3.11.3 Measuring the Lithuanian accrued-to-date pension liabilities

The aim of our calculation is to quantify pension entitlements accrued-to-date which can be further differentiated into pension payments to present pensioners and to future pensioners. The current total pension expenditures represent an appropriate starting point for our calculations since they indicate how much is spent for present pensioners. Table 40 displays the aggregated pension benefits of the two pension schemes in Lithuania – social security and state pensions.

Table 40: Social security and government employer pension payments Lithuania (in million EUR)

Type of pension	Pension payments		
	2005	2006	2007
Social security pensions	1,278.09	1,439.40	2,071.83
Old age pensions	917.54	1,037.27	1,511.48
Disability pensions	285.66	325.40	446.79
Survivor pensions	74.89	76.73	113.56
State pensions	110.41	118.00	137.56
Total	1,388.50	1,557.40	2,209.39

Source: Statistics Lithuania (2008)

Table 40 illustrates that total pension expenditures in Lithuania amounted to 1.56 bn. EUR in 2006, which corresponds to 6.5 per cent of GDP. In comparison to most other European countries these pension expenditures are relatively small. Therefore, one could assume that the Lithuanian ADL are comparably small as well. This is only a presumption since other factors such as the demographic development, the indexation of future pensions as well as recent pension reforms can have significant impacts on the ADL results. With   Table 41 we want to take a look at the actual outcomes for the year 2006, applying the PBO approach first.[140]

---

[140] The supplementary tables for the year 2007 can be found in the appendix of this survey.

Table 41: Supplementary table Lithuania 2006 PBO
(in bn. EUR)

				Non-core national accounts (figures in bn. EUR)	
				General Government	Social Security
				G	H
			Opening Balance Sheet		
		1	Pension entitlements	**3.25**	**35.68**
			Changes in pension entitlements due to transactions		
Sum 2.1 to 2.4		2	**Increase in pension entitlements due to social contributions**	**0.33**	**3.56**
		2.1	*Employer actual social contributions*		1.51
		2.2	*Employer imputed social contributions*	0.16	
		2.3	*Household actual social contributions*		0.16
		2.4	*Household social contribution supplements*	0.17	1.89
		3	Other (actuarial) increase of pension entitlements		2.23
		4	Reduction in pension entitlements due to payment of pension benefits	0.12	1.44
2 + 3 - 4		5	Change in pension entitlements due to social contributions and pension benefits	0.21	4.35
		6	Transfers of entitlements between schemes	0.00	0.00
		7	Changes in pension entitlements due to other transactions	0.00	0.00
			Changes in pension entitlements due to other economic flows		
		8	Changes in entitlements due to revaluations	0.00	0.00
		9	Changes in entitlements due to other changes in volume	0.00	0.00
			Closing Balance Sheet		
		10	Pension entitlements	3.46	40.03
			Pension entitlements (% of GDP 2006)	14.44	166.92
		11	Output		
		12	Assets held at the end of the period to meet pensions		

Source: Own calculations

Starting with the social security pension scheme (in column H) entitlements add up to 35.68 bn. EUR in the beginning of 2006. On the one hand this value decreases in 2006 by aggregated pension payments of 1.44 bn. EUR. On the other hand pension entitlements increase due to household social contributions supplements (1.89 bn. EUR) and other actuarial increases of pension entitlements (2.23 bn. EUR). At the end of 2006 final pension entitlements add up to 40.03 bn. EUR, equal to almost 167 per cent of GDP in 2006. Results for the state pensions are displayed in a similar manner in column G. Adding social contributions (0.33 bn. EUR) to and subtracting pension payments (0.12 bn. EUR) from the opening balance (3.25 bn. EUR) result in final entitlements of the state pensions (3.46 bn. EUR) which is equal to around 14 per cent of GDP in 2006. As expected, the level of total pension expenditures is relatively small in Lithuania compared to the other countries examined in this survey.

The same calculations have been conducted using the ABO approach. Since this method – in contrast to the PBO approach – does not take into account future wage growth, the results tend to be considerably smaller. Table 42 shows the respective outcomes.

Table 42: Supplementary table Lithuania 2006 ABO
(in bn. EUR)

				Non-core national accounts (figures in bn. EUR)	
				General Government	Social Security
				G	H
			Opening Balance Sheet		
		1	Pension entitlements	**2.83**	**31.21**
			Changes in pension entitlements due to transactions		
Sum 2.1 to 2.4		2	Increase in pension entitlements due to social contributions	**0.30**	**3.33**
		2.1	*Employer actual social contributions*		1.51
		2 2	*Employer imputed social contributions*	0.16	
		2.3	*Household actual social contributions*		0.16
		2.4	*Household social contribution supplements*	0.15	1.66
		3	Other (actuarial) increase of pension entitlements		1.91
		4	Reduction in pension entitlements due to payment of pension benefits	0.12	1.44
2 + 3 - 4		5	Change in pension entitlements due to social contributions and pension benefits	**0.18**	**3.79**
		6	Transfers of entitlements between schemes		0.00
		7	Changes in pension entitlements due to other transactions		0.00
			Changes in pension entitlements due to other economic flows		
		8	Changes in entitlements due to revaluations	**0.00**	**0.00**
		9	Changes in entitlements due to other changes in volume		0.00
			Closing Balance Sheet		
		10	Pension entitlements	**3.01**	**35.01**
			Pension entitlements (% of GDP 2006)	**12.55**	**145.98**
		11	Output		
		12	Assets held at the end of the period to meet pensions		

Source: Own calculations

The opening pension entitlements as well as the closing pension entitlements turn out to be about twelve per cent lower than the respective PBO results. Thus, the entitlements of the social security pension (state pension) scheme amount to 35.01 (3.01) bn. EUR at the end of 2006, corresponding to roughly 146 (13) per cent of GDP.

3.12 LV – Latvia

Latvia has a population of 2.29 million inhabitants.[141] The national currency is the Latvian Lats (LVL), the rate of exchange to the Euro comes to 0.6972 LVL.[142] The GDP in 2006 amounted to 11.2 bn. LVL which corresponds to 16.0 bn. EUR. The per capita GDP added up to 4,900 LVL or 7,000 EUR in 2006. Since the year 2000 Latvia has had one of the highest GDP growth rates in Europe. In 2006, annual GDP growth was 11.9 per cent and inflation was 6.2 per cent; unemployment rate added up to 8.5 per cent – almost unchanged compared to the previous two years. However, it has recently dropped to 6.1 per cent, partly due to active economic migration, mostly to Ireland and the United Kingdom. Latvia plans to introduce the Euro as the country's currency but, due to the high inflation rate not meeting the Maastricht criteria, this is not expected to happen before 2012.

3.12.1 The demographic development in Latvia

As most other Central- and East-European countries, Latvia faces a fertility rate well below replacement level (~ 2.1 children per woman). In 2006, the Latvian fertility rate showed a value of 1.35 children per woman. Figure 30 demonstrates the age-specific population structure of Latvia in 2006.

A strong reduction of births can be seen around the age cohorts of 15 to 20. This can most probably be ascribed to the times of Glasnost under Mikhail Gorbachev in the beginning of the 1990s, when Latvia gained its independence. The impact of unsecure political situations and changes on fertility rates can often be monitored; Latvia is another good example for this.[143]

Furthermore, the impact of World War II and the following Soviet occupation can especially be noticed at the age cohorts of around 60 which are much smaller than the ones above.

---

[141] Figure as at January 1st, 2006. We display country data for 2006 since this is a main base year for our calculations.

[142] Exchange rate as at December 29th, 2006.

[143] Compare the case of Lithuania in section 3.11.1 of this survey.

Figure 30: Population structure in Latvia (2006)
age groups 0 to 100 years

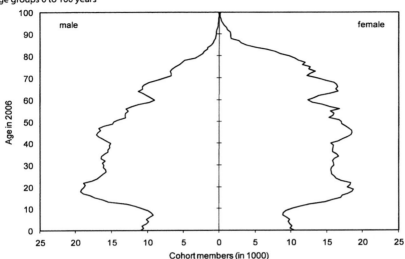

Source: Own calculations based on Eurostat (2009)

The life expectancy of Latvia is well below EU average. A male (female) born in 2006 can expect to reach an age of 65.4 (76.3) years. The difference between life expectancies of men and women is remarkable. It amounts to almost eleven years, whereas in countries like Germany a difference of less than six years can be observed. Life expectancy at birth in Latvia is assumed to rise up to 74.3 (82.5) until 2050 for males (females) which means that especially male life expectancy will undergo considerable growth. Figure 31 shows the numerical development of elderly persons in Latvia until 2050.

It turns out that – different from many European countries – the number of elderly people in Latvia will rise very slowly in the future. In the first years up to 2010, the number will even decrease slightly. Up to 2040, it will grow by less than 20 per cent compared to the base year 2006. As we will see later in this chapter, this development will have a dampening impact on the Latvian pension liabilities.

Figure 31: Development of elderly persons (aged 60+) in Latvia
indexed to 100 in 2006

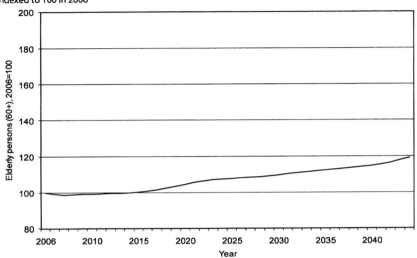

Source: Own calculations based on Eurostat (2009)

3.12.2 The Latvian pension system

3.12.2.1 The principles of the Latvian pension system

The pension system in general consists of a state pension scheme composed of an earnings-related pension financed on a PAYG basis through notional individual accounts (NDC), a fully funded, defined contribution mandatory pension scheme, and private voluntary occupational and individual pension arrangements.

Old age pensions are calculated by dividing the amount accumulated in the notional account (contributions uprated in line with the covered wage bill) by projected cohort unisex life expectancy at retirement (calculated annually using projected life expectancy at retirement age with a unisex life table). The average benefit is directly dependent on the actual pension age, number of years worked as well as dynamics of contribution base (growth of the contribution wage sum in Latvia), which determines the rate of return for the NDC pension capital. Pensions granted before 1996 were not revised according to the rules of the NDC scheme. The indexation of existing pensions is differentiated according to the amount of the pension. Small pensions are indexed considering the actual CPI and 50 per cent of the real growth of contribution wage sum. Other pensions are indexed with CPI.[144]

Benefits can be claimed at any time from the retirement age. The transition to the retirement age of 62 is carried out on a step-by-step basis, i.e. by six months each year. Men have already reached the retirement age of 62 since 2003, but women will reach it in 2008. In 2006, legal retirement age for women was 61 years. Up to mid-2008 (early retirement will be eliminated after this date), the legislation provides for a possibility to retire two years before the age of 62 for men and two years before the increasing schedule to 62 for women, if persons insurance record is 30 years or more. In 2003, the average age of retirement was 61.1 for men and 57.7 for women.

3.12.2.2 Recent reforms of the Latvian pension system

In 1995, Latvia was the first country in Central and Eastern Europe to legislate a NDC reform.[145] The reform consists of two components: The non-financial defined contribution (NDC) part was implemented on January 1st, 1996; a financial defined contribution (FDC) part came into force on Juli 1st, 2001. People who reach the minimum pension age are guaranteed a minimum pension which is financed by revenues outside the overall contribution of 20 per cent. Rights acquired in the old scheme were converted to NDC capital.[146]

3.12.3 Measuring the Latvian accrued-to-date pension liabilities

The results of our calculations regarding the pension liabilities of the social security pension scheme in Latvia are based on the following pension expenditures from 2005, 2006 and 2007, which are shown in Table 43:

---

[144] Due to a lack of further information, we assumed an average indexation rate of CPI plus 25 per cent of wage growth.

[145] The functioning of the NDC system is described in the previous section. The idea of NDC originally goes back to Buchanan (1968).

[146] For a comprehensive description of the Latvian NDC pension system, see Palmer et al. (2006).

Table 43: Social security pension payments Latvia
(in million LVL)

Type of pension	Pension payments		
	2005	2006	2007
Old age pensions	465.95	567.46	654.23
Disability pensions	63.65	66.82	70.17
Survivor pensions	18.48	21.54	22.36
Total	548.08	655.82	746.76

Source: Latvijas Statistika (2008)

Naturally, the old age pension payments make up the biggest part of the pension expenditures in all three years. Expenditures sum up to a total of 548.081 million (m.) LVL in 2005, 655.823 m. LVL in 2006 and 746.759 m. LVL in 2007. Expressed as a fraction of the GDP in the respective years, pension payments add up to 6.0 per cent in 2005, 5.9 per cent in 2006 and 5.4 per cent in 2007. We will discover later in section 3.20 that these figures are rather small compared to other European countries. Table 44 contains the results of our calculations for the year 2006 using the PBO approach first. [147]

As Table 44 shows, the balance starts with pension entitlements of 11.42 bn. LVL. These entitlements are increased by social contributions of 2.27 bn. LVL and decreased by pension payments (row 4) of 0.66 bn. LVL. The residual shows an increase of pension entitlements amounting to 0.92 bn. LVL. The closing balance adds up to pension entitlements of 13.95 bn. LVL at the end of 2006, corresponding to nearly 125 per cent of GDP in 2006.

---

[147] The supplementary tables for the year 2007 can be found in the appendix of this survey.

Table 44: Supplementary table Latvia 2006 PBO
(in bn. LVL)

				Non-core national accounts (figures in bn. LVL)	
				General Government	Social Security
				G	H
			Opening Balance Sheet		
		1	Pension entitlements		**11.42**
			Changes in pension entitlements due to transactions		
Sum 2.1 to 2.4		2	Increase in pension entitlements due to social contributions		**2.27**
	2.1		*Employer actual social contributions*		1.64
	2.2		*Employer imputed social contributions*		▬
	2 3		*Household actual social contributions*		
	2.4		*Household social contribution supplements*		0.63
		3	Other (actuarial) increase of pension entitlements		0.92
		4	Reduction in pension entitlements due to payment of pension benefits		0.66
2 + 3 - 4		5	Change in pension entitlements due to social contributions and pension benefits		**2.53**
		6	Transfers of entitlements between schemes		*0.00*
		7	Changes in pension entitlements due to other transactions		*0.00*
			Changes in pension entitlements due to other economic flows		
		8	Changes in entitlements due to revaluations		*0.00*
		9	Changes in entitlements due to other changes in volume		*0.00*
			Closing Balance Sheet		
		10	Pension entitlements		*13.95*
			Pension entitlements (% of GDP 2006)		*124.86*
		11	Output		
		12	Assets held at the end of the period to meet pensions		

Source: Own calculations

The pension liabilities applying the ABO approach are shown in Table 45. The opening balance adds up to pension entitlements of 9.86 bn. LVL. Social contributions amount to 2.18 bn. LVL, pension benefits account for 0.66 bn. LVL. The total change in pension entitlements comes up to 2.13 bn. LVL which leads to the closing balance of 11.99 bn. LVL, equal to some 107 per cent of Latvia's GDP in 2006.

Accrued-to-date liabilities of 19 EU countries

Table 45: Supplementary table Latvia 2006 ABO
(in bn. LVL)

			Non-core national accounts (figures in bn. LVL)	
			General Government	Social Security
			G	H
		Opening Balance Sheet		
	1	Pension entitlements		*9.86*
		Changes in pension entitlements due to transactions		
Sum 2.1 to 2.4	2	**Increase in pension entitlements due to social contributions**		*2.18*
	2.1	*Employer actual social contributions*		1.64
	2.2	*Employer imputed social contributions*		
	2.3	*Household actual social contributions*		0.00
	2.4	*Household social contribution supplements*		0.55
	3	Other (actuarial) increase of pension entitlements		0.60
	4	Reduction in pension entitlements due to payment of pension benefits		0.66
2 + 3 - 4	5	**Change in pension entitlements due to social contributions and pension benefits**		*2.13*
	6	Transfers of entitlements between schemes		*0.00*
	7	Changes in pension entitlements due to other transactions		*0.00*
		Changes in pension entitlements due to other economic flows		
	8	Changes in entitlements due to revaluations		*0.00*
	9	Changes in entitlements due to other changes in volume		*0.00*
		Closing Balance Sheet		
	10	Pension entitlements		*11.99*
		Pension entitlements (% of GDP 2006)		*107.31*
	11	Output		
	12	Assets held at the end of the period to meet pensions		

Source: Own calculations

3.13 MT – Malta[148]

Malta is the smallest country in the Euro currency area with a population of 0.40 million inhabitants.[149] It became a member of the Euro area in 2008 having joined the European Union in May 2004. The Maltese GDP amounted to 5.1 bn. EUR in 2006 which corresponds to 12,500 EUR per capita.

3.13.1 The demographic development in Malta

Malta's demography is – similar to most other European populations – strongly affected by a double ageing process. In other words, not only total fertility rates declined significantly in Malta in the past two decades – reaching a level of 1.41 in 2006 – but also life expectancies increased considerably in the past years. While a female (male) born in 1980 could expect to live 72.8 (68.0) years, this value increased up to 81.9 (77.0) in 2006. As a result the Maltese population pyramid considerably changed its appearance in the past decades. An overview of the age-specific population structure in 2006 is given in the following Figure 32.

Owing to the demographic changes mentioned above the population structure resembles a tree truncated down half way. However, this tree reflects also historic events such as the impact of the Second World War. Between 1940 and 1943 – due to its important strategic position in the Mediterranean – Malta was under siege and severely bombarded. Not only were numerous Maltese killed during this time but also fewer babies were born, leading to the cut at the cohorts aged around 65. As in most European countries, numerically strong post-war generations are now reaching the retirement age in Malta. This has significant impacts on future pension expenditures and therefore on our calculations.

---

[148] We would like to thank Clyde Caruana and his colleagues from the Maltese National Statistics Office for valuable comments on this chapter.

[149] Figure as at January 1st, 2006. We display country data for 2006 since this is a main base year for our calculations.

Figure 32: Population structure in Malta (2006)
age groups 0 to 100 years

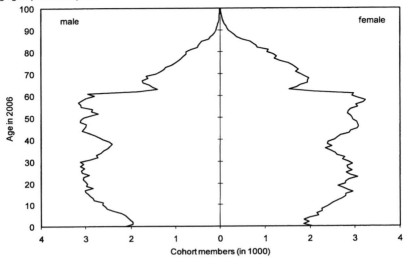

Source: Own calculations based on Eurostat (2009)

The quantitative development of elderly people – persons who are 60 years and older – is displayed in Figure 33. Starting from base year 2006 a rather steep rise in the number of elderly people can be observed in Malta. In 2025 the number of people aged 60 years and over will have increased by 60 per cent. It should be noted that this is one of the biggest growth rates in elderly people in comparison to other countries examined in this survey. This rise can be traced back to the large cohorts aged 40 to 60 in the base year 2006 as well as to the future rise in the life expectancy of the Maltese people. According to the assumptions of Eurostat a new-born Maltese male (female) in 2050 can expect to live five (three) years longer than its counterpart born in 2006. After 2025 this increase in the number of elderly people will significantly slow down. However, regarding the quantification of the Maltese ADL the development from 2006 to 2025 is more significant. To explain this fact one specific and important characteristic of the ADL approach shall be pointed out. Age groups which retire in the near future (next 20 years) have accrued more entitlements than the cohorts which receive a pension in the later future (after the next 20 years). This is due to the fact that the latter are of younger age today and therefore have contributed for a shorter period to the pension system.

Figure 33: Development of elderly persons (aged 60+) in Malta
indexed to 100 in 2006

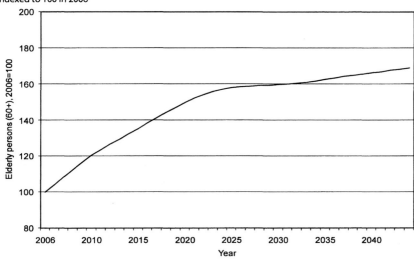

Source: Own calculations based on Eurostat (2009)

3.13.2 The Maltese pension system

3.13.2.1 The principles of the Maltese pension system

In line with the majority of Mediterranean countries the corner stone of the Maltese pension system is represented by the first pillar. An occupational second pillar does not exist in Malta, with the only exception being that of civil servants employed before 1979. Individual savings – the third pillar – only play a minor role in Maltese old age provisions. Nevertheless, they are expected to become more important for the income of future pensioners.

Since the first pillar is the focus of our analysis we shall describe it further. The first (public and mandatory) pillar practically covers the entire Maltese population and is financed as common by a PAYG system. It consists of a non-contributory as well as a contributory scheme. The former scheme is a means-tested, flat rate benefit, securing a minimum pension to people over age 61 for men and 60 for women. Its benefits are indexed to inflation. The contributory scheme is named the "two-thirds" pension since it amounts to two-thirds of the average reference wage. In the case of employees (self-employed) the two thirds pension is calculated on the basis of the average basic wages (net-income) during the best three (ten) out of the last ten years prior to retirement. For the calculation of the pension, past wages (net-incomes) are generally indexed with the relative cost of living increases. A full pension of two-thirds is payable to persons who have paid or have been credited with 30 years of contributions (with a yearly average of 50 contributions). Fewer years of contributions result in linearly reduced pensions with the minimum years of contributions amounting to nine.

The two-thirds pension covers all employees, self employed as well as civil servants employed after 1979. However, civil servants appointed before 1979, persons enrolled in the police force (after 25 years of service or 55 years of age), and members of the army are entitled to receive the so-called Treasury Pension.[150]

Regarding the adjustment of pensions the Maltese pension system differentiates between persons born before and after 1962. Pensions of the former group are adjusted on the highest of either the cost of living adjustment (COLA) or the increase in wages awarded to the present occupant of the last post occupied by the pensioner. According to the Maltese National Statistics Office pensions are indexed in practice by about 90 per cent according to wage growth and ten per cent according to the COLA increase. This proportion has been used in our calculations. Pensions of people born after 1962 are indexed by 70 per cent by the growth of the national average wage and 30 per cent by inflation. However, this new indexation rule will not apply before 2012. The statutory retirement age for women (men) in Malta is 60 (61) years in 2006. This value will gradually increase to 65.

3.13.2.2 Recent reforms of the Maltese pension system

Under the pressure of budget deficits and the demographic development described above Malta adopted a rather profound pension reform in 2006. The most significant reform steps and their implication for the ADL shall be outlined in the following section. According to the new 2006 legislation the statutory pension age will be gradually raised (in the period 2014 to 2023) to 65 for men and women likewise. According to our calculations this reform step reduces the Maltese pension liabilities by about seven per cent of GDP in 2006. Furthermore, the necessary period of contribution to receive a full two-thirds pension will be increased from 30 to 40 years (for people born after 1962). A further reform affects the pension calculation of persons born after 1962. Their pension shall be determined on the

---

[150] According to the Maltese National Statistics Office the last civil servants to benefit from Treasury Pension will retire in 2020. Knowing that civil servants presently represent about 75 per cent of beneficiaries of Treasury Pensions, one can expect that total expenditures of this pension scheme will decrease considerably in the coming decades.

best ten basic wages within the last forty years prior to retirement. According to our calculations this change will lead to a reduction of the pension level of six (four) per cent for men (women). For this calculation it is assumed that the relative profile of the insurable income stays constant over time, the per capita wage growth amounts to 1.5 per cent and the average old age retirement age for both sexes is 61 years (and gradually increases to 65).[151] However, it should be noted that this reduction factor represents only a rough estimation. In particular, future changes in the wage profile due to higher employment participation rates of elderly workers are difficult to predict.

With the reform of 2006 the possibility to receive an early pension will be restricted to those in employment. Moreover, the reform envisages that child-rearing periods are partly credited by the pension system. Although it can be assumed that this reform step will slightly raise total pension entitlements, we are not able to quantify the impact of this specific change in the pension legislation.

3.13.3 Measuring the Maltese accrued-to-date pension liabilities

ADL consist of all pension entitlements which have been accrued to the present by living generations. These entitlements result in respective present and future pension payments. As a starting point we want to take a look at the present pension payments in the base years 2005-2007 illustrated in Table 46. These pension expenditures do not include non-contributory pension payments.[152]

Overall, aggregated pension payments in Malta in the years 2005-2007 amounted to about 8.7 per cent of the respective GDPs. The biggest share of expenditures is represented by the social security pensions – and namely the two-thirds pension. Pensions which can be classified as government employer pensions, the Treasury Pensions, play only a minor role in Malta representing about 1.5 of the respective GDP.

---

[151] At present, average gross wages after the age of 61 decline tremendously. This might be due to the fact that elderly people work only part time. For our calculation we assume that the relative wage profile of the last ten years before retiring stays constant. In other words, somebody who retires in the future at the increased statutory retirement age of 65 is expected to have the same relative wage profile – with respect to the last ten years – as somebody who retires at the present statutory retirement age of 61.

[152] Since in Malta non-contributory pension benefits have the character of a social assistance scheme they have been excluded in our calculations. For 2007 and 2005 we have no data about the aggregated non-contributory pension payments. Therefore we assumed that the proportion of non-contributory pension of the aggregated budget in 2007 and 2005 is equal to the year 2006.

Table 46: Social security and government employer pension payments Malta
(in million EUR)

Type of pension	Pension payments		
	2005	2006	2007
Social security pensions	345.66	370.74	394.34
Old age pensions	225.24	245.63	266.64
Disability pensions	38.17	38.31	37.53
Survivor pensions	82.25	86.80	90.17
Treasury pensions	73.32	74.82	76.16
Total	418.98	445.56	470.50

Source: National Statistics Office Malta (2008)

The application of the methodology of calculating ADL for the Maltese pension system produces the following results for the year 2006, presented in the supplementary table.[153]

First of all, it should be noted that the results shown in Table 47 reflect the PBO approach which is described precisely in section 2.2.2.2 of this survey. Starting with the opening balance, pension entitlements of the Maltese social security (column H) add up to 12.82 bn. EUR at the beginning of 2006. These entitlements are increased by social contributions from employers', employees' as well as household social contributions amounting in total to 0.89 bn. EUR during 2006. Nevertheless, pension entitlements diminish considerably in 2006. This reduction has two major causes. One is the payment of pension benefits (0.37 bn. EUR). The other is the adopted pension reform in 2006. We estimate that the later reform brought a reduction of 1.59 bn. EUR in the entitlements, equal to about 31 percentage points of the GDP in 2006. The resulting pension liabilities of social security pensions at the end of 2006 sum up to 11.53 bn. EUR, which represents some 226 per cent of GDP. Lower outcomes have been generated for the government employer pension scheme. Its total pension liabilities at the end of 2006 amount to 2.18 bn. EUR, which is equal to almost 43 per cent of the Maltese GDP in 2006.[154] Different results can be observed when applying the ABO approach:

---

[153] The supplementary tables for the year 2007 can be found in the appendix of this survey.

[154] It should be noted that the results of the social security pensions in contrast to government employer pensions could be calculated more precisely. This is due to the fact that we had only age- and sex-specific pension profiles for the social security pensions.

Table 47: Supplementary table Malta 2006 PBO
(in bn. EUR)

			Non-core national accounts (figures in bn. EUR)	
			General Government	Social Security
			G	H
		Opening Balance Sheet		
	1	Pension entitlements	**2.15**	**12.82**
		Changes in pension entitlements due to transactions		
Sum 2.1 to 2.4	2	Increase in pension entitlements due to social contributions	**0.12**	**0.89**
	2.1	*Employer actual social contributions*		0.14
	2.2	*Employer imputed social contributions*	0.01	
	2 3	*Household actual social contributions*		0.14
	2 4	*Household social contribution supplements*	0.11	0.61
	3	Other (actuarial) increase of pension entitlements		-0.24
	4	Reduction in pension entitlements due to payment of pension benefits	0.08	0.37
2 + 3 - 4	5	Change in pension entitlements due to social contributions and pension benefits	0.05	0.28
	6	Transfers of entitlements between schemes	**0.00**	**0.00**
	7	Changes in pension entitlements due to other transactions	**-0.02**	**-1.57**
		Changes in pension entitlements due to other economic flows		
	8	Changes in entitlements due to revaluations	**0.00**	**0.00**
	9	Changes in entitlements due to other changes in volume	**0.00**	**0.00**
		Closing Balance Sheet		
	10	Pension entitlements	**2.18**	**11.53**
		Pension entitlements (% of GDP 2006)	**42.72**	**226.25**
	11	Output		
	12	Assets held at the end of the period to meet pensions		

Source: Own calculations

Comparing Table 47 and Table 48, one can clearly see the differences in results using both approaches (PBO and ABO). The actual contributions paid by employers and households stay the same – these are statistical figures that do not depend on the choice between ABO and PBO. However, rather significant changes can be observed when looking at pension entitlements in the opening and closing balance sheet. Using the ABO (PBO) approach, pension entitlements at the beginning of 2006 add up to 11.32 (12.82) bn. EUR and at the end of 2006 they amount to 10.37 (11.53) bn. EUR. Since the ABO approach does not take into account future wage growth, the respective outcomes turn out to be about ten per cent lower when applying the ABO approach. Also, in the case of ABO the entitlements are considerably reduced due to the 2006 pension reform. We estimate that this reduction amounted to 1.40 bn. EUR or 27 percentage points of the GDP in 2006.

It should be mentioned that the PBO/ABO choice also has an impact on the household social contribution supplements as well as on the other (actuarial) increase of pension entitlements. The contribution supplements are affected because the average of opening and closing pension liabilities is the basis for estimating this figure. Changing pension liabilities will therefore always change contribution supplements in the same time.

Table 48: Supplementary table Malta 2006 ABO
(in bn. EUR)

				Non-core national accounts (figures in bn. EUR)	
				General Government	Social Security
				G	H
			Opening Balance Sheet		
		1	Pension entitlements	2.06	11.32
			Changes in pension entitlements due to transactions		
Sum 2.1 to 2.4		2	Increase in pension entitlements due to social contributions	0.13	0.82
	2.1		*Employer actual social contributions*		0.14
	2.2		*Employer imputed social contributions*	0.03	
	2.3		*Household actual social contributions*		0.14
	2.4		*Household social contribution supplements*	0.10	0.54
		3	Other (actuarial) increase of pension entitlements		-0.01
		4	Reduction in pension entitlements due to payment of pension benefits	0.08	0.37
2 + 3 - 4		5	Change in pension entitlements due to social contributions and pension benefits	0.05	0.44
		6	Transfers of entitlements between schemes		0.00
		7	Changes in pension entitlements due to other transactions	-0.01	-1.39
			Changes in pension entitlements due to other economic flows		
		8	Changes in entitlements due to revaluations	0.00	0.00
		9	Changes in entitlements due to other changes in volume	0.00	0.00
			Closing Balance Sheet		
		10	Pension entitlements	2.10	10.37
			Pension entitlements (% of GDP 2006)	41.16	203.46
		11	Output		
		12	Assets held at the end of the period to meet pensions		

Source: Own calculations

Furthermore, the entitlements of the government employer pensions turn out to be lower applying the ABO approach. At the end of 2006 they add up to 2.10 bn. EUR, which corresponds to roughly 41 per cent of GDP in 2006.

3.14 NL – Netherlands

The Netherlands has a population of 16.33 million inhabitants.[155] It has a prosperous and open economy, which depends heavily on trade. Due to its location it is a major European transportation hub and trans-shipment centre. The Dutch economy is noted for its secure framework with low inflation and unemployment as well as stable industrial relations. It is one of the twelve countries which introduced the Euro currency on January 1st, 2002. Its GDP in the year 2006 added up to 539.9 bn. EUR, the per capita GDP amounted 33,000 EUR. The economy draws from a labour force of 7.5 million people. The labour force participation lies with 73.2 per cent well above the average of the EU25 (63.8 per cent) and the EU15 (65.2 per cent). Employment statistics further show a relatively low 5.5 per cent unemployment rate.

3.14.1 The demographic development in the Netherlands

Like most industrialized countries, the Netherlands' demography is characterized by increasing longevity and decreasing birth rates. As a starting point, we look at the population structure of the Netherlands in 2006 – Figure 34 shows the cohorts of male and female persons aged zero to 100 years.

Two special features can be observed when looking at the Dutch population pyramid. The first one is the peak around the age group of 60-year olds; this must be ascribed to the special effects caused by World War II. Most probably in many cases the desire to have children was postponed to the postwar period which is the reason for the numerically strong cohorts born in 1947 and afterwards. Between 1950 and 1965 the total fertility rate always ranged above 3.0 children per woman. The other feature is the decline in numbers of age groups 30 to 35 years old in 2006. This can clearly be traced back to the drop in birth rate due to the pill which is observable in the majority of industrialized countries at that time. However, the fertility rate in the Netherlands recovered slowly as can be seen at the cohorts aged zero to 20 years in 2006. In fact, after the total fertility rate began its decline starting at a rate of 3.19 in 1963 on, it dropped below the replacement rate of ~ 2.1 in 1973 and reached its minimum of 1.47 children per woman in 1983. After this it rose slowly to 1.7 children per woman in 2006.

---

[155] Figure as at January 1st, 2006. We display country data for 2006 since this is a main base year for our calculations.

Figure 34: Population structure in the Netherlands (2006)
age groups 0 to 100 years

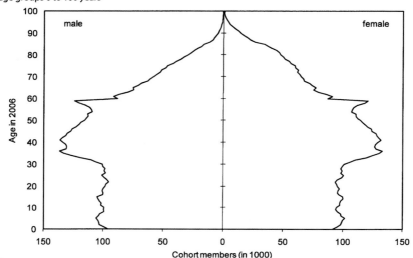

Source: Own calculations based on Eurostat (2009)

Life expectancy for persons born in 2006 amounted to 77.7 years for men and 82.0 years for women. For persons born in 2050 this value is assumed to increase to 80.2 years for men and 83.6 for women. Figure 35 illustrates the quantitative development of persons aged 60 or more.

Similar to the other countries examined, the Netherlands faces a substantial future increase of elderly persons. From 2006 until 2035 a steady growth can be observed. Only after 2035, the number of elderly persons decreases due to the fact that the cohorts aged 20 to 30 years in 2006 enter the group of elderly persons at that time. Since these age groups are relatively small in numbers, the number of elderly persons diminishes. But even in 2045 this number will be around 60 per cent higher than it was in 2006.

Figure 35: Development of elderly persons (aged 60+) in the Netherlands
indexed to100 in 2006

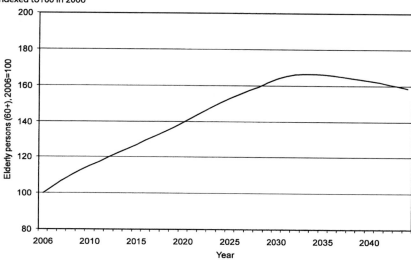

Source: Own calculations based on Eurostat (2009)

3.14.2 The Dutch pension system

3.14.2.1 The principles of the Dutch pension system

The public old age pension is part of the three pillars old age pension system of the Netherlands and makes up roughly half of the retirement income. The other pillars are the funded occupational pensions and the private provisions. The "Algemene Oulderdom Wet" (AOW) is the statutory old age pension scheme of the Netherlands. It was introduced in the General Old Age Act of 1956. The AOW provides flat rate benefits from age 65. These benefits do not depend on a means test nor are they affected by other forms of income or contributions paid prior to retirement. AOW entitlement is accrued at a rate of two per cent for every year of residence between the age of 15 and 65. Individuals who fully meet the requirements receive 70 per cent of the net minimum wage or 100 per cent as a couple if married or living together. The statutory minimum wage equals in net terms 55 per cent of the average wage. It is adjusted in line with average wage growth twice a year. The Conditional Indexing Adjustment Act, introduced in 1992, can however suspend indexation if the dependency rate was to deteriorate rapidly. Indexation was suspended in 1992 and 1995 but has been fully restored ever since. Residents who are not entitled to the full AOW benefits and whose total income, including other sources of income, lies beneath the subsistence level (i.e. less than 70 per cent of the legal minimum wage) are entitled to receive social assistance.

The statutory pension scheme can be described as a PAYG system since present contributors provide the pension payments made to present pensioners. The AOW pensions are financed through contributions depending on taxable income, with premiums levied as a part of the personal income tax. The administrative body for the AOW is the social insurance bank (Soziale Verzekeringsbank – SVB). The SVB is independent of the government in its day-to-day operations.

3.14.2.2 Recent reforms of the Dutch pension system

There are no reforms currently implemented in the AOW.

3.14.3 Measuring the Dutch accrued-to-date pension liabilities

Although there are separate pension schemes for civil servants in the Netherlands, this survey only takes into account the social security pension scheme (AOW). This is due to the fact that all other (employer) pension schemes are organized on a funded basis, therefore they are already shown in national accounts and there is no need for further estimations. Table 49 shows the pension payments made by the AOW in 2005, 2006 and 2007.

Table 49: Social security pension payments Netherlands
(in bn. EUR)

Type of pension	Pension payments		
	2005	2006	2007
Old age pensions	23.37	24.17	25.20
Disability pensions	8.52	8.75	9.39
Survivor pensions	1.43	1.36	1.37
Total	**33.32**	**34.28**	**35.96**

Source: Statistics Netherlands (2008)

The social security pension payments in the Netherlands belong – in relation to the respective GDP – to the lowest of all countries examined, especially when it comes to Western European countries. They add up to only 6.3 per cent of the Dutch GDP in 2006. Applying the method of calculating ADL described in section 2.2.2 of this study, Table 50 demonstrates the generated results for the year 2006, beginning with the results from the PBO approach:[156]

Table 50: Supplementary table Netherlands 2006 PBO
(in bn. EUR)

			Non-core national accounts (figures in bn. EUR)	
			General Government	Social Security
			G	H
		Opening Balance Sheet		
	1	Pension entitlements		1,280.28
		Changes in pension entitlements due to transactions		
Sum 2.1 to 2.4	2	Increase in pension entitlements due to social contributions		81.26
	2 1	*Employer actual social contributions*		
	2.2	*Employer imputed social contributions*		
	2 3	*Household actual social contributions*		17.36
	2 4	*Household social contribution supplements*		63.90
	3	Other (actuarial) increase of pension entitlements		-51.63
	4	Reduction in pension entitlements due to payment of pension benefits		34.28
2 + 3 - 4	5	Change in pension entitlements due to social contributions and pension benefits		-4.64
	6	Transfers of entitlements between schemes		0.00
	7	Changes in pension entitlements due to other transactions		0.00
		Changes in pension entitlements due to other economic flows		
	8	Changes in entitlements due to revaluations		0.00
	9	Changes in entitlements due to other changes in volume		0.00
		Closing Balance Sheet		
	10	Pension entitlements		1,275.64
		Pension entitlements (% of GDP 2006)		236.26
	11	Output		
	12	Assets held at the end of the period to meet pensions		

Source: Own calculations

The opening balance of the social security scheme shows pension entitlements of 1,280.28 bn. EUR. Social contributions increase this figure by 81.26 bn. EUR while the residual in row 3 shows a negative value of -51.63 bn. EUR. There is in fact a whole set of possible explanations why the residual in this case turns out to be negative. One possible reason could be the absence of subsidies in the pension scheme (unlike the German social security scheme, for instance). Another explanation could be the generous nature of total pension entitlements in relation to pension rights earned in the base year. If this is the case, the *household social contribution supplements* which are estimated by applying an interest rate of five per cent to the pension liabilities, blow up the total social contributions tremendously. This has to be balanced by the residual in row 3.

---

[156] The supplementary tables for the year 2007 can be found in the appendix of this survey.

Pensions paid from this scheme in 2006 accrue to 34.28 bn. EUR which results in a closing balance of pension entitlements of 1,275.64 bn. EUR, equal to around 236 per cent of GDP in 2006. Admittedly, this is a rather low outcome compared to other Western European countries due to the the fact that the AOW in the Netherlands is only a basic pension scheme. It grants benefits which do not depend on the amount of contributions paid prior to retirement. However, bearing in mind the extremely low pension expenditures of only 6.3 per cent of GDP, one could expect lower ADL than the ones shown above. The fact that the Dutch ADL do not belong to the lowest of all countries examined despite their small pension expenditures can be traced back to high pension indexation and non-appearance of any pension reforms so far.

Analogous to the calculations conducted for pension schemes of the other countries, the results of the ABO approach are considerably lower than those of the PBO approach. These results are displayed in Table 51:

Table 51: Supplementary table Netherlands 2006 ABO
(in bn. EUR)

				Non-core national accounts (figures in bn. EUR)	
				General Government	Social Security
				G	H
			Opening Balance Sheet		
		1	Pension entitlements		1,280.28
			Changes in pension entitlements due to transactions		
Sum 2.1 to 2.4		2	Increase in pension entitlements due to social contributions		81.26
		2.1	Employer actual social contributions		0.00
		2.2	Employer imputed social contributions		
		2.3	Household actual social contributions		17.36
		2.4	Household social contribution supplements		63.90
		3	Other (actuarial) increase of pension entitlements		-51.63
		4	Reduction in pension entitlements due to payment of pension benefits		34.28
2 + 3 - 4		5	Change in pension entitlements due to social contributions and pension benefits		-4.64
		6	Transfers of entitlements between schemes		0.00
		7	Changes in pension entitlements due to other transactions		0.00
			Changes in pension entitlements due to other economic flows		
		8	Changes in entitlements due to revaluations		0.00
		9	Changes in entitlements due to other changes in volume		0.00
			Closing Balance Sheet		
		10	Pension entitlements		1,275.64
			Pension entitlements (% of GDP 2006)		236.26
		11	Output		
		12	Assets held at the end of the period to meet pensions		

Source: Own calculations

The closing balance for the social security pension scheme adds up to 1,275.64 bn. EUR, respectively around 236 per cent of GDP in 2006. This means that the ABO outcome is exactly the same as the PBO result. This finding makes sense bearing in mind that future pension payments in the Dutch AOW scheme do not depend on the magnitude of future contributions. See section 2.2.2.2 for further explanations. Generally there should be no difference between ABO and PBO outcomes when pension schemes are examined which feature a flat-rate payment independent of contributions paid to the scheme prior to retirement.

3.15 PL – Poland

Poland has a population of 38.16 million inhabitants.[157] The national currency is the Polish Zloty (PLN), the rate of exchange to the Euro is 3.831 PLN.[158] The GDP in 2006 amounted up to 1,060.0 bn. PLN which corresponds to 272.1 bn. EUR. The per capita GDP was 27,800 PLN or 7,100 EUR. The Polish economy is largely dominated by the service sector which accounts for about 64 per cent of GDP compared to about 32 per cent in the industrial sector. Poland became a member of the European Union in 2004 and thus is obliged to introduce the Euro in due course. However, Poland currently belongs to the seven countries for which adoption is not yet scheduled since convergence criteria are not met.

3.15.1 The demographic development in Poland

Poland's demographic history after World War II is characterized by high fertility rates which decreased only after the opening of the Iron Curtain after 1989. Figure 36 illustrates the age-specific population structure for cohorts aged zero to 100 years in 2006.

The impact of World War II on the number of births in Poland can clearly be identified when looking at the generations born between 1941 and 1946. This is the cohort aged 60 to 65 in the year 2006. After the end of World War II the fertility rate recovered quite rapidly which led to numerically large cohorts aged 45 to 60. Between 1960 and 1970, the total fertility rate decreased from nearly 3.0 to 2.2 children per woman. This explains the decline in births which can be observed around the age group of 40 in 2006. The recurring gains in birth numbers afterwards can be traced back to the fact that these cohorts were born by those aged 45 to 55 in 2006. Due to the fact that these are quite large in numbers, their children are numerous as well – this is sometimes referred to as the "echo-effect".

---

[157] Figure as at January 1st, 2006. We display country data for 2006 since this is a main base year for our calculations.

[158] Exchange rate for as at December 29th, 2006.

Figure 36: Population structure in Poland (2006)
age groups 0 to 100 years

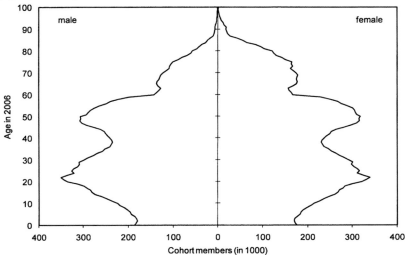

Source: Own calculations based on Eurostat (2009)

Not surprisingly, the life expectancy in Poland shows a trend similar to the countries described before. An average male (female) born in 2006 can expect to live for 70.9 (79.7) years. This value is assumed to rise to 79.1 (84.4) for males (females) born in 2050. Figure 37 demonstrates the prospective development of persons aged 60 or more years.

The development of elderly persons reflects well the age structure in 2006 shown in Figure 36. In the first years after 2006 a comparatively high number of persons will enter the age group of "60+". These are the numerically large cohorts aged 45 to 58 years in 2006. After 2020, the growth of the monitored age group will slow down, due to the smaller groups aged 35 to 45 in 2006 entering the group of elderly people. But this slowdown is only temporary; after 2030 this group grows at a higher speed again. In conclusion it has to be emphasized that between 2006 and 2045 Poland features one of the biggest numerical increases in elderly persons, compared to the other countries examined in this survey.

Figure 37: Development of elderly persons (aged 60+) in Poland
indexed to 100 in 2006

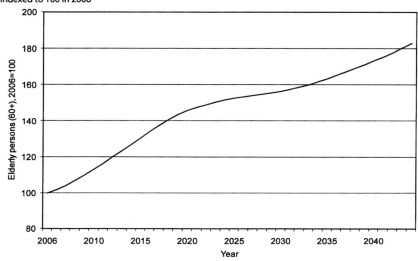

Source: Own calculations based on Eurostat (2009)

3.15.2 The Polish pension system

3.15.2.1 The principles of the Polish pension system

The Polish system is split into three different parts: There are institutionally distinguished schemes for private sector employees, farmers and a number of civil servants groups which are all financed at least in parts out of the official budget. The private sector scheme is the only one relying significantly on contributions; a defined contribution scheme by now.

The private sector scheme

The Polish pension system is currently in a transition phase after the reform of 1999 which changed the general pension system from a defined benefit scheme to a non-financial defined contribution (NDC) scheme. The pure new scheme under which all workers born after 1968 will retire is designed as follows: The contribution is defined at 19.52 per cent of gross earnings with payment equally split between employers and employees. 12.22 per cent are credited to individual accounts at the central insurance institution (ZUS) with a rate of return equal to the wage sum growth of that year after controlling for inflation, and the remaining 7.3 per cent are invested into private funds with an individual and variable rate of return. As contributions to this system only started in 1999 there was an account value set for all people employed at that time which is to represent their contributions up to 1998. After retirement, account values are converted into an annuity which is based on the average unisex life expectancy of the age group at the age of retirement. Retirement age is 65 years for men and 60 years for women with no institutional early-retirement plans. Due to the system change, workers born before 1969 do not have the financial pillar in their accounts so that their total contribution is indexed at real wage growth. People born before 1949 still receive their pension from a defined benefit scheme, which grants them 24 per cent flat of the average wage. This amount is incremented by a proportion of an average out of the best ten years in a row chosen from the last 20 years of working. The proportion is 1.3 per cent per year of contribution. If pension benefits fall below some defined threshold there is a supplement paid out of tax accounts. In general, existing pensions are indexed with inflation rate plus 20 per cent of real wage growth.[159]

Pension system for farmers

Pensions for farmers are paid mainly out of the state budget; the contribution ratio is only about ten per cent. Farmers pay contributions equal to 30 per cent of the minimum old age pension and are eligible to the ages of 60/65 years (women/men), provided they have paid contributions for at least 25 years. The indexation of pensions corresponds to the one used for the general private sector scheme.

Scheme for civil servants

The civil servants' scheme is not financed by contributions at all. A pension can be claimed after a minimum service time of 15 years. Pension benefits are calculated as a proportion of the final salary received with the replacement rate being 2.6 percentage points per year of service and a maximum replacement rate of 75 per cent. Similar to the pension schemes described above, the indexation follows the inflation plus 20 per cent real salary growth.

3.15.2.2 Recent reforms of the Polish pension system

In 1999 the whole Polish social security system and with it the pension system underwent a fundamental reform. Before 1999 there was a monolithic contribution rate of 36.59 per cent to all social security schemes which did not take into account the burdens of the different institutions. The system was defined benefit, granting

---

[159] For a detailed description of the Polish pension system see European Commission (2007), p.270 et sqq.

workers a percentage of the average of their best three years in a row as a pension. In contrast to the new system there were possibilities of retirement as early as 55 years of age in some cases. Due to perceived immediate necessity of reform there was practically no phasing in. Only people born before 1949 are exempt from the new rules since they had already acquired considerable claims in the old system.[160]

3.15.3 Measuring the Polish accrued-to-date pension liabilities

Analogous to what was conducted in the previous countries' estimates, the aggregated pension payments for the years 2005, 2006 and 2007 provide a starting point for our calculations. Pension benefits from the social security pension schemes are shown in Table 52.

Table 52: Social security pension payments Poland
(in bn. PLN)

Institution	Pension payments		
	2005	2006	2007
Social insurance scheme (FUS)	**96.10**	**104.00**	**108.40**
Old age pensions	58.80	68.30	72.80
Disability pensions	21.00	18.10	17.60
Survivor pensions	16.30	17.60	18.00
Pension scheme for farmers (FER)	**14.96**	**13.25**	**12.98**
Old age pensions	12.11	10.78	10.59
Disability pensions	2.44	2.47	2.39
Survivor pensions	0.41	./.	./.
Total	**111.06**	**117.25**	**121.38**

Source: Narodowy Bank Polski (2008)

Changes according to the pension reform in 1999 are taken into account in the following manner: First it has to be made clear that in this survey we only consider the liabilities based on notional accounts. This means in reverse that future pensions paid from the funded pillar introduced in the pension reform 1999 are not taken into account. We then assume that individuals born after 1968 pay only 50 per cent of their contributions in the notional fund. For persons older than those born in 1968 we gradually phase in the contributions until reaching 100 per cent for the individuals born in 1949.

---

[160] A detailed description of the NDC system in Poland can be found in Chłón-Dominczak and Góra (2006).

A second feature of the reform which has to be taken into account in our calculations is the fact that the pension a person receives when he/she retires depends on his/her further life expectancy at that time. We considered this issue by taking the assumptions of Eurostat regarding life expectancy of a new-born person in 2050 as a basis and in a second step carrying out own calculations for further life expectancies of 62 year old persons for the period between 2006 and 2050. This was done by using unisex life expectancy tables. According to these tables, further unisex life expectancy at the age of 62 rises from 20.3 years in 2006 up to 23.5 years in 2050.

Pension benefits for civil servants are paid from two different institutions. The first is the social insurance scheme for non-military personnel which is responsible for all non-military uniformed services like police, fire service, prison officers etc. The second one is the social insurance scheme for military. Payments from both of these government employer pension schemes are shown in Table 53.

Table 53: Government employer pension payments Poland [161]
(in bn. PLN)

Institution	Pension payments		
	2005	2006	2007
Social insurance scheme for non-military	4.60	4.75	5.74
Old age pensions	3.34	3.45	./.
Disability pensions	0.39	0.40	./.
Survivor pensions	0.87	0.90	./.
Social insurance scheme for military	4.68	4.84	4.65
Old age pensions	2.67	2.76	./.
Disability pensions	0.63	0.65	./.
Survivor pensions	1.38	1.43	./.
Total	9.28	9.59	10.39

Source: Narodowy Bank Polski (2008)

It is worth mentioning that the sum of pension benefits paid in 2006 adds up to 126.845 bn. PLN which corresponds to a value of 12.0 per cent of GDP in 2006. We will discover later in section 3.20 that this value is relatively high compared to other countries examined here.

---

[161] Unfortunately no further breakdown was given for the year 2007.

Applying the method of the Freiburg model described in section 2.2.2 the following results have been generated for the year 2006, shown in Table 54. As with the results presented in the previous country chapters, we start by applying the PBO approach:[162]

Table 54: Supplementary table Poland 2006 PBO
(in bn. PLN)

			Non-core national accounts (figures in bn. PLN)	
			General Government	Social Security
			G	H
		Opening Balance Sheet		
	1	Pension entitlements	286.18	3,428.81
		Changes in pension entitlements due to transactions		
Sum 2.1 to 2.4	2	Increase in pension entitlements due to social contributions	12.91	246.35
	2.1	*Employer actual social contributions*	0.00	30.37
	2.2	*Employer imputed social contributions*	-1.49	■
	2.3	*Household actual social contributions*	0.00	41.80
	2.4	*Household social contribution supplements*	14.39	174.18
	3	Other (actuanal) increase of pension entitlements	■	-19.49
	4	Reduction in pension entitlements due to payment of pension benefits	9.59	117.25
2 + 3 - 4	5	Change in pension entitlements due to social contributions and pension benefits	3.31	109.61
	6	Transfers of entitlements between schemes	0.00	0.00
	7	Changes in pension entitlements due to other transactions	0.00	0.00
		Changes in pension entitlements due to other economic flows		
	8	Changes in entitlements due to revaluations	0.00	0.00
	9	Changes in entitlements due to other changes in volume	0.00	0.00
		Closing Balance Sheet		
	10	Pension entitlements	289.50	3,538.42
		Pension entitlements (% of GDP 2006)	27.31	333.81
	11	Output		
	12	Assets held at the end of the period to meet pensions		

Source: Own calculations

Column G represents the liabilities for military and non-military general government employees. It shows opening pension entitlements of 286.18 bn. PLN. There are no employer or household actual social contributions in this pension scheme, thus social contributions consist of imputed social contributions of -1.49 bn. PLN and household social contributions supplements of 14.39 bn. PLN only. Contributions accumulate to a value of 12.91 bn. PLN. Pension benefits paid in 2006 add up to 9.59 bn. PLN, thus the change in pension entitlements amounts to 3.31 bn. PLN. The closing balance of pension entitlements comes up to 289.50 bn. PLN, equal to roughly 27 per cent of GDP in 2006.

---

[162] The supplementary tables for the year 2007 can be found in the appendix.

The opening pension entitlements for the social security pension scheme accrue to a value of 3,428.81 bn. PLN. Employer actual social contributions are 30.37 bn. PLN, those from households add up to 41.80 bn. PLN. Household social contribution supplements sum to 174.18 bn. PLN. These figures lead to an increase in pension entitlements due to social contributions of 246.35 bn. PLN. Row 3 represents the residual figure and amounts to -19.49 bn. PLN; pension benefits paid out in 2006 reduce the entitlements by 117.25 bn. PLN. Finally the closing pension entitlements add up to a value of 3,538.42 bn. PLN which is equal to almost 334 per cent of the GDP. Adding up the pension entitlements of column G and H Poland shows pension entitlements to the amount of more than 360 per cent of the GDP in 2006. When comparing the results of the various countries in section 3.20 we will discover that this is one of the highest outcomes of all countries examined.

Table 55: Supplementary table Poland 2006 ABO
(in bn. PLN)

			Non-core national accounts (figures in bn. PLN)	
			General Government	Social Security
			G	H
		Opening Balance Sheet		
	1	Pension entitlements	250.62	3,002.73
		Changes in pension entitlements due to transactions		
Sum 2.1 to 2.4	2	Increase in pension entitlements due to social contributions	12.62	224.74
	2.1	*Employer actual social contributions*	0.00	30.37
	2.2	*Employer imputed social contributions*	0.01	
	2.3	*Household actual social contributions*	0.00	41.80
	2.4	*Household social contribution supplements*	12.61	152.57
	3	Other (actuarial) increase of pension entitlements		-10.02
	4	Reduction in pension entitlements due to payment of pension benefits	9.59	117.25
2 + 3 - 4	5	Change in pension entitlements due to social contributions and pension benefits	3.02	97.48
	6	Transfers of entitlements between schemes	0.00	0.00
	7	Changes in pension entitlements due to other transactions	0.00	0.00
		Changes in pension entitlements due to other economic flows		
	8	Changes in entitlements due to revaluations	0.00	0.00
	9	Changes in entitlements due to other changes in volume	0.00	0.00
		Closing Balance Sheet		
	10	Pension entitlements	253.64	3,100.20
		Pension entitlements (% of GDP 2006)	23.93	292.47
	11	Output		
	12	Assets held at the end of the period to meet pensions		

Source: Own calculations

Table 55 presents the results in case of following the ABO approach. As expected, the entitlements turn out to be significantly lower than the PBO outcomes. Closing pension entitlements of the general government employer pension scheme add up to 253.64 bn. PLN or nearly 24 per cent of GDP in 2006. Entitlements of the social security pension scheme come up to 3,100.20 bn. PLN, equal to some 292 per cent of GDP in 2006. Compared to the results using the PBO approach, figures have decreased by more than twelve per cent.

3.16 PT – Portugal[163]

Portugal has a population of 10.57 million inhabitants.[164] In 1986, it joined the European Community alongside Spain and was in the group of the first eleven countries to adopt the Euro in 1999. With the economic integration into the EU the Portuguese economy has been steadily growing especially in the service industry. In 2006 its GDP amounted to 155.5 bn. EUR, corresponding to about 14,700 EUR per capita.

3.16.1 The demographic development in Portugal

Demography reflects to a huge degree the history of the respective country. Going 60 years back Portugal unlike most central European countries had a neutral position during the Second World War – like its Iberian neighbour Spain. This fact can still be recognized today looking at Figure 38. As one can see the cohort aged 60 years and older is relatively numerously represented in Portugal. Despite the large number of elderly people, the Portuguese demography cannot be compared with the classical pyramid but rather with the shape of a tree. Its narrow trunk is represented by the cohorts of the zero to 20 year olds. This form can be traced back to the decline of fertility rates beginning at the end of the 1970s. Stated in numbers, the total fertility rate in Portugal sank from a level of around 2.8 in 1970 per woman to 2.2 in 1980 and declining further until today with a level of 1.35 (2006). The impact of international migration on the population dynamics as well as on the labour force resources is not negligible, particularly in countries like Portugal where the migration is a major determinant of demographic change. However, since we calculate entitlements of the present Portuguese population or more precisely of the present Portuguese contributors, the level of future migration has no implication for our results.

As in the rest of Europe the Portuguese population enjoyed an increase of life expectancy in recent decades. While a male (female) born in 1970 could expect to live 64.0 (70.3) years, this value rose over the last decades to 75.5 (82.3) in 2006. According to the assumptions of Eurostat this trend will continue with life expectancies in 2050 of 80.4 (86.6) for males (females). Figure 39 quantitatively

---

[163] We would like to thank Maria Teresa Ferreira from Statistics Portugal for valuable comments and comprehensive updates of this chapter.

[164] Figure as at January 1st, 2006. We display country data for 2006 since this is a main base year for our calculations.

illustrates this process showing the development of persons aged 60 years and older in the coming decades.

Figure 38: Population structure in Portugal (2006)
age groups 0 to 100 years

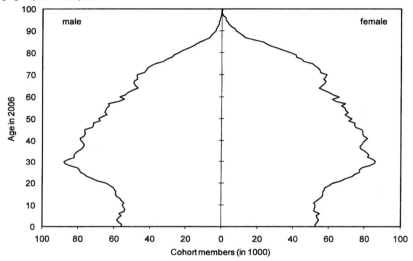

Source: Own calculations based on Eurostat (2009)

Taking the year 2006 as a benchmark, the number of elderly persons is expected to grow significantly. In 2030 there will be nearly 40 per cent more representatives of the age group of 60 years and older. By 2045 it can be assumed that this number will have further increased to 50 per cent. This development represents an important factor for our calculations since future pension expenditures – paid to present and future pensioners – are ranged with our estimate of the respective ADL.

Figure 39: Development of elderly persons (aged 60+) in Portugal
indexed to 100 in 2006

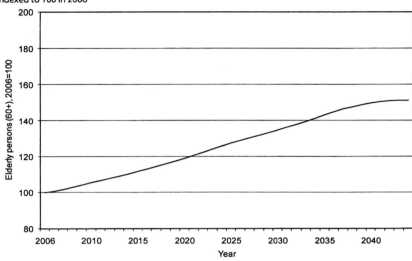

Source: Own calculations based on Eurostat (2009)

3.16.2 The Portuguese pension system

3.16.2.1 The principles of the Portuguese pension system

Under the conventional taxonomy of three pillars, one can describe the Portuguese pension system as having a predominant first pillar, a second pillar represented by private occupational schemes which play a significant role in some sectors (such as banking, insurance and communication) and an increasingly significant third pillar (but still representing a smaller share of the Portuguese private pension's schemes). Within the mandatory, publicly run first pillar, private sector workers and civil servants have had, until recently, different pension schemes. Since the beginning of 2006 new employees in the public sector are incorporated in the social security system.

The social security system comprises a general regime (the so called "Regime Geral" which applies to nearly all workers, including the self-employed), [165] a non-

---

[165] There are special regimes for miners, longshoremen, fishermen, merchant seamen, civil aviation workers, air traffic controllers and dancers. Special regimes are gradually being unified within the general regime.

contributory regime and a special regime for agricultural workers. The latter is closed to new contributors since 1986 and is expected to be phased out by 2045.

The general regime can be characterized as a defined benefit system working on a PAYG financing basis. It entitles old age pensioners with at least 15 years of earnings registration to an earnings-related pension.

The non-contributory regime, apart from attributing social pensions to those who have never contributed to the social security system or are not eligible for a earnings-related pension (because they have less than 15 years of earnings registration), also works on a complementary basis of the contributive regime: every year a minimum threshold is set according to the length of workers contributory career and if the pension benefit formula falls under that threshold, the non-contributory regime covers the rest.

3.16.2.2 Recent reforms of the Portuguese pension system

Like most European countries Portugal is facing the challenges of an ageing society which put substantial pressure on the Portuguese pension system – especially from a long term perspective. Therefore the Portuguese government reacted with a number of reforms in the last decade. Major reforms were taken in 2002 and 2006.

In 2002 the government introduced a new benefit formula for old age pensions in order to take into account individual lifetime contributions. Under the old calculation formula the highest-earning ten years out of the last 15 years were considered and an accrual rate of two per cent was applied irrespective of the length of the workers career. Under the new formula lifetime wages (up to a maximum of 40 years) are accounted for and accrual rates (ranging from two per cent and 2.3 per cent) are set according to the workers' wages and the length of their contributory career. These new rules will not only lead to a stronger link between contributions and benefits but also to a reduction of future pensions.

Additionally, in 2006 a tripartite agreement on the reform of social security was signed, enabling the introduction of new measures and the reinforcement of the measures already taken in 2002. In fact, due to the long transition rules established within the 2002 reform the expected impact upon the social security system would be very slow. In that sense, one of the measures taken within the 2006 reform was the introduction of new rules enabling a faster transition to the new pension benefit formula. Another significant measure was the establishment of a new rule-of-law regarding the annual increases of pensions, abandoning the indexation to the national minimum wage in favor of price indexation. The new indexation of pensions is now linked to CPI as well as to the real GDP growth. Furthermore, the indexation of pensions differs depending on the amount of the pension.[166] Another significant step taken in 2006 was the introduction of a sustainability factor which adjusts pensions (from 2008 onwards) in accordance with changes in the life expectancy. Other measures introduced within the 2006 reform consisted in: reinforcing the mechanisms for the protection of long contributory careers; introducing a ceiling to higher pensions; and promoting active ageing (giving bonuses to those who decide to extend their working lives beyond the legal retirement age and increasing penalties for early retirements).[167]

The 2006 tripartite agreement on the reform of social security also determines that the above mentioned measures – namely, the sustainability factor, the indexing rules, the incentives to prolong the working life and the penalties for early retirement – should be adopted in a framework of convergence between different social protection schemes. Regarding the convergence between the public employee pension system, the so-called Caixa Geral de Aposentações (CGA) and the social security pension system, a gradual increase (until 2015) of the statutory retirement age for civil servants from 60 to 65 is in force.[168] Furthermore, within this reform the pension benefit calculation has been changed. Similar to the general scheme the average wage of the entire career – for those appointed after 1993 – will be accounted for in the pension calculation. For civil servants appointed before 1993 the pension calculation will be conducted as a weighted average of the last monthly wage and the average wage since 2006, with the weights being the career length before and after 2006. According to our calculations the change in the reference period to the whole working life will lead to a reduction of the pension level of about twelve per cent.

---

[166] In our calculations we assume that future pensions will increase in accordance with the development of CPI and therefore stay constant in real terms. This scenario is based on the assumption that most of the pensions will amount to the range of 1.5 to six times the social support index (IAS) and the average growth rate of GDP will be between two and three per cent.

[167] Due to a lack of data we could not implement the above mentioned other measures in our calculations.

[168] In our calculations we assume that this reform step leads to an average reduction of pension payments of eleven per cent – comparing pensions in 2015 and 2006. Hereby we first of all take the assumption that the effective retirement age stays constant. Secondly we suppose that half of the civil servants will not have collected the necessary 30 years of contribution at the age of 55 in order to receive a penalty free early retirement. Therefore this group is confronted with a pension reduction of 4.5 per cent per year of increase in retirement age. This assumption is based on information – given by Statistics Portugal – that in 2006 the average years of contribution at the age of 55 amounted to 26.

Moreover, the other main measures of the social security reform were also applied to the CGA system from 2008, namely the introduction of the sustainability factor, the new indexation rule for pension's updates and the promotion of active ageing. Besides, the divisor in the pension formula will be gradually increased from 36 to 40 (until 2013) which will reduce the pension benefits of civil servants by about nine per cent. The pension reform of 2006 also introduced augmentations (reductions) for deferred (early) retirement which will be set according to the length of the pensioner´s contributory career. In the following section it will be shown that the 2006 reform significantly reduced the Portuguese pension liabilities.

3.16.3 Measuring the Portuguese accrued-to-date pension liabilities

For the description of our results it is essential to first of all look at present aggregated pension payments (illustrated in Table 56). Our calculations show that the ADL of a certain pension scheme to a high degree consist of payments to already present pensioners and only to a minor degree to future pensioners. Thus, the present pension budget – which indicates the amount of annually pension payments paid to present pensioners – is rather decisive for our results.

Table 56: Social security and government employer pension payments Portugal (in bn. EUR)

Institution/ type of pension	Pension payments		
	2005	2006	2007
Regime Geral	8.96	9.77	10.49
Old age pensions	6.62	7.31	7.91
Disability pensions	1.06	1.09	1.12
Survivor pensions	1.28	1.37	1.46
Public employee pensions (CGA)	6.35	6.77	7.18
Old age & disability pensions	5.73	6.13	6.50
Survivor pensions	0.62	0.64	0.68
Total	15.31	16.54	17.67

Source: Banco de Portugal (2008)

In total Portugal spent 16.54 bn. EUR in 2006 for pensions in the social security scheme which is equal to 10.6 per cent of GDP in 2006. We will see in section 3.20 that this is a relatively high value in comparison to other EU countries. Due to recent reform steps taken – as described above – these pension expenditures will decrease considerably in the future. Nevertheless, the present extensive volume of pension has a significant impact on our results. Table 57 displays the outcomes for the year 2006, applying the PBO approach first.[169]

Table 57: Supplementary table Portugal 2006 PBO
(in bn. EUR)

			Non-core national accounts (figures in bn. EUR)	
			General Government	Social Security
			H	I
		Opening Balance Sheet		
	1	Pension entitlements		450.30
		Changes in pension entitlements due to transactions		
Sum 2.1 to 2.4	2	Increase in pension entitlements due to social contributions		40.45
	2 1	*Employer actual social contributions*		11.49
	2 2	*Employer imputed social contributions*	▮▮▮	
	2 3	*Household actual social contributions*		6.11
	2.4	*Household social contribution supplements*		22.85
	3	Other (actuarial) increase of pension entitlements	▮▮▮	13.84
	4	Reduction in pension entitlements due to payment of pension benefits		16.54
2 + 3 - 4	5	Change in pension entitlements due to social contributions and pension benefits		37.75
	6	Transfers of entitlements between schemes		0.00
	7	Changes in pension entitlements due to other transactions		-24.30
		Changes in pension entitlements due to other economic flows		
	8	Changes in entitlements due to revaluations		0.00
	9	Changes in entitlements due to other changes in volume		0.00
		Closing Balance Sheet		
	10	Pension entitlements		463.75
		Pension entitlements (% of GDP 2006)		298.33
	11	Output		
	12	Assets held at the end of the period to meet pensions		

Source: Own calculations

At the beginning of the year 2006 social security pension entitlements amount to 450.30 bn. EUR. On the one hand these pension entitlements are increased by actual social contributions from employers (11.49 bn. EUR) and employees (6.11 bn. EUR). On the other hand pension entitlements are reduced by pension payments in 2006 summing up to 16.54 bn. EUR as well as by the pension reform of 2006 described above. As displayed in row 7 this reform causes a decrease in entitlements of 24.30 bn. EUR.[170] As a result, pension entitlements of the

---

[169] The supplementary tables for the year 2007 can be found in the appendix of this survey.

[170] This reduction is based to about two-thirds on the reform of the public employee pension system.

Portuguese social security add up to 463.75 bn. EUR at the end of 2006 – using the PBO approach. This corresponds to around 298 per cent of GDP in 2006. [171]

However, the results change if one holds constant today's salaries using the ABO approach. Table 58 illustrates the respective outcomes.

Table 58: Supplementary table Portugal 2006 ABO
(in bn. EUR)

				Non-core national accounts	
				(figures in bn. EUR)	
				General Government	Social Security
				H	I
			Opening Balance Sheet		
		1	Pension entitlements		378.48
			Changes in pension entitlements due to transactions		
Sum 2.1 to 2.4		2	Increase in pension entitlements due to social contributions		36.86
		2.1	*Employer actual social contributions*		11.49
		2.2	*Employer imputed social contributions*		
		2.3	*Household actual social contributions*		6.11
		2.4	*Household social contribution supplements*		19.26
		3	Other (actuarial) increase of pension entitlements		10.71
		4	Reduction in pension entitlements due to payment of pension benefits		16.54
2 + 3 - 4		5	Change in pension entitlements due to social contributions and pension benefits		31.03
		6	Transfers of entitlements between schemes		0.00
		7	Changes in pension entitlements due to other transactions		-17.58
		8	Changes in entitlements due to revaluations		0.00
		9	Changes in entitlements due to other changes in volume		0.00
			Closing Balance Sheet		
		10	Pension entitlements		391.93
			Pension entitlements (% of GDP 2006)		252.13
		11	Output		
		12	Assets held at the end of the period to meet pensions		

Source: Own calculations

While all statistical figures from national accounts are unaffected by the choice between ABO and PBO, pension entitlements can change significantly. This is also the case in Portugal. Pension entitlements of the opening and closing balance turn out to be 16 per cent smaller using the ABO approach. The reform of 2006 changes as well; according to our calculations, ABO entitlements are reduced due to this

---

[171] We assumed in our calculations that the age structure of civil servants is the same as the age-specific composition of the Portuguese population. This presumption was taken due to a lack of data. Campos and Pereira (2008, p. 114), however, state that a large number of people entered the public sector following the April 25th, 1974 Revolution. Hence, it can be expected that in the coming 15 years a number higher than the average of the Portuguese population will retire in the CGA. Under these circumstances we would underestimate the Portuguese pension liabilities in our calculations.

reform by 17.58 bn. EUR. In total Portuguese pension entitlements accrue to 391.93 bn. EUR at the end of 2006 applying the ABO approach. This corresponds to roughly 252 per cent of the Portuguese GDP in 2006.

3.17 SE – Sweden

Sweden had a population of 9.05 million inhabitants as of January 1ˢᵗ, 2006.[172] The national currency is the Swedish Crown (SEK), which had an exchange rate of 9.0404 SEK to the EUR as at December 29ᵗʰ, 2006. The GDP in Sweden was 2,900.8 bn. SEK in 2006, equal to a value of 313.5 bn. EUR. This corresponds to a per capita GDP of 319,400 SEK or 34,500 EUR.

The Swedish economy is largely dominated by the services sector which accounts for about 60 per cent of GDP (excluding state sector) compared to about 27 per cent in manufacturing. About 20 per cent of services are financial services; another 50 per cent are trade related. This high trade dependence, particularly the high export dependence, might have been a major incentive for the Swedish to vote against the adoption of the Euro in the 2003 referendum, in order to keep a competitive exchange rate position. In contrast to Denmark and the UK, Sweden is bound to the adoption by the accession treaty so that adoption can only be delayed. The delay is achieved through an exchange rate policy which does not satisfy the criteria of European Exchange Rate Mechanism (ERM) II.

3.17.1 The demographic development in Sweden

Sweden's demographic history is characterized by increased life expectancy, considerable immigration during and after World War II, and decreased fertility rates since the mid 1960s. Figure 40 illustrates the age-specific population structure of Sweden in 2006.

The numerical peak observable at the cohort aged around 60 can be traced back to rising fertility rates after World War II. Nevertheless, age cohorts between 45 and 55 years amount to slightly lower figures, due to lower fertility rates between 1950 and 1960. The generation aged 40 years in 2006 features the largest group of all age cohorts – this can be attributed to two effects: On the one hand, after 1960 fertility rates in Sweden began to rise again until they reached the maximum of 2.48 in 1964. Secondly, an effect often referred to as the "echo-effect" accounts for the quantitative large cohorts observed here.[173]

---

[172] We display country data for 2006 since this is a main base year for our calculations.

[173] Assuming constant fertility rates, it is straightforward that a numerically large age cohort will cause a higher number of children than a small one. Seeing the relatively large number of persons aged 60 years in 2006 in Figure 44, the high number of persons aged around 40 can be explained.

Figure 40: Population structure in Sweden (2006)
age groups 0 to 100 years

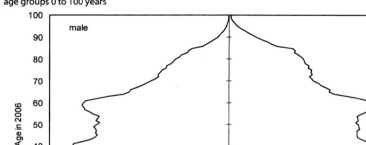

Source: Own calculations based on Eurostat (2009)

After the peak in 1964, fertility rates decreased again to a value of 1.6 children per woman in 1978. Unlike the development in other industrialized countries, the rate did not stay on this low level, but increased to a value of 2.13 in 1990. After slight declines, in 2006 the total fertility rate amounted to 1.85 children per woman which is a rather high value compared to most other EU member countries.

As mentioned above, Sweden faced considerable rises of life expectancy in the past, and this development is assumed to continue in the future. In figures, a male (female) born in 2006 can expect to live for 78.8 (83.1) years in Sweden. This figure is assumed to rise to 83.3 (86.5) years for males (females) born in 2050. Figure 41 demonstrates the future relative numbers of persons aged 60 or older in Sweden. The future numerical rise of elderly persons in Sweden turns out to be rather modest. Until 2035, this age group will increase by around 37 per cent and will then even decline again due to smaller age cohorts entering the group of elderly persons at that time. In contrast to other countries examined in this survey, Sweden does not seem to face a major increase of elderly persons in the future.

Figure 41: Development of elderly persons (aged 60+) in Sweden
indexed to 100 in 2006

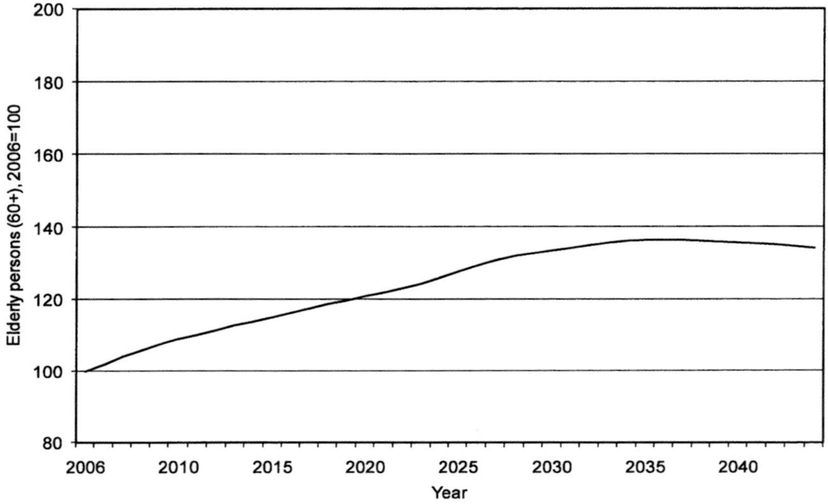

Source: Own calculations based on Eurostat (2009)

3.17.2 The Swedish pension system

3.17.2.1 The principles of the Swedish pension system

The Swedish old age pension scheme does not discriminate between privately and publicly employed workers; both groups are covered by the same social security system.

In 1998 the current Swedish pension system was legislated. This system is income-related and has two pillars of which the first is a notional defined contribution (NDC) PAYG scheme and the second one is a privately managed financially funded defined contribution (FDC) scheme. Altogether 18.5 per cent of pensionable income is paid into these schemes.

Each working person contributes 16 per cent of pensionable income to the first pillar, which is credited to a personal account indexed to wage growth per capita.[174]

---

[174] An automatic mechanism using a balance ratio which relates the pension system's assets (including the rate of return of the buffer funds) to its liabilities abandons indexation by average per capita wage growth in case the stability of the system is in danger. See Könberg et al (2006).

The account is notional since current pension obligations are paid out of current contributions so that capital is not actually accumulated in the account.

In the second pillar every working person has to invest 2.5 per cent of pensionable income into market funds among which they have a freedom of choice. Until recently the fund transactions were managed by a state clearing house as a broker but upon request by Eurostat these transactions are managed by private brokers since 2007. If a person does not choose one or several funds of her own, the money is invested into a public fund composed of bonds, domestic and foreign equities. Please note that only the first pillar is subject to the calculations presented later in this chapter, as the second pillar does not meet the requirements of the pension schemes examined in this survey.

At the end of the working career the accumulated capital augmented by compensations for periods of no employment for particular reasons (e.g. childbirth) is transformed into an annuity by dividing the balance in the notional account by an annuity divisor. This divisor is determined by further unisex life expectancy at retirement for a given cohort at age 65 and an imputed real rate of return of 1.6 per cent (which corresponds to a long-term real growth rate of the economy assumed by the policy makers). Benefits are adjusted each year for inflation.[175]

3.17.2.2 Recent reforms of the Swedish pension system

Before 1999 the Swedish system was a combination of a flat-rate pension called folkepension (at the initial level of today's guarantee) and an earnings-related part which was defined benefit as opposed to the new defined contribution scheme. The benefit was a proportion of the average wage of the best 15 years of the working career. Full eligibility was achieved with 30 years of covered earnings at age 65; maximum pension age was 67.

The system is currently – until 2015 – in a transition period. Those born in 1937 or earlier are still in the old system with the exception of the guarantee, where the new regulation is already applied. Those born in 1938 receive 20 per cent of their pension from the old system and 80 per cent from the new, with accounts being created from historical files. The share of the new system payments increases by five

---

[175] Benefits are also wage-indexed, but only with the difference between the assumed long-term wage growth of 1.6 per cent and the actual per capita real wages (for further details, see Könberg et al (2006)). Therefore the system is in principle CPI-indexed but has a "sustainability-factor" in case that economic growth deviates from an assumed "norm" of 1.6 per cent. For reasons of simplicity, we assumed CPI indexation for our calculations.

percentage points per year up to birth year 1953. All people born 1954 or later are fully covered by the new system. As described above, future pensions besides other factors depend on the development of life expectancy at the age of 65. This has been taken into account in our calculations by taking the assumptions of Eurostat for persons born in 2050 as a starting point and estimating the further life expectancy at the age of 65 years accordingly.

3.17.3 Measuring the Swedish accrued-to-date pension liabilities

As there is no special pension scheme for civil servants in Sweden because these persons are integrated in the NDC system, only the social security pension scheme will be examined. The aggregated pension benefits paid out in 2005, 2006 and 2007 are given in Table 59.

Table 59: Social security pension payments Sweden
(in bn. SEK)

Type of pension	Pension payments		
	2005	2006	2007
Old age pensions	192.93	199.32	208.67
Disability pensions	56.45	56.39	56.55
Survivor pensions	16.73	16.59	16.43
Total	266.11	272.30	281.65

Source: Statistics Sweden (2008)

As this table indicates, pension payments in Sweden add up to 9.7 per cent of GDP in 2005, 9.4 per cent of GDP in 2006 and 9.2 per cent of GDP in 2007. In other words, the quota pension payments to GDP faced a small decrease between 2005 and 2007. Taking the pension benefits shown above as a starting point, the following outcomes for the year 2006 have been generated, beginning with the figures of the PBO approach:[176]

---

[176] The supplementary tables for the year 2007 can be found in the appendix.

Table 60: Supplementary table Sweden 2006 PBO
(in bn. SEK)

			Non-core national accounts (figures in bn. SEK)	
			General Government G	Social Security H
		Opening Balance Sheet		
	1	Pension entitlements		*8,302.12*
		Changes in pension entitlements due to transactions		
Sum 2.1 to 2.4	2	Increase in pension entitlements due to social contributions		*600.12*
	2.1	*Employer actual social contributions*		108.94
	2.2	*Employer imputed social contributions*		▬
	2.3	*Household actual social contributions*		77.40
	2.4	*Household social contribution supplements*		413.79
	3	Other (actuarial) increase of pension entitlements		-380.61
	4	Reduction in pension entitlements due to payment of pension benefits		272.30
2 + 3 - 4	5	Change in pension entitlements due to social contributions and pension benefits		-52.80
	6	Transfers of entitlements between schemes		0.00
	7	Changes in pension entitlements due to other transactions		0.00
		Changes in pension entitlements due to other economic flows		
	8	Changes in entitlements due to revaluations		0.00
	9	Changes in entitlements due to other changes in volume		0.00
		Closing Balance Sheet		
	10	Pension entitlements		*8,249.32*
		Pension entitlements (% of GDP 2006)		*284.49*
	11	Output		
	12	Assets held at the end of the period to meet pensions		

Source: Own calculations

The opening balance indicates pension entitlements of 8,302.12 bn. SEK. Actual contributions to the amount of 108.84 bn. SEK (employer) and 77.40 bn. SEK (households) and household social contribution supplements adding up to 413.79 bn. SEK lead to a total of 600.12 bn. SEK of social contributions. The residual figure of other (actuarial) increase of pension entitlements in row 3 turns out to be negative in this case (-380.61 bn. SEK). As with the Netherlands in chapter 1, there are many possible explanations for this phenomenon. It could be traced back to the fact that the social security pension scheme in Sweden is a NDC system which possesses a notional rate of return lower than the applied rate of five per cent to estimate the household contribution supplements in row 2.4. Another reason for the negative residual might be the absence of subsidies in this autonomous scheme.

Pension benefits paid out in 2006 amount to 272.30 bn. SEK which cause a decline in pension entitlements of 52.80 bn. SEK (row 5). Pension entitlements at the end of 2006 accrue to 8,249.32 bn. SEK which corresponds to around 284 per cent of GDP in 2006.[177] Analogous to the procedure followed in the previous chapters, the pension entitlements have also been calculated applying the ABO approach. The respective results are shown in Table 61:

Table 61: Supplementary table Sweden 2006 ABO
(in bn. SEK)

				Non-core national accounts (figures in bn. SEK)	
				General Government	Social Security
				G	H
			Opening Balance Sheet		
		1	Pension entitlements		7,164.74
			Changes in pension entitlements due to transactions		
Sum 2.1 to 2.4		2	Increase in pension entitlements due to social contributions		543.98
	2.1		Employer actual social contributions		108.94
	2.2		Employer imputed social contributions		
	2.3		Household actual social contributions		77.40
	2.4		Household social contribution supplements		357.65
	3		Other (actuarial) increase of pension entitlements		-295.09
	4		Reduction in pension entitlements due to payment of pension benefits		272.30
2 + 3 - 4		5	Change in pension entitlements due to social contributions and pension benefits		-23.41
	6		Transfers of entitlements between schemes		0.00
	7		Changes in pension entitlements due to other transactions		0.00
			Changes in pension entitlements due to other economic flows		
	8		Changes in entitlements due to revaluations		0.00
	9		Changes in entitlements due to other changes in volume		0.00
			Closing Balance Sheet		
	10		Pension entitlements		7,141.32
			Pension entitlements (% of GDP 2006)		246.28
	11		Output		
	12		Assets held at the end of the period to meet pensions		

Source: Own calculations

Unsurprisingly, figures decrease when using the ABO approach. This holds for the opening pension entitlements (7,164.74 bn. SEK) as well as the household contribution supplements (357.65 bn. SEK) and the residual decrease (295.09 bn. SEK). Pension entitlements at the end of the year come up to 7,141.32 bn. SEK, equal to roughly 246 per cent of GDP in 2006. This means that the pension liabilities of the ABO approach come up to a value approximately 13 per cent lower than the outcomes using the PBO approach.

---

[177] The pension entitlements of Sweden indicated here are considerably higher than the ones shown in Heidler, Raffelhüschen and Weddige (2008), p. 76 et sqq. The main reason for this is the fact that in this survey old age pensions, disability pensions and survivor pensions have been taken into account while Heidler, Raffelhüschen and Weddige (2008) included old age pensions only.

3.18 SK – Slovakia[178]

Slovakia´s population amounted to 5.39 million inhabitants in 2006.[179] After the fall of the Iron Curtain it has undergone a profound transformation from a centrally planned to a market based economy. Slovakia was in the first group of the Eastern European countries to join the EU in 2004. A further integration-step into the European Union was taken in 2009 with the adoption of the Euro. Up to this point the official currency was the Slovakian Koruna (SKK).[180] Slovakia experienced considerable economic growth rates in the last years, resulting in a GDP of 1,659.4 bn. SKK in 2006 which corresponds to 44.6 bn. EUR. The resulting per capita GDP added up to about 8,300 EUR.

3.18.1 The demographic development in Slovakia

As observed in all European countries the Slovakian population is steadily growing older. However, the ageing process in Slovakia differs from that of most other EU countries. Total fertility rates as the major factor behind this development have been extremely low and amounted to 1.24 in 2006. Moreover, life expectancy has increased considerably in recent years. While a female (male) born in 1980 could expect to live 74.4 (66.7) years, this number increased until the year 2006 to 78.4 (70.4) for women (men). According to the estimations of Eurostat life expectancy will rise further until the year 2050 to a value of 83.4 (77.7) years for women (men). The age-specific population structure for Slovakia in 2006 is illustrated in Figure 42.

The picture shows that the population structure can be partly regarded as a historic mirror mostly influenced by past fertility, migration and mortality rates. In this line one can also detect past events in the present Slovakian demography such as the Prague Spring in 1968. This politically uncertain period was accompanied by considerably low birth rates. Thus, the cohorts born around 1968 – the 35 to 39 year olds – are relatively under-represented in 2006. Two cohorts are relatively numerously represented in Slovakia. One is the group aged 20-35. The other group is represented by the cohorts aged 40-55 years. The cohort of elderly being already

---

[178] We would like to thank Zuzana Durcenkova from Narodna banka Slovenska (National Bank of Slovakia) for valuable comments on this chapter.

[179] Figure as at January 1st, 2006. We display country data for 2006 since this is a main base year for our calculations.

[180] The exchange rate was 34.435 SKK to the Euro as at December 29th, 2006.

eligible to an old age pension – aged 60 and older – is comparably small.[181] However, the development of elderly people will significantly change in the coming decades as displayed in Figure 43.

Figure 42: Population structure in Slovakia (2006)
age groups 0 to 100 years

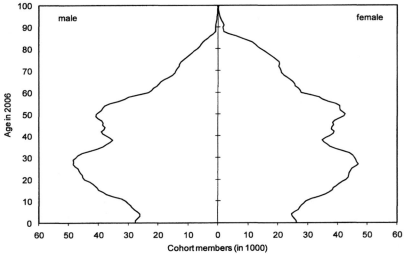

Source: Own calculations based on Eurostat (2009)

In the coming years the large cohorts aged 40-55 will enter the age-group of elderly persons ("60+"). This means that as early as 2025 there will be 50 per cent more representatives of potential retirees. After a short slow-down of this trend due to the smaller cohorts aged 35-40 in 2006 this figure will further increase to almost 100 per cent in 2045. Summing up, Slovakia´s population presently has a relatively small group of people being 60 years and older and therefore eligible to an old age pension. This situation will, however, change tremendously in the coming decades with one of the fastest growth of elderly people examined in this survey.

---

[181] This is one reason why the Slovakian total pension expenditures in 2006 amounted to a modest level of 7.2 per cent of GDP. For our calculations this fact will play an important role since the entitlements of present pensioners commonly represent a considerable indicator for the size of the respective ADL.

Figure 43: Development of elderly persons (aged 60+) In Slovakia
indexed to 100 in 2006

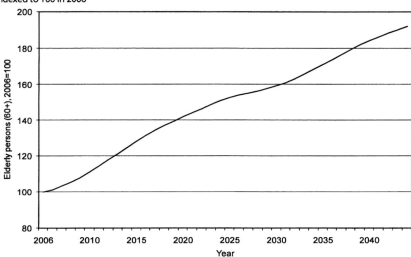

Source: Own calculations based on Eurostat (2009)

3.18.2 The Slovakian pension system

3.18.2.1 The principles of the Slovakian pension system

The Slovakian pension system is based on three main pillars plus an additional special system for civil servants working as members of the police, military forces, Slovak intelligence agency, national security office, prison guards, the railways police and custom officers.

The first pillar is represented by the mandatory, general government sponsored and un-funded social security pension system which has been inherited from the former Czechoslovakia and is based on a PAYG financing. The second pillar is a defined contributory fully funded scheme and has been introduced in 2005. It was originally mandatory for individuals who did not participate in the first pillar yet and were entering the labour market for the first time after the year 2004, and self-employed people. In 2007 the government decided to eliminate its mandatory character and introduced the element of voluntariness for entering the second pension pillar. The supplementary pension scheme and other financial products form the third pillar of the Slovakian pension system. It is voluntary and also fully funded. The special pension system for civil servants is sponsored by general government, based on a PAYG principle. The system is obligatory for all civil servants.

3.18.2.2 Recent reforms of the Slovakian pension system

In the course of the transition of the Slovakian economy its pension system went under severe financial pressure. With high unemployment rates and low motivation of the economically active population to contribute to the pension system, expenditures exceeded revenues in years prior to the first major reform in 2003. Furthermore, it became clear in recent years that the financial sustainability of the Slovakian pension system would be considerably challenged by a fast ageing society, as illustrated above. For these reasons the Slovak Republic embraced major reform steps adopted in 2003, 2004 and 2007 and implemented them in the respective following years 2004, 2005 and 2008.

Until the reform of 2004, the retirement age was set to 57 (60) years for women (men). According to the old legislation this age was further reduced by one year for each child raised, down to a minimum of 53 years (for women). With the reform of 2004 statutory retirement ages have been gradually increased by nine months per year to 62 years for both sexes equally – without taking further regard to the number of raised children. Furthermore, reduced retirement ages which depended on the type of occupation have been abolished with the reform of 2004. In order to increase revenues of the pension system the maximum payment base has been changed to three multiples of the average salary in the economy with the reform of 2003.[182] Besides that, new elements have been introduced which allow pensioners to retire before (after) the retirement age. In such cases old age pensions have been reduced (increased) by six per cent per year. Furthermore, the option to work while drawing a pension has been implemented. Another main element of the reform in 2004 was the introduction of a new pension formula. While the old system consisted of different elements of redistribution the new point system creates a more direct link between contributions and benefits. Similar to the German pension system, contributors who earn the average wage receive one point per year of insurance. For the benefit calculation one point stands for the equivalent of providing workers with 1.16 per cent of their average lifetime wage. Last but not least the reform of 2004 implemented a new indexation of pensions. According to

---

[182] Due to a lack of data about the distribution of salaries in Slovakia we were not able to consider the change of the payment base in our calculations.

these new rules pensions are adjusted annually by one half of the growth in CPI and one half to the growth of the average salary in the economy.[183]

The main cornerstone of the reform implemented in 2005 was the introduction of a mandatory funded second pillar. According to this new legislation contributions by both employees and employers to the old age pension insurance are split. Half is transferred to the first pillar and the other half to the funded second pillar on individual accounts. While current contributors were free to switch to this mixed system for a limited time period, all new entrants to the labour market are automatically obliged to pay contributions according to these new rules. With the reform of 2005 unfunded pension entitlements in Slovakia will decrease significantly in the long run. However, for the calculation of the present ADL – which consider only contributions up to the base year – this recent reform has only a minor impact. Taking the year 2006 as the base year we assume that the ADL will be reduced by about three per cent of GDP (2006) due to the reform of 2005.[184]

After the reform of 2005 further changes of the pension system have been adopted in 2007 and implemented in 2008. These include the tightening of rules for early retirement, increase of minimum time of contributions entitling for a pension from ten to 15 years as well as a further increase of the payment base for contributions to four multiples of average salary while maintaining the old restrictions for calculation of pension benefits. Furthermore the second pillar has been temporarily opened for the first half of the year 2008 for people to switch back to the first pillar or enter the second pillar, and the element of optionality has been introduced for those entering the labor market for the first time after the year 2007. In September 2008 the government decided to reopen the second pillar for the period from November 15th, 2008 till the end of June 2009. These second pillar reform measures have been adopted to increase the revenues of the first pillar. They represent a reversal of recent approaches to strengthen the second pillar.

---

[183] The indexation of pensions of the military which are increased according to the growth of an average service salary of professional soldiers is an exception of this rule. Due to a lack of information we did not consider this specific indexation rule.

[184] For this comparison we presume that all Slovakian contributors younger than 40 years have chosen to take part in the new second pillar. This seems quite reasonable since about 1.5 million of all insured persons (roughly 2.6 million) in Slovakia have had contributed to the second pillar at the end of 2006.

3.18.3 Measuring the Slovakian accrued-to-date pension liabilities

For the calculation of the Slovakian pension liabilities, social security pensions as well as government employer pensions have to be taken into account. Government employer pensions consist of pension payments for military forces as well as pension payments for police and fire forces. Table 59 illustrates the respective aggregated pension payments for the years 2005 to 2007.

Table 62: Social security and government employer pension payments Slovakia (in bn. SKK)

Institution/ Type of pension	Pension payments		
	2005	2006	2007
Social security[185]	104.60	115.13	126.52
Old age pensions	79.30	87.68	96.15
Disability pensions	12.71	13.87	15.38
Survivor pensions	12.59	13.58	14.99
Military forces[186]	2.48	2.71	3.21
Old age pensions	2.31	2.52	2.97
Disability pensions	0.03	0.03	0.03
Survivor pensions	0.14	0.16	0.21
Police and fire services[187]	1.64	1.81	2.03
Old Age pensions	1.53	1.68	1.88
Disability pensions	0.01	0.01	0.01
Survivor pensions	0.10	0.12	0.14
Total	108.72	119.65	131.76

Source: Narodna banka Slovenska (2008)

The following Table 63 displays the outcomes of calculating the Slovakian ADL for the year 2006 (beginning with the PBO approach):[188]

---

[185] Source of data: Social Insurance Agency Slovakia.

[186] Source of data: Military Offices for Social Insurance Slovakia.

[187] Source of data: Ministry of Interior Slovakia.

[188] The supplementary tables for 2007 can be found in the appendix of this survey.

Table 63: Supplementary table Slovakia 2006 PBO
(in bn. SKK)

			Non-core national accounts (figures in bn. SKK)	
			General Government	Social Security
			G	H
		Opening Balance Sheet		
	1	Pension entitlements	*135.76*	*3,114.51*
		Changes in pension entitlements due to transactions		
Sum 2.1 to 2.4	2	Increase in pension entitlements due to social contributions	*25.79*	*259.79*
	2.1	*Employer actual social contributions*	1.96	67.46
	2.2	*Employer imputed social contributions*	15.74	
	2 3	*Household actual social contributions*	0.77	31.07
	2 4	*Household social contribution supplements*	7.32	161.26
	3	Other (actuarial) increase of pension entitlements		76.89
	4	Reduction in pension entitlements due to payment of pension benefits	4.52	115.13
2 + 3 - 4	5	Change in pension entitlements due to social contributions and pension benefits	*21.27*	*221.55*
	6	Transfers of entitlements between schemes	*0.00*	*0.00*
	7	Changes in pension entitlements due to other transactions	*0.00*	*0.00*
		Changes in pension entitlements due to other economic flows		
	8	Changes in entitlements due to revaluations	*0.00*	*0.00*
	9	Changes in entitlements due to other changes in volume	*0.00*	*0.00*
		Closing Balance Sheet		
	10	Pension entitlements	*157.04*	*3,336.06*
		Pension entitlements (% of GDP 2006)	*9.47*	*201.09*
	11	Output		
	12	Assets held at the end of the period to meet pensions		

Source: Own calculations

In the government employer pension scheme (column G) pension entitlements in the beginning of 2006 amount to 135.76 bn. SKK. On the one hand these pension entitlements are reduced due to pension payments of 4.52 bn. SKK in 2006. On the other hand this figure is increased due to actual contributions (1.96 bn. SKK) and actual household social contributions (0.77 bn. SKK) in 2006. Furthermore employer imputed social contributions (15.74 bn. SKK) significantly increase pension entitlements. Overall pension entitlements of the government employer pension scheme amount to 157.04 bn. SKK at the end of 2006. This is equal to some nine per cent of GDP in 2006.

Looking at the social security pension scheme (column H) the opening account of pension entitlements shows a value of 3,114.51 bn. SKK in 2006. Actual contributions account for 67.46 (employer) and 31.07 (employee) bn. SKK. The household contribution supplement comes up to 161.26 bn. SKK, the residual value adds up to 76.89 bn. SKK. Pension benefits in 2006 amount to 115.13 bn. SKK which overall leads to a change in pension entitlements of 221.55 bn. SKK. As a result, the closing stock of pension entitlements shows 3,336.06 bn. SKK, corresponding to about 201 per cent of GDP in 2006.

The same calculations have been conducted using the ABO approach. Table 64 illustrates the respective results.

Table 64: Supplementary table Slovakia 2006 ABO
(in bn. SKK)

| | | | Non-core national accounts (figures in bn. SKK) | |
			General Government G	Social Security H
		Opening Balance Sheet		
	1	Pension entitlements	*121.20*	*2,764.60*
		Changes in pension entitlements due to transactions		
Sum 2.1 to 2.4	2	Increase in pension entitlements due to social contributions	*23.73*	*241.94*
	2.1	*Employer actual social contributions*	1.96	67.46
	2 2	*Employer imputed social contributions*	14.46	
	2.3	*Household actual social contributions*	0.77	31.07
	2 4	*Household social contribution supplements*	6.54	143.41
	3	Other (actuarial) increase of pension entitlements		80.33
	4	Reduction in pension entitlements due to payment of pension benefits	4.52	115.13
2 + 3 - 4	5	Change in pension entitlements due to social contributions and pension benefits	*19.20*	*207.14*
	6	Transfers of entitlements between schemes		*0.00*
	7	Changes in pension entitlements due to other transactions		*0.00*
		Changes in pension entitlements due to other economic flows		
	8	Changes in entitlements due to revaluations	*0.00*	*0.00*
	9	Changes in entitlements due to other changes in volume		*0.00*
		Closing Balance Sheet		
	10	Pension entitlements	*140.40*	*2,971.75*
		Pension entitlements (% of GDP 2006)	*8.46*	*179.13*
	11	Output		
	12	Assets held at the end of the period to meet pensions		

Source: Own calculations

All numbers which have been taken from the national accounts, values in row 2.1, row 2.3 and row 4 stay constant. As expected, the other numbers are considerably lower when using the ABO approach in comparison to the method of PBO. Opening pension entitlements are lowered to 121.20 bn. SKK (column G) and 2,764.60 bn. SKK (column H). The closing pension entitlements likewise turn out to be smaller using the ABO approach. For the government employer pension scheme they accrue to 140.40 bn. SKK, corresponding to around eight per cent of GDP in 2006. The respective figure for the social security pension scheme adds up to 2,971.75 bn. SKK or in other words roughly 179 per cent of GDP. Comparing PBO and ABO results, the latter one turns out to be about eleven per cent lower than the respective PBO outcomes. We will see in section 3.20 that the size of Slovakian pension liabilities is relatively low in comparison to other countries examined in this survey.

3.19 UK – United Kingdom

The United Kingdom is a unitary state consisting of four countries: England, Northern Ireland, Scotland and Wales. The national currency is the Pound Sterling (GBP), with an exchange rate of 0.6715 GBP to the Euro in 2006.[189] In terms of nominal GDP, the United Kingdom is the fifth largest economy in the world. In 2006, the GDP added up to 1,321.9 bn. GBP, equal to a value of 1,939.0 bn. EUR. This corresponds to a per capita GDP of 21,800 GBP or approximately 32,000 EUR. The United Kingdom has a population of 60.43 million inhabitants as of January 1st, 2006.[190]

3.19.1 The demographic development in the UK

The United Kingdom's demographic development in the past is characterized by two features: Birth rates have decreased since the late 1960s while life expectancy has increased continuously over the last decades. Figure 44 shows the age-specific population structure of the UK in 2006, with men displayed on the left side and women on the right.

Some special features can be identified when examining the age pyramid of the UK. For one thing, the peak at the age group close to 60 is noticeable. This can most probably be traced back to a sudden increase in birth rates after the end of World War II. Apart from that, the age cohorts of the baby boom generation can clearly be identified. These are the age groups from 35 to 45 years in 2006. Younger age groups are numerically smaller which can be ascribed to the drop in birth rates at the end of the 1960s. Over the course of time the fertility rate started to recover, yet reached its absolute minimum 2001 with an average of only 1.63 births per woman. Recently, the births rates show a positive development; the fertility rate in 2006 amounted to 1.84. This progress can also be identified in the figure shown above at the age groups of zero to five years.

---

[189] Exchange rate as at December 29th, 2006.

[190] We display country data for 2006 since this is a main base year for our calculations.

Figure 44: Population structure In the UK (2006)
age groups 0 to 100 years

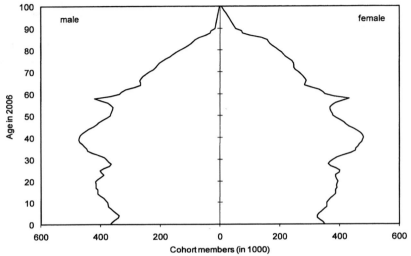

Source: Own calculations based on Eurostat (2009)

As mentioned previously, life expectancy in the UK has increased considerably in the last decades. In 2005, it added up to 77.1 years for males and 81.1 for females. This value is assumed to increase further to 82.9 for males and 86.6 for females born in the year 2050. Figure 45 shows the consequences of this increase by outlining the numerical development of elderly persons (persons aged 60 or older) between 2006 and 2045.

Compared to other EU member states, the numerical rise of elderly people in the UK turns out to be rather high. In the year 2025, elderly persons will have outnumbered the ones from 2006 by close to 40 per cent. Accordingly, the number will continue to rise which means that the UK faces high numbers of potential retirees in the future.

Figure 45: Development of elderly persons (aged 60+) in the UK
indexed to 100 in 2006

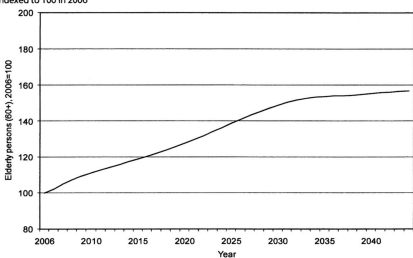

Source: Own calculations based on Eurostat (2009)

3.19.2 The UK pension system

3.19.2.1 The principles of the UK pension system

Britain features a rather complex pension system with elements of public and private provision. The public scheme consists of two tiers, a flat-rate basic pension and an earnings-related additional pension. It is possible to "contract out" of the earnings-related pension into private pensions of different types. To qualify for the basic state pensions, people need to pay social security contributions or have credits for nine-tenths of their potential working lives (44 years). Those who do not meet these requirements will receive a reduced pension. The benefit value for the earnings-related pension is calculated applying the average lifetime salary; earlier salaries are uprated in line with general average earnings. After retirement, the pensions are price-indexed. In 2003, the pension credit was introduced. Its target is to guarantee a pension level above the basic state pension. Unlike the basic state pension, it is means-tested. [191]

---

[191] For a short summary of the UK pension system see OECD (2007), p. 198-201. European Commission (2007) contains a more detailed description (p. 361 et sqq.).

3.19.2.2 Recent reforms of the UK pension system

The UK pension system underwent various modifications in the last years. In 2003, the pension credit was introduced which is an entitlement for people aged 60 and over, replacing the former Minimum Income Guarantee (MIG). It guarantees everyone aged 60 and over a minimum pension. The last pension reform took place in 2007 when some changes to the basic state pension were decided including:

- reducing the number of qualifying years needed for a full basic state pension to 30 for people who will reach state pension age on or after April 6th, 2010,
- any number of qualifying years will give entitlement to at least some basic state pension,
- people who have fewer than 30 qualifying years will get 1/30 of full basic state pension for each qualifying year they have,
- increasing basic state pension in line with earnings, rather than prices, which means it should rise more quickly each year than it does now (not before 2012).

Furthermore, some changes to the earnings-related pension have been conducted and the state pension age for women will increase from 60 to 65 so that it will be the same for both men and women by 2020. This change will be phased in from 2010. For both men and women retirement age is to rise further from 65 to 68 in stages between 2024 and 2046.

3.19.3 Measuring the UK accrued-to-date pension liabilities

In contrast to all other countries examined in this survey except Austria, we did not receive any data supply from the UK. The age-sex-specific micro data for the pension system stems from the Department for Work and Pensions (DWP, 2008) in the UK. The respective profile figures can be found in the appendix of this survey. Pension expenditures for 2005-07 were derived by simply multiplying the average pension payments per person with the caseload. These figures are displayed in Table 65:

Table 65: Social security pension payments United Kingdom
(in bn. GBP)

Type of pensions	Pension payments		
	2005	2006	2007
Old age pensions	51.18	53.68	57.25

Source: Department for Work and Pensions (2008)

Unfortunately only figures for old age pensions of the basic state pension scheme were available. They add up to 4.1 per cent of GDP in 2005, 2006 and 2007. It is worth mentioning that this share of GDP accounts for the lowest of all examined countries in this survey. Applying the above mentioned data to the methodology of the Freiburg model, the following outcomes are generated. We start with the PBO approach, depicted in Table 66:

Table 66: Supplementary table United Kingdom 2006 PBO (in bn. GBP)

			Non-core national accounts (figures in bn. GBP)	
			General Government	Social Security
			G	H
		Opening Balance Sheet		
	1	Pension entitlements		1,141.21
		Changes in pension entitlements due to transactions		
Sum 2.1 to 2.4	2	Increase in pension entitlements due to social contributions		58.66
	2.1	*Employer actual social contributions*		
	2.2	*Employer imputed social contributions*		
	2.3	*Household actual social contributions*		
	2.4	*Household social contribution supplements*		58.66
	3	Other (actuarial) increase of pension entitlements		58.95
	4	Reduction in pension entitlements due to payment of pension benefits		53.68
2 + 3 - 4	5	Change in pension entitlements due to social contributions and pension benefits		63.93
	6	Transfers of entitlements between schemes		0.00
	7	Changes in pension entitlements due to other transactions		0.00
		Changes in pension entitlements due to other economic flows		
	8	Changes in entitlements due to revaluations		0.00
	9	Changes in entitlements due to other changes in volume		0.00
		Closing Balance Sheet		
	10	Pension entitlements		1,205.14
		Pension entitlements (% of GDP 2006)		90.92
	11	Output		
	12	Assets held at the end of the period to meet pensions		

Source: Own calculations

Due to the fact that no actual social contributions were supplied, the supplementary table does not show a complete picture of the social security pension. However, the opening balance adds up to pension entitlements of 1,141.21 bn. GBP which are reduced by pension benefits in 2006 to the amount of 53.68 bn. GBP. Entitlements at the end of 2006 add up to 1,205.14 bn. GBP, corresponding to almost 91 per cent of the GDP. As expected, this value is the lowest of all examined countries due to the minor size of pension benefits. Due to lack of data regarding age-sex-specific earnings during lifetime, it was not possible to compute the ABO pension liabilities in an adequate way in the case of the UK. Therefore the supplementary table for the ABO approach is not displayed here.

3.20 Cross-country comparison

This section gives an overview of the pension liabilities of the 19 countries examined in this study. The sum of accrued-to-date liabilities (ADL) from the government employer pension scheme (column G of the supplementary table) and the social security pension scheme (column H) at the end of 2006 will be taken as a basis. To allow meaningful comparisons across the countries examined, liabilities are related to countries' respective GDP in 2006. In a second step, we will identify the main determining factors for the level of pension liabilities.

It must be emphasized in advance that the ranking of a certain country is not necessarily connected to the financial shape of the country's pension scheme. In other words: The level of pension liabilities is not related to the sustainability of the pension scheme.[192] Even if a pension scheme features considerably high liabilities, these could possibly be compensated by future contributors. But as future contributions are not taken into account when estimating ADL, no statement can be made concerning sustainability or necessary reforms of the pension system. However, even if we assume that the extent of ADL will not be mixed up with the extent of sustainability, there is a clear political danger in presenting a cross-country comparison. For example, some governments, especially in countries with a high explicit debt-GDP ratio, fear that the publication of a cross-country comparison of ADL – not to mention the inclusion of ADL in the system of national accounts (SNA) – could be a first step towards the integration of ADL to explicit public debt. In the light of the Maastricht criteria, this fear is of course understandable. Nevertheless, for reasons mentioned in section 2.1 of this study, ADL cannot be equated to explicit debt.

To assure comparability, all pension liabilities shown in this chapter have been calculated on the same basis, which is PBO in our case. Figure 46 displays a cross-country comparison of pension liabilities in 2006 related to the respective countries' GDP. In case the country features a government employer pension scheme and a social security pension scheme, both schemes are added to a total of ADL.

---

[192] See section 2.1 for further details. In general, a pension scheme is considered sustainable if neither future contributions nor benefits have to be adjusted to generate financial balance, taking into account future demographic and economic circumstances. For a detailed description of fiscal sustainability, see Bonin (2001), p. 54 et sqq.

Figure 46: Cross-country comparison of ADL in 2006
(in per cent of GDP 2006, PBO)

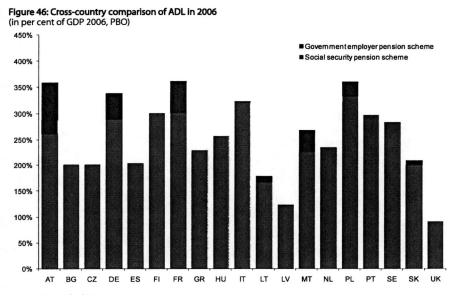

Source: Own calculations

As shown above, the largest pension liabilities in per cent of GDP can be found in France (362.2), Poland (361.1) and Austria (359.9), followed by Germany (338.6) and Italy (323.1). It might be a coincidence that all these countries possess a special pension scheme for civil servants but even without these schemes they rank among the highest figures observed. Most of the other countries show pension liabilities in the range of 200 to about 300 per cent of GDP. These are Finland (301.4), Portugal (298.3) and Sweden (284.5) followed by Malta (269.0), Hungary (257.5), the Netherlands (236.2) and Greece (230.7). Slovakia (210.5), Spain (204.2), Bulgaria (201.8) and the Czech Republic (201.4) can be regarded as having a medium level of pension liabilities. The lowest liabilities have been calculated for the United Kingdom (91.2), followed by Latvia (124.8) and Lithuania (179.9).

In the next part, a brief attempt is made to identify the main determining factors for the different results. We start with the initial levels of expenditures in the base year 2006. These can be detected in Figure 47:

189

Figure 47: Cross-country comparison of pension expenditures in 2006
(in per cent of GDP 2006)

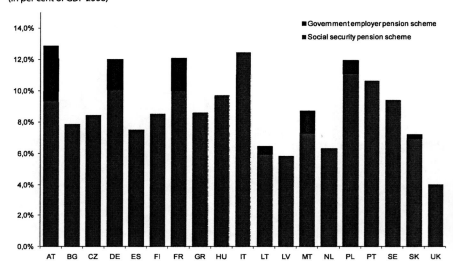

Source: Own calculations

Figure 47 displays the size of public pension expenditures related to the corresponding GDPs in 2006. Austria (12.9), Italy (12.4), France (12.1), Germany (12.0) and Poland (12.0) show the highest expenditures in 2006, amounting to twelve per cent of GDP and above. Having in mind that these five countries dispose of the highest pension liabilities in total as well, a first determining factor might have been found already. The majority of countries surveyed in this study show pension expenditures in the range of about seven to ten per cent of GDP. These are the Southern European countries except Italy (Portugal (10.6), Greece (8.6), Spain (7.5) and Malta (8.7)), most of the Eastern European countries (Hungary (9.7), Czech Republic (8.5), Bulgaria (7.9) and Slovakia (7.2)) along with the Scandinavian countries (Sweden (9.4) and Finland (8.5)). Rather low expenditures can be observed in the two Baltic countries Lithuania (6.5) and Latvia (5.9) as well as in the Netherlands (6.3). The UK shows by far the lowest expenditures (4.1).[193]

---

[193] It should be noted that budget data for the UK only includes a part of the public pension, the basic state pension. Thus, it does not cover the whole public pension system. Besides this, the pension system of the UK features a strong third pillar, and the social security pension scheme can be characterized as a minimum pension scheme.

To sum up, the first determining factor is given by the present level of expenditures of a country's pension scheme. Ceteris paribus, it can be stated that the higher the initial pension expenditures of a country are, the higher their pension liabilities accrued-to-date will be.[194] However, the question arises to which factor the different levels of pension expenditures in the base year can be ascribed to. If a country shows high pension expenditures, this can basically be traced back to two reasons: either the generosity of the system or the age-structure of the population. Two countries might guarantee the same level of per-capita pensions; still the one showing a higher average age will be forced to spend more. In order to check if different expenditure levels shown in Figure 47 are correlated to the age-structure of the corresponding countries, we now take a look at the old-age dependency ratios (OADR) of the examined countries. These are supposed to serve as a proxy for the age structure of each country. Figure 48 shows the OADR60[195] in a cross-country comparison. As this figure shows, the ranking of OADR60 does not follow the ranking of the level of pension expenditures. Poland as the country with one of the highest expenditure levels holds a rather low dependency ratio. In contrast to this, Hungary shows the highest OADR60 even though its pension expenditures does not belong to the highest in this country selection. However, there are other examples which support the assumption of a correlation between pension expenditures and old age dependency ratios. Germany and Italy both show rather high OADR60 and high pension expenditures. To sum up, it can be stated that the cross-country differences in age-structure cannot satisfyingly explain the differences in pension expenditures. Thus, we presume that generosity or – in other words – the replacement rate plays an important role.

---

[194] Holzmann et al. (2004, p. 25) come to similar findings. However, although they make out a positive correlation between the level of liabilities and the level of pension expenditures, the current pension spending of a country does not seem to be a reliable predictor of pension liabilities from their point of view. It is worth mentioning that Holzmann et al. examine 35 low and middle income countries which – unlike the countries examined in this survey – in many cases do not show a mature pension scheme. Especially in case of rather young pension schemes the level of pension expenditures might be low despite high pension liabilities. Thus, in those cases the explanatory power of the amount of initial pension expenditures is limited.

[195] The OADR60 expresses the share of the population aged 60 and more in relation to the share of population aged 20 to 59.

Accrued-to-date liabilities of 19 EU countries

Figure 48: Cross-country comparison of old age dependency ratios (OADR60) in 2006
(share of people aged 60 and more to people aged 20 to 59)

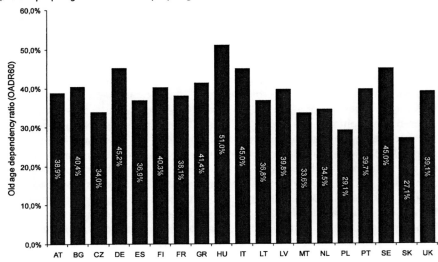

Source: Own calculations based on Eurostat (2009)

A second factor determining pension liabilities might very well be the future development of elderly persons. Figure 49 and Figure 50 show a cross-country comparison of the development of elderly persons (defined as persons aged 60 or older). In order to ensure some clearness, the 19 countries examined have been classified in Euro and non–Euro countries.

It can be discovered at first sight that in all observed countries the number of elderly persons (60+) is expected to rise in the future. For our purposes, the development of this age group in the first 20 to 30 years is of higher interest than the final level in 2045, simply due to the fact that persons entering the observed age group after 2040 have not had the chance to earn a considerable amount of pension rights until 2006.[196] Thus, they are of less interest than persons entering the "60+" age group in the near future. Figure 49 and Figure 50 show that the largest increase is assumed to take place in Malta, Slovakia, Poland and the Netherlands followed by France and Finland in the first 30 years after 2006. This might explain why Poland shows slightly higher pension liabilities than Austria despite featuring

---

[196] Furthermore, pension benefits in 2040 are highly discounted. Therefore they have a minor impact on our outcomes.

lower pension expenditures in 2006 than their Austrian counterparts. Developments on a rather low level can be observed in Hungary, Bulgaria, Lithuania and especially Latvia. All other countries feature a medium rise in the number of elderly people.

Figure 49: Cross-country comparison of the development of elderly persons (60+), Euro area 2006 to 2045 (2006 = 100)

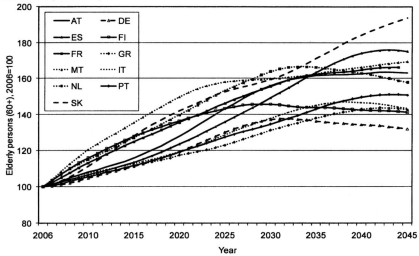

Source: Own calculations based on Eurostat (2009)

Other important factors are the indexations of pensions as well as deductions of future pensions due to pension reforms already enacted. Figure 51 (Euro countries) and Figure 52 (non-Euro countries) demonstrate how the expenditures in the various countries will develop in the future.

Figure 50: Cross-country comparison of the development of elderly persons (60+), non-Euro area 2006 to 2045 (2006 = 100)

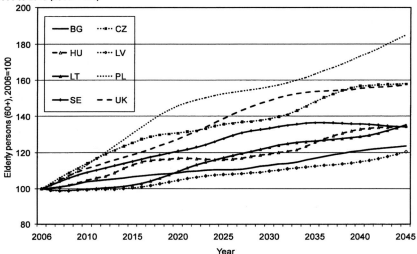

Source: Own calculations based on Eurostat (2009)

Due to the fact that the expenditures are discounted to the present value of 2006, almost all graphs minimize over time. Nevertheless, expenditures in Malta and Finland increase in the first years after 2006. This can be mainly traced back to the demographic development in these countries.

As an example, we choose two countries which start at the same level of expenditures – Greece and Malta. It can be seen that Greece's future expenditures constantly stay below that of the Maltese. One reason for this – besides the ageing development – might be the indexation of pensions. While pension benefits in Greece are in general only adjusted to the growth of the CPI, pensions in Malta are mainly indexed to wage growth.

Figure 51: Cross-country comparison of public pension expenditures 2006 to 2055, Euro area
(present value 2006, in per cent of GDP 2006, PBO)

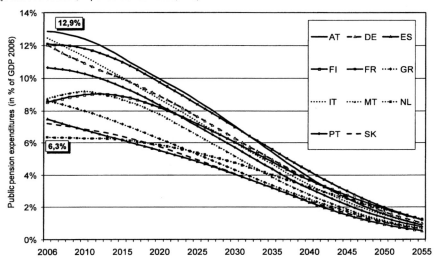

Source: Own calculations

Another interesting example is given by the comparison between Slovakia and the Netherlands. Although Slovakian pension expenditures start at a higher level than their Dutch counterparts, their pension liabilities rank below the ones from the Netherlands. In terms of demography they show a similar ageing process; their indexation rules do not differ remarkably from each other either. Hence, the different liability levels might be ascribed to the fact that there have not been any major pension reforms in the Netherlands in recent years, while the legal retirement age in Slovakia was raised by three years for men and even six years for women. Furthermore, Slovakia introduced a second funded pillar in 2005 which will partly replace its unfunded counterpart and therefore reduce future expenditures. Recapitulating these examples, the influence of indexation and recent pension reforms on the level of pension liabilities might not be as strong as the initial level of pension expenditures, but it does seem to play a significant role.

After examining the development of elderly age groups as well as the impact of reforms and the pension indexation, the initial level still seems to be the most important determining factor regarding the level of pension liabilities of a certain country. Table 67 summarizes our findings and gives an overview of the main determining factors detected.

Figure 52: Cross-country comparison of public pension expenditures 2006 to 2055, non-Euro area (present value 2006, in per cent of GDP 2006, PBO)

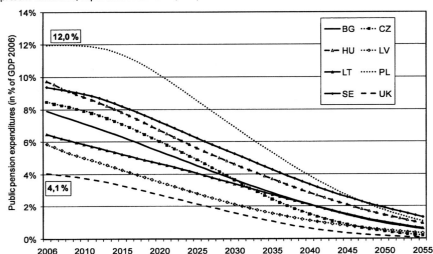

Source: Own calculations

Three points (•••) indicate that the respective factor will considerably increase pension liabilities. One point (•) on the contrary implies the opposite and two points (••) a degree in between. This approach shall be illustrated by an example: Finland shows relatively high (•••) initial pension expenditures as well as a relatively high (•••) increase in the development of elderly people. Furthermore, the Finnish indexation of pensions can be regarded as quite low (•/••) but not very low (•) and it has introduced modest pension reforms (••) in recent years.[197] Overall, Finland features the 6th highest pension liabilities in terms of GDP. Hence, it can be stated that the fewer points a country shows in total, the smaller are its pension liabilities in terms of GDP. However, it should be kept in mind in this context that the initial level of pensions apparently is the main determining factor for the level of pension liabilities.

---

[197] Since we compare pension liabilities at the end of 2006 only pension reforms legislated up to this point have been considered in Table 67.

Table 67: Main determining factors of pension liabilities in the EU

	Initial level of pension expenditures in % of GDP	Development of elderly persons (60+)	Pension Indexation	Recent pension reforms: *Profound* (•), *Moderate* (••), *None* (•••)	Ranking of pension liabilities
AT (Austria)	•••	••	•	•	3
BG (Bulgaria)	••	•	••	••	15
CZ (Czech Republic)	••	••	••	•	16
DE (Germany)	•••	••	•••	•/••	4
ES (Spain)	••	••	•	•••	14
FI (Finland)	•••	•••	•/••	••	6
FR (France)	•••	•••	•	••	1
GR (Greece)	••	•/••	•	••	12
HU (Hungary)	••	•	••	••	10
IT (Italy)	•••	••	•	•	5
LT (Lithuania)	•	•	•••	••	17
LV (Latvia)	•	•	•/••	•	18
MT (Malta)	••	•••	•••	•	9
NL (Netherlands)	•	•••	•••	•••	11
PL (Poland)	•••	•••	•/••	•	2
PT (Portugal)	•••	••	•	•/••	7
SE (Sweden)	••	••	•	•	8
SK (Slovakia)	••	•••	••	••	13
UK (United Kingdom)	•	••	•	•/••	19

Source: Own illustration

Picking up Feldstein's (1974) argument presented in section 2.1 of this text, in the following part a brief attempt is made to check if the design of a public pension scheme or – more precisely – the extent of ADL of that scheme has an impact on the saving behaviour of the examined country. Figure 53 shows a cross-country comparison of ADL and gross household savings for all countries examined in this chapter.[198]

The order of the countries follows the ranking of the ADL.[199] Unlike our previous procedure, we now express the ADL (and the gross household saving rate) in relation to the gross disposable income (GDI) instead of the gross domestic product (GDP). Thus, the results shown above differ from the ones presented in Figure 46. The ADL of the different countries are displayed as grey bars with the related scale on the left side of the figure; the data labelling is white. The saving rates are marked

---

[198] Only Malta has been left out as no gross household saving rate has been available for Malta.

[199] The government employer pension schemes are not shown in Figure 53 as Feldstein's (1974) argumentation includes social security pension schemes only.

as black squares with data indicated in black colour and the corresponding scale on the right side.

Figure 53: Cross-country comparison of ADL and gross household savings 2006
(in per cent of GDI 2006, PBO)

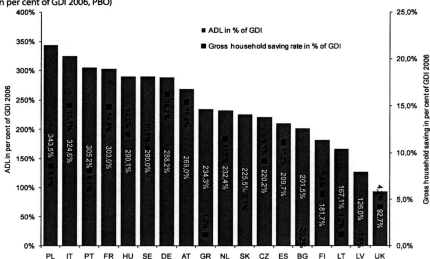

Source: Own calculations, Eurostat (2009), Leetmaa et al (2009)

Feldstein (1974, 1996) empirically showed that the existence of a social security pension scheme reduces private savings. Thus, we presume that this also applies for the countries of the EU. We are fully aware of the fact that in order to comprehensively test if Feldstein's findings for the United States also apply to European countries, time series of ADL and private savings should be used instead of a discrete point in time. However, for lack of these time series, the figure shown above may serve as a first indicator for this analysis.

At first sight it becomes apparent that there is no clear correlation between the ADL and the gross savings of a country. Though Poland as the country ranked first in terms of ADL indicates relatively low savings, the subsequent countries show high ADL as well as high private savings. The lowest saving rates of all countries presented can be found in Latvia (-3.6 per cent of GDI) and Bulgaria (-29.2 per cent of GDI). However, in contrast to our presumption, these countries show rather low ADL in relation to their GDI.

Besides different designs of pension schemes as a possible criterion, varying private saving rates across Europe may be traced back to the following factors:[200] Generally, higher income leads to a higher saving rate (income effect). Gains/losses on assets may lead to changing saving rates while the imcome stays constant (wealth effect). Furthermore, better credit facilities may cause lower saving rates as consumption credits are easier to obtain. Last but not least, cultural and social differences among countries may also result in diverse saving behaviour.

---

[200] See Leetmaa et al. (2009), p. 2.

4 Open-system net liabilities of four selected countries

In chapter 3 the accrued-to-date liabilities (ADL) of the public pension schemes of 19 EU member countries were presented. The corresponding calculations were conducted in order to receive some benchmark results for pension liabilities which are going to be included in the revised system of national accounts. As pointed out earlier, the concept of ADL does not allow for a judgement of sustainability of a pension scheme (or of any other scheme examined). In fact, the size of ADL can even lead to wrong assessments regarding the sustainability of a pension scheme, especially when it comes to cross-country comparisons. Taking the evaluation of Figure 46 as an example, one might come to the conclusion that the pension system of countries like Poland or Austria are in an unfavourable situation in terms of sustainability while countries like Lithuania or Latvia seem to be in a relatively comfortable position. This view is certainly wrong, and it can be shown that the ranking of Figure 46 could even be inverted when sustainability enters the picture. The reason for this is twofold: First, in the concept of ADL only the pension rights which have been earned until the base year are taken into consideration. That means that only a part of future pension expenditures is covered by ADL. Secondly, the concept of ADL merely includes expenditures; assets like future contributions or possibly some kind of capitalized funds are not taken into account. In other words, ADL represent a purely gross concept.

As has been shown previously in section 2.1, the concept of open-system net liabilities (OSNL) on the one hand considers future pension payments derived from pension rights which have been accrued prior to as well as after the base year. On the other hand, when calculating OSNL, future pension expenditures are confronted with future contributions. For this reasons, OSNL are a suitable indicator for assessing the sustainability of a pension scheme. The present value of all future deficits quantifies the discrepancy to a sustainable situation.

This chapter contains a sustainability analysis for the social security pension schemes of four selected member countries of the European Union. In contrast to the procedure in chapter 3 where general social security pension schemes as well as government-sponsored employer schemes have been taken into account, this chapter will focus on general social security schemes only. The countries examined are Germany, Lithuania, the Netherlands and Sweden. They cover a considerable range of different features regarding diverging designs of the corresponding public pension schemes as well as demographic peculiarities in Europe: Germany is a good example for a Bismarckian pension system of the defined benefit type while the Netherlands show a Beveridgean pension system with only basic coverage, benefits which are independent from contributions paid before and a traditionally strong second pillar of occupational pensions. The social security system of Sweden represents an example for a social security system with a Scandinavian character, while as a matter of exception in Scandinavia, Sweden was the first country to introduce a so-called notional defined contribution (NDC) pension scheme. Lithuania as one of the Baltic states and the first Soviet republic to declare its independence in 1990 has implemented a social security system which has recently been adjusted to future demographic challenges.

In terms of demographic peculiarities, Sweden and the Netherlands show relatively high birth rates, while Germany and Lithuania belong to the European countries with the lowest fertility rates. Life expectancies in Germany, the Netherlands and Sweden are quite similar with Sweden ranking first followed by Germany and the Netherlands; however, Lithuania's male/female citizens in average die twelve/ five years earlier than their North and Western European counterparts. Furthermore it is worth mentioning that the gap between male and female life expectancy in Lithuania is considerably higher than in any other EU member states (except Latvia and Estonia). This special feature which can be observed in most former Soviet republics can probably be traced back to lifestyle choices and industrial labour of the male population in those countries.

We will proceed by examining the four countries mentioned previously. The first country to be surveyed will be Germany, followed by Lithuania, the Netherlands and Sweden. We will start by presenting the future demographic development of the population whereas we will focus on the future demographic age structure and the relation between the old and the young. In this context we will present a population projection for each country. Although population projections were already produced in the course of the ADL chapter, we have to recalculate them for our OSNL calculations since in this chapter migration is included. Furthermore, we apply two projection scenarios, as will be shown later in this chapter.

The corresponding pension schemes will be described only briefly since this has been done already in the respective sections of chapter 3. Moreover, age-sex-specific pension profiles are identical to the ones used in chapter 3 unless indicated otherwise. Contribution profiles for the four countries examined will be shown in the appendix of this survey. Aggregate data for the various countries generally stems from the corresponding members of the Eurostat/ECB Contact Group on Pensions.

4.1   DE – Germany

The general social security pension scheme in Germany, the *Gesetzliche Rentenversicherung* (GRV, statutory pension insurance) is by far the biggest pension scheme in Germany. It encompasses some 20 million beneficiaries and about 35 million actively insured persons.[201] The total expenditures in 2006 added up to 230.76 bn. EUR which corresponds to 9.9 per cent of GDP in 2006. These expenditures were financed by social contributions to the amount of 148.71 bn. EUR and a taxed-financed federal subsidy of 82.05 bn. EUR. Expressed in another way, one third of all pension payments in 2006 have been paid out of taxes.[202] The profiles which have been applied for distributing the aggregate sums to the age cohorts in the base year can be found in the appendix of this study.[203]

4.1.1   Future demographic development

Analogous to chapter 3, we will begin with an assessment of the demographic situation in Germany. In contrast to our former procedure, we now calculate two population projections which are based on the assumptions of the recent population projections of Eurostat, Europop2004 and Europop2008.[204] In doing so, we are able to show how demographic assumptions – especially regarding life expectancy – have changed considerably between the last two projections of Eurostat. Furthermore, we will demonstrate the impact of varying demographic scenarios on our results. It is worth noticing that in contrast to chapter 3 we now integrate future migration into our projections as in this chapter pension schemes are considered to be open. This enables individuals to enter the scheme in the future and earn some pension entitlements. Table 68 presents the central assumptions of the German population projection.

---

[201] Statistics as of December 31ˢᵗ, 2006. Source: Deutsche Rentenversicherung Bund (2007b, 2008).

[202] Source: Statistisches Bundesamt (2008).

[203] See Figure 82 and Figure 83.

[204] For the Europop2008 scenario, we deploy the assumptions of Europop2008, convergence scenario, convergence year 2150. For the Europop2004 scenario, we use the assumptions of Europop2004, trend scenario, national level, baseline variant. This is valid for all countries examined in this chapter. All details regarding Europop2008 and Europop2004 are available on Eurostat's webpages (http://epp.eurostat.ec.europa.eu). Comparing these two scenarios, one comes to the conclusion that Europop2008 represents a scenario of an older population relative to Europop2004 due to higher life expectancy and lower net migration. Please note that we regard Europop2008 as the more realistic scenario because it is the most recent projection of Eurostat. Hence we will focus on Europop2008 in case we take only one scenario into consideration.

Table 68: Central assumptions of the German population projection

Parameter	Year	Scenarios	
		Europop2004	Europop2008
Total fertility rate	2006	1.34	1.34
	2050	1.45	1.49
Life expectancy at birth for females/males in years	2006	82.4/ 77.2	82.4/ 77.2
	2050	86.9/ 82.0	88.0/ 83.6
Net migration	2006	22,791	22,791
	2050	179,196	135,726

Source: Eurostat (2009)

The table shows that the total fertility rate in Germany is expected to rise from a level of 1.34 to 1.45 (1.49) until 2050 in the Europop2004 (Europop2008) scenario, hence the two scenarios do not differ substantially from each other in this regard. The life expectancy in Germany is supposed to change as well. According to Europop2004, it will rise to 86.9 years for women and 82.0 years for men born in 2050. This means a considerable increase of 4.5 years for women and 4.8 years for men. In Europop2008, even higher yields of life expectancy are expected; here, an increase of 5.6 years for women and 6.4 years for men is assumed. In other words, in four years time the assumptions regarding life expectancy of individuals born in 2050 increase by 1.1 years for women and even 1.6 years for men. Net migration also varies considerably between the two scenarios, in Europop2004 net migration in 2050 is expected to be about one third higher than in Europop2008. However, both scenarios expect an extensive increase of net migration in relation to 2006.

When examining the impact of future demographic development on PAYG pension schemes, the total size of future population is less important than the possible change of the age structure. Figure 54 shows the age structure of the German population in 2005 and 2050 (Europop2004 and Europop2008).

The age structure in 2006 has been extensively discussed in section 3.4.1 of this study. Therefore, we will now put the focus on the changes of age structure in 2050. It can clearly be seen in Figure 54 that regardless which scenario is chosen all cohorts up to the age of 55 will have decreased in the year 2050. The biggest loss compared to 2006 can be detected in the age groups of around 35 to 45 which represented the baby-boomer generation in 2006. The different course of the two scenarios Europop2004 and Europop2008 can be traced back to two differences: Europop2004 shows bigger cohorts in the younger part of the population in 2050; this is due to higher assumptions regarding future net migration. However, Europop2008 shows higher results at the age groups being 70 years or older in 2050 which can be ascribed to higher assumptions regarding future life expectancy.

Figure 54: Population structure in Germany (2006 and 2050)

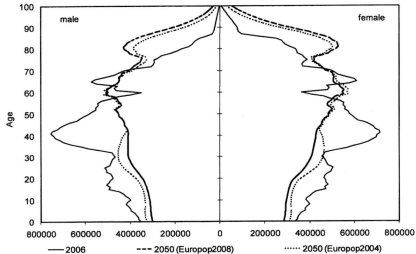

Source: Own calculations based on Eurostat (2009)

When we examined accrued-to-date liabilities (ADL) of various pension schemes in chapter 3 of this study, no future contributions have been taken into consideration which means that our results have not been affected by the development of future contributors. Thus, the only demographic indicator relevant for the extent of ADL was the future development of elderly people.[205] However, when assessing open-system net liabilities, the situation changes. As mentioned previously, the size of the total population or the number of elderly people is not the only component which affects the results. It is rather the future relation between retirees and contributors which counts. The old-age dependency ratio (OADR) expresses the share of old people (usually 65 and older or 60 and older) to young people (usually 20 to 64 or 20 to 59).[206] It represents a good proxy for the future share of beneficiaries to contributors, as it indicates the number of potential beneficiaries in relation to potential

---

[205] See for example Figure 13 of this study.

[206] The share of people aged 65 and more to people aged 20 to 64 will be called OADR 65. Similar to section 3.20, the share of people aged 60 and more to people aged 20 to 59 will be called OADR 60.

contributors. If the OADR stays constant over time, no adjustments in terms of contribution rates or pension levels will have to be made in a pension scheme financed on a PAYG basis. The question which of the two ratios shall be uses preferably for evaluating the future population depends on the average retirement age of the relevant pension scheme. Figure 55 shows the development of the OADR65 and OADR60 in Germany, using both demographic scenarios described previously.

Figure 55: Development of the old-age dependency ratio in Germany until 2070

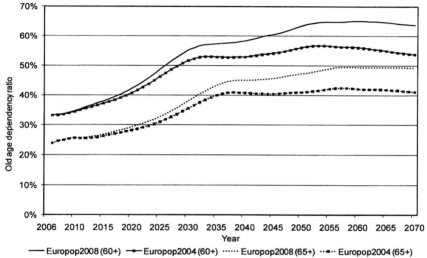

Source: Own calculations based on Eurostat (2009)

Taking a look at the OADR60 in the Europop2008 scenario first, the ratio rises from some 33 per cent in 2006 up to 55 per cent in 2030 and continues rising up to a level of nearly 64 per cent in 2050. In other words, the OADR60 in 2050 will almost be twice as high as it was in 2006. Changing to the Europop2004 scenario, things seem to look less alarming. The OADR60 in 2030 comes off nearly four points lower at a ratio of some 51 per cent. In 2050 the gap will have increased even more to a value of more than seven points (56 per cent). The differences between these two indicators can be traced back to the different assumptions of both scenarios; higher net migration causes a higher number of young persons in Europop2004 while higher life expectancy accounts for a higher number of elderly persons in Europop2008.

The OADR65 draws a similar picture, but it is worth mentioning that the differences between both scenarios are not as large as in the case of OADR60. From a starting point of nearly 24 per cent both scenarios follow almost the same path until in 2015 the rate of growth begins to differ. In 2030 the Europop2008 scenario shows a value of 38 per cent, respectively 35 per cent for Europop2004. Eventually in 2050 almost the same gap as in the case of the OADR60 can be detected, Europop2008 amounts to 47 per cent while Europop2004 indicates a value of 41 per cent.

To sum up it can be said that the share of elderly persons in relation to persons of employable age in Germany will rise considerably in the future. However, the extent strongly depends on the indicator applied and the underlying assumptions. It varies from an increase of 69 per cent (OADR65, Europop2004) between 2006 and 2050 to 98 per cent (OADR65, Europop2008). In the following section we will demonstrate how this development affects the results of our calculations.

4.1.2   Results

Analogous to our procedure in chapter 3 we applied a real wage growth rate of 1.5 per cent and a real discount rate of 3.0 per cent. However, at this point it is worth highlighting that there are certain differences between the way accrued-to-date liabilities and open-system net liabilities have been calculated in this survey. This refers to a case when reforms of the pension system have been established after the base year but prior to the time of calculation. When accounting for accrued-to-date liabilities, only those legal changes are considered which are adopted until the end of the base year. In the concept of generational accounting as the methodology applied for estimating open-system net liabilities in this study all legal changes up to the time of calculation are taken into consideration. In the case of Germany this refers to the increase of the legal retirement age from 65 to 67 in 2007, the so-called catch-up factor in 2007 which makes up prior pension deductions not realized previously and the suspension of the temporary modification of the pension formula in 2008. All these reforms have been included in our calculations. Table 69 gives an overview of the corresponding results:

Table 69: Open-system net liabilities of the German statutory pension insurance in 2006

Demographic scenarios	Open-system net liabilities	
	In bn. EUR	In % of GDP 2006
Europop2004	2,241.41	96.6 %
Europop2008	3,276.22	141.1 %

Source: Own calculations

The main finding of our calculations is the following: The German statutory pension scheme is not sustainable. However, Table 69 indicates that the extent of non-sustainability heavily depends on which demographic scenario is applied. The open-system net liabilities with Europop2004 add up to some 96 per cent of GDP in 2006 while the (more realistic) scenario of Europop2008 amounts to some 140 per cent of GDP. In other words, Europop2008 produces a result nearly 50 per cent higher than Europop2004. This can be ascribed to the fact that on the one hand, in Europop2008 the net migration is assumed to be lower than in Europop2004 and thus there will be less contributors to pay into the system (admittedly, there will also be less retirees to receive pensions in the long run, but this effect turns out to be rather small due to high discounting). On the other hand, life expectancy is assumed to grow faster in Europop2008, thus retirees will receive their pensions for a longer period of time.

In order to allow a better classification of the former result, we will now take a look at the pension level of future retirees. We set the initial pension level of the base year to 100 and compare the average future pension to the corresponding growth-adjusted wage level. Figure 56 shows how the pension level of an average German male retiree develops over time.

The image clearly shows that future pensions in Germany will not grow as fast as wages. In 2020, retirees will receive 88 per cent of what a retiree in 2006 has been paid related to the corresponding wage of that year. This value will even decrease to 81 per cent in 2030 and 77 per cent in 2050. Generally the indexation of pensions should follow the per-capita wage growth rate. However, a couple of pension reforms mentioned above cause considerable cuts of the pension indexation. In fact, the development of the pension level shows how future retirees are affected by recent pension reforms. In a short excursion we will show that without these reforms, the pension system in Germany would face a much more unfavourable situation in terms of sustainability.[207] Figure 57 demonstrates the path from a situation without pension reforms in 2001 to the current situation much closer to sustainability.[208]

---

[207] Heidler (2009) provides similar estimations (see p. 134). However, the total outcomes differ from the ones presented in this study due to a different base year, different profiles and other demographic assumptions.

[208] For these calculations the Europop2008 scenario has been deployed. However, applying the Europop2004 scenario, results qualitatively stay the same.

Figure 56: Average gross pension level In Germany 2006 to 2070[209]
indexed to 100 in 2006

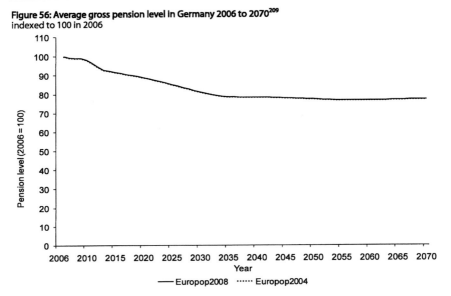

Source: Own calculations

It can be seen that the Riester reform in 2001, which introduced a new pension for-mula, reduced the OSNL by 28 percentage points of GDP in 2006. The biggest cut-back took place in 2004 when the sustainability factor was decided. It reduced the OSNL by 76 percentage points of GDP. The last major pension reform in 2007 was the gradual increase of the legal retirement age from 65 to 67, starting in 2011. This reform lessened the OSNL by another 27 percentage points; hence the current status quo amounts to 141 per cent of GDP. In other words, the sustainability gap of the German pension scheme has been close to halved thanks to pension reforms since 2001.[210]

---

[209] Due to simplification, this figure only refers to male retirees. However, pensions for female reti-rees follow the same growth path. This counts for the pension levels of all countries examined in this chapter.

[210] It is worth mentioning that our analysis does not simulate a situation where none of the above-mentioned pension reforms has ever come into force. This is not possible due to the fact that the past impacts of the reforms are implicitly included in the budget of the base year. For this reason, we rather picture a scenario where all pension reforms are abolished in the base year 2006.

Figure 57: Open-system net liabilities of the German statutory pension insurance in 2006 before and after pension reforms (Europop2008), in per cent of GDP

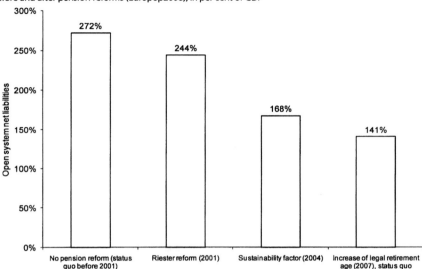

Source: Own calculations

As emphasized previously, one of the main assumptions of generational accounting is a constant continuation of current fiscal policy. In the case of the pension sector, this inter alia implies constant contribution rates.[211] We now change this assumption by illustrating what will happen if policy makers immediately adjust the contribution rate in case of an unbalanced budget. Put differently, we calculate endogenous contribution rate which in every period ensure fiscal balance. By doing so, it can be demonstrated how future contributors will be incriminated if deficits are financed by contribution boost instead of taxes. Figure 58 illustrates the course of these contribution rates:

---

[211] This is certainly not a realistic scenario since in a non-balanced situation contribution rates are often subject to change. However, please note that generational accounting is not a forecasting tool. It is rather supposed to unfold hidden debts and shows the consequences of what will happen if policy makers do not react.

Figure 58: Future endogenous pension contribution rates in Germany, 2006 to 2070

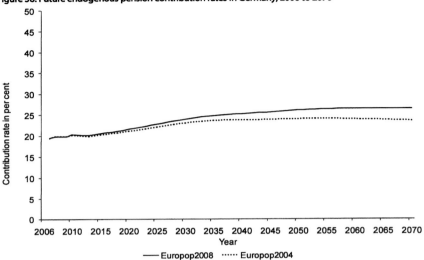

Source: Own calculations

Not surprisingly, in the long run endogenous growth rates turn out to be considerably higher in case Europop2008 is applied. Consequently, the growth paths of both Europop2004 and Europop2008 follow the growth path of the old-age dependency ratio presented in Figure 55. The differences between the course of contribution rates and the old-age dependency ratio can be traced back to the decreasing pension level shown in Figure 56. Expressed in numbers, contribution rates rise from a level of 19.5 per cent to 23.1 per cent in 2030 and 24.1 per cent in 2050 (Europop2004), respectively 24.0 per cent in 2030 and 26.1 per cent in 2050 (Europop2008).

4.2   LT – Lithuania

The total expenditures of the Lithuanian social security pension scheme in the base year 2006 amounted to a value of 1.44 bn. EUR.[212] This corresponds to 6.0 per cent of GDP in 2006. Total revenues from social pension contributions came up to a value of 1.73 bn. EUR.[213] Thus, the Lithuanian pension scheme could record a surplus of 0.29 bn. EUR in 2006.[214] The profiles which have been applied for distributing the aggregate sums to the age cohorts in the base year can be found in the appendix of this study.[215]

4.2.1   Future demographic development

In the following section we will supply a brief outline of the future demographic development in Lithuania. Analogous to the previous section we will start by comparing the central assumptions of the official population projections of Eurostat. Table 70 gives an overview of these assumptions:

Table 70: Central assumptions of the Lithuanian population projection

Parameter	Year	Scenarios	
		Europop2004	Europop2008
Total fertility rate	2006	1.35	1.35
	2050	1.60	1.51
Life expectancy at birth for females/males in years	2006	77.0/ 65.3	77.0/ 65.3
	2050	83.7/ 75.5	85.3/ 78.1
Net migration	2006	-4,857	-4,857
	2050	4,322	1,151

Source: Eurostat (2009)

---

[212] We are aware of the fact that the national currency of Lithuania is the Lithuanian Litas (LTL). However, since figures supplied by Statistics Lithuania are indicated in EUR, we follow this manner.

[213] This figure has been derived from the number of total social contributions in 2006. According to the Ministry of Social Security and Labour (2007, p. 75) in Lithuania total contributions in 2006 amounted to 7.8 bn. LTL. As pensions account for 26.1 percentage points of the total contribution rate of 34.0 per cent, the aggregate of pension contributions amounted to 5.9 bn. LTL. Applying the 2006 exchange rate of 3.4528 LTL to the Euro, total contributions of 1.734 bn. EUR come out.

[214] However, in order to achieve a balanced budget in the base year we made the assumption that the surplus is directly transferred to the private pension fund which has been established in 2004. Thus, the contributions relevant for financing pension payments in the base year amount to 1.439 bn. EUR.

[215] See Figure 93 and Figure 94.

The Lithuanian total fertility rate belongs to the lowest fertility rates in Europe. In 2006, it amounted to 1.35 children per woman. According to Eurostat assumptions, this rate can expected to rise until 2050 to 1.6 in Europop2004, respectively 1.51 in Europop2008. It is worth mentioning that in both scenarios Lithuania will face higher fertility rates in 2050 than Germany, even though fertility rates in Lithuania lie below the German level in 2006.

As described in section 3.11.1 of this study, the difference between male and female life expectancy is considerably high in Lithuania. In fact, this feature can be observed in all three Baltic states. Women born in 2006 can expect to live for 77.0 years while their average male counterparts face a life expectancy of only 65.3 years. However, due to Eurostat scenarios, this discrepancy in sex-specific mortality is going to be reduced in the future. According to Europop2004, female life expectancy will increase by 6.7 years until it reaches a level of 83.7 years in 2050. Moreover, male life expectancy is assumed to increase by 10.2 years and is supposed to reach a level of 75.5 years in 2050. This means that the discrepancy in male and female life expectancy will diminish from 11.7 years in 2006 to 8.2 years in 2050. However, according to Europop2008, mortality in 2050 will even be lower than in the corresponding assumptions of Europop2004. In this scenario, female individuals born in 2050 are expected to reach an average age of 85.3 years, equal to an increase of 8.3 years of life expectancy. Their male counterparts will face a life expectancy of 78.1 years in 2050. In other words, the differences in assumptions regarding life expectancy amount to 1.6 years for women and 2.6 years for men.

As mentioned before, the crucial demographic criterion in terms of sustainability for pension schemes is not the future total size of population but rather the age structure of future populations. Figure 59 illustrates the age structure of the Lithuanian population in 2006 and 2050. For the projection until 2050, both scenarios Europop2004 and Europop2008 have been calculated.

The depicted chart clearly shows the future change in age structure of the Lithuanian population. In 2006, the age group of 20-year-olds is by far the largest while there is another peak at the age group of around 45. In contrast to 2006, in the year 2050 the cohorts around 60 show the biggest size. Low fertility rates and a net migration close to zero (especially in the case of Europop2008) cause considerable decreases of younger age groups. At this point it is also worth mentioning that until 2050 the total number of Lithuanian citizens will drop by more than 20 per cent.

Figure 59: Population structure in Lithuania (2006 and 2050)

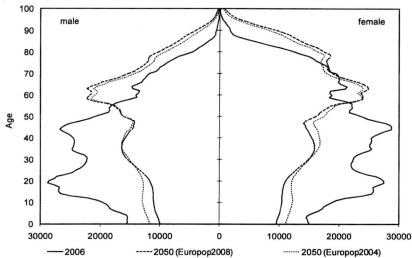

Source: Own calculations based on Eurostat (2009)

As Figure 59 indicates, future labour force will go down substantially while the number of elderly persons will grow as Lithuanian baby boomers grow older and life expectancy increases. Figure 60 will quantify this transformation by depicting the old-age dependency ration (OADR) until 2070.

Beginning with the OADR60, for the year 2006 a rather low value of some 26 per cent can be observed. Until 2030, both projection scenarios follow a similar growth path up to a value of some 39 per cent. After that year the growth paths begin to vary from each other; Europop2008 shows an OADR60 of about 61 per cent in 2050 while Europop2004 indicates a value of only 53 per cent in 2050 and is supposed to decrease after 2055 while in the Europop2008 scenario it will continue to increase. The reasons for these different courses are differing assumptions regarding future net migration and life expectancy. However, both scenarios show considerable relative enhancements. In Europop2004 the OADR60 increases by 108 per cent between 2006 and 2050; Europop2008 indicates an increase of even 138 per cent in the same period of time. Expressed differently, from 2006 up to 2050 the number of potential retirees in relation to potential contributors will in any case be more than doubled. The following section will show the impact of these developments on our results.

213

Figure 60: Development of the old-age dependency ratio in Lithuania until 2070

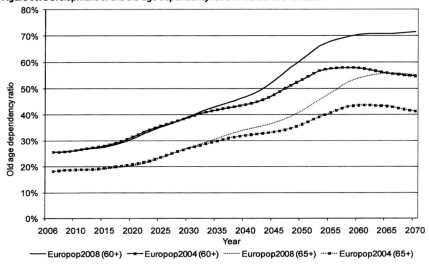

Source: Own calculations based on Eurostat (2009)

4.2.2 Results

For calculating the open-system net liabilities (OSNL) of the Lithuanian social security pension scheme certain assumptions regarding the impact of the last pension reform in Lithuania on future pension payments had to be made. We assumed that from 2007 on, contributors in Lithuania choose to direct the maximum possible rate of 5.5 percentage points of the contribution rate (26.1 per cent in 2006) into the privately managed pension fund. As we measure merely the PAYG part of the social security pension, this means in return that the future pension level will eventually be reduced by some 21 per cent. We defined a transition period for this reduction which lasts from 2007 to 2047.

Furthermore, we applied a real per-capita growth rate of 1.5 per cent and a real discount rate of 3.0 per cent. We are aware of the fact that country-specific growth and discount rates might vary from these assumptions which are used in general for all calculations in this study. However, to ensure better comparability between the outcomes for different countries, from our point of view a general constant assumption regarding wage growth and discount rates seems quite helpful.[216] Table 71 indicates the main results of our evaluation.

Table 71: Open-system net liabilities of the Lithuanian social security pension scheme in 2006

Demographic scenarios	Open-system net liabilities	
	In bn EUR	In % of GDP 2006
Europop2004	12.92	53.9 %
Europop2008	18.37	76.6 %

Source: Own calculations

The table indicates that the Lithuanian pension scheme faces OSNL to the amount of nearly 54 per cent of GDP in the Europop2004 scenario and about 76 per cent in the Europop2008 scenario. Compared to the results for the German pension scheme presented in the previous section, one feature stands out. Despite a more unfavourable future demographic development, Lithuania faces lower liabilities than Germany. This can mainly be ascribed to the lower level of initial pension expenditures in relation to GDP.

Analogous to our proceeding in the previous section, we will now take a look at the future pension level in Lithuania. As a starting point we defined the pension level in 2006 and set this to 100. Figure 61 demonstrates how pensions in Lithuania will develop in relation to respective per-capita wages. Regarding the development of wages over time, a per-capita growth rate of 1.5 per cent in real terms has been assumed.

The chart shown above indicates that the future pension level will decrease considerably. In 2030, pensions will have reached a level of some 88 per cent compared to the pension level in 2006 whereas in 2050 the pension level will have been decreased to nearly 78 per cent. This reduction can be traced back to the fact that in the future contributions will partly be directed to private funds. Bearing in mind the pension reform mentioned previously, Lithuanian policymakers seem to have reacted timely on the demographic challenges. Since benefits from the privately managed pension fund have not been taken into account in our calculations, one can assume that the level of total future pensions will not drop considerably in the future. However, as Table 71 indicates, the pension scheme of Lithuania is not in a

---

[216] Our sensitivity analysis in the appendix shows the impact of varying growth and discount rates on our outcomes.

sustainable situation yet. Figure 62 shows how contribution rates would develop if contributors were to immediately adjust future deficits of the pension scheme:

Figure 61: Future gross pension level in Lithuania 2006 to 2070
indexed to 100 in 2006

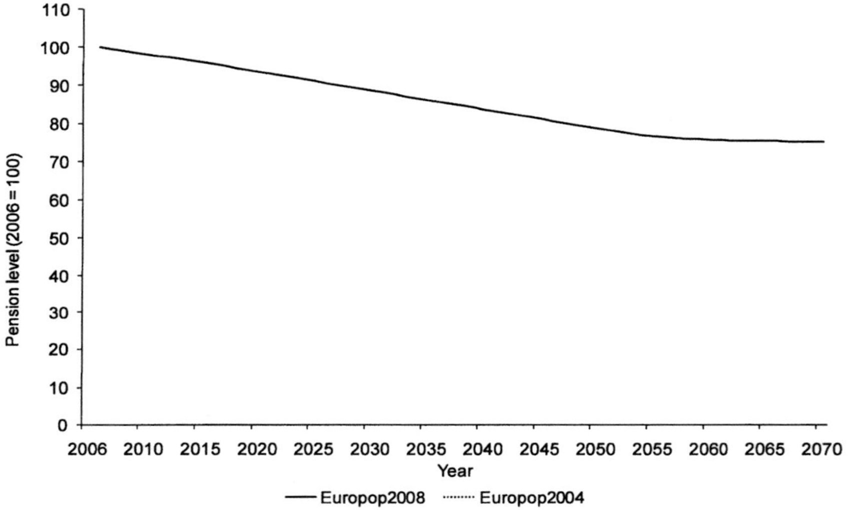

Source: Own calculations

Figure 62 clearly illustrates that endogenous contribution rates will rise substantially. Due to a higher old-age dependency ratio, Europop2008 shows higher contribution rates. In 2030, it reaches a level of 31.0 per cent compared to 30.7 per cent in the Europop2004 scenario. Thereafter the growth paths of the scenarios diverge; applying Europop2008 the contribution rate in 2050 comes up to 40.0 per cent, which is equivalent to an increase of 53 per cent compared to 2006. Switching to Europop2004, contribution rates in 2050 reach a value of 36.7 per cent, corresponding to an increase of 40 per cent in relation to 2006.

How can the substantial rise of endogenous contribution rates be explained in the context of a rather modest level of ONSL? First, the future pension budget deficits will have to be financed by a small number of contributors due to the declining number of young individuals. Second, relatively high contribution rates can only be observed in the far future from the year 2030 on. This means that the pension budget deficits will occur rather late which leads to high discounting of these deficits. Hence, these deficits have a large impact on future contribution rates, but a low impact on the present value of ONSL.

Figure 62: Future endogenous pension contribution rates in Lithuania, 2006 to 2070

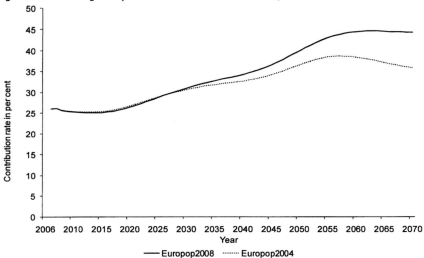

Source: Own calculations

To sum up, it is safe to say that even though some efforts have been made to pre-pare the Lithuanian social security pension scheme for the demographic challenges of the future, there are still some adjustments to be set up. Otherwise future wage earners will have to face substantially higher contribution rates.

4.3   NL – Netherlands

The Dutch social security pension scheme (AOW – Algemene Ouderdomswet) can be characterized as a typical Beveridgean pension system. As described in-depth in section 3.14.2.1of this study, it provides merely a basic pension which does not depend on the amount of contributions paid prior to retirement. The Dutch pension system disposes of a large second pillar due to traditionally extensive occupational pensions. However, these benefits are not included in our calculations as they do not belong to the public pension system. Total public pension expenditures in the base year 2006 amounted to 34.28 bn. EUR, which corresponds to 6.3 per cent of GDP. These were levelled by total contributions coming up to 27.94 bn. EUR and tax-financed subsidies amounting to a residual of 6.34 bn. EUR. The age-sex-specific profiles applied for distributing these aggregate figures among the various age cohorts in the base year can be found in the appendix of this study.[217]

4.3.1   Future demographic development

In order to get an idea of the impact of different demographic assumptions on the level of open-system net liabilities (OSNL), we have applied two scenarios for the population projection of the Netherlands. The central assumptions for these scenarios are indicated in Table 72.

Table 72: Central assumptions of the Dutch population projection

Parameter	Year	Scenarios	
		Europop2004	Europop2008
Total fertility rate	2006	1.72	1.72
	2050	1.75	1.76
Life expectancy at birth for females/males in years	2006	82.0/ 77.7	82.0/ 77.7
	2050	83.6/ 80.2	87.8/ 83.7
Net migration	2006	10,122	10,122
	2050	31,096	7,176

Source: Eurostat (2009)

In terms of future fertility, Europop2004 and Europop2008 both expect a slight increase up to 2050. The difference between the two scenarios is negligible, and in both cases we can in principle speak of an assumed constant total fertility rate. It is worth mentioning that fertility in the Netherlands is considerably higher than in the

---

[217] See Figure 97 and Figure 98.

first two countries examined in this chapter. However, the Netherlands does not reach the replacement level of 2.1 either.

In contrast to fertility, mortality is expected to substantially change in the future. However, on closer inspection only the Europop2008 scenario shows considerable increases in life expectancy. In this scenario, life expectancy is assumed to rise from 82.0 years for women und 77.7 years for men in 2006 up to 87.8 for women and 83.7 years for men in 2050. In other words, an increase of 5.8 years for women and 6.0 years for men is expected. The assumptions of Europop2004 are rather conservative compared to Europop2008. Female life expectancy is assumed to step up only 1.6 years until 2050 while male citizens born in 2050 can expect to live 2.5 years longer than their counterparts born in 2006.

Moreover, assumed future net migration also differs considerably between both scenarios. While in Europop2004 numbers are supposed to substantially rise from some 10,000 net migrants in the base year to more than 31,000 in 2050, net migration in Europop2008 is expected to even drop to a value of about 7,000 in 2050. Figure 63 demonstrates the consequences of the different assumptions on the future population structure:

Figure 63: Population structure of the Netherlands (2006 and 2050)

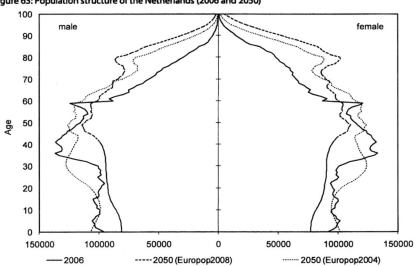

Source: Own calculations based on Eurostat (2009)

We will not discuss the age structure in the base year here as this has been done extensively in section 3.14.1 of this study. At first sight it can be stated that the change in population structure does not seem to be as extensive as seen in the countries examined previously. Especially the age structure of Europop2004 shows similar numbers in the cohorts of the younger generations. However, the number of old-aged people in 2050 outnumbers its counterpart in 2006 significantly due to minor increases of life expectancy. Unlike Europop2004, Europop2008 indicates considerable losses in the younger generations, especially in the cohorts aged 35 to 50. This is due to the low net migration assumed. In contrast to that, age cohorts of old-aged people show large gains in relation to 2006. Figure 64 will illustrate the resulting old-age dependency ratios (OADR) for both Europop2004 and Europop2008:

Figure 64: Development of the old-age dependency ratio in the Netherlands until 2070

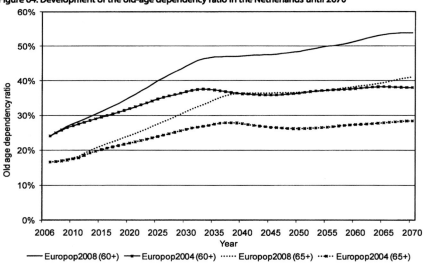

Source: Own calculations based on Eurostat (2009)

Starting with the OADR60[218] a large deviation of the growth paths of Europop2004 and Europop2008 can be detected. The Europop2004 scenario indicates a value of some 37 per cent for the year 2030 compared to 24 per cent in the base year 2006. Between 2030 and 2050 the ratio stays nearly constant and even shows some de-

---

[218] For a definition of the different old-age dependency ratios see footnote 206.

creases, until it reaches a value of about 36 per cent in 2050. The rather modest development especially after 2030 can be traced back to the assumptions of high net migration and low rises in life expectancy. Changing the perspective to Europop2008, the situation becomes more dramatic. In 2030, the OADR60 will already have reached a level of some 44 per cent, which will even have increased up to about 48 per cent in 2050. In other words, the ratio in 2030 will be 84 per cent higher than in 2006. Comparing 2050 with the base year 2006, the rate of increase comes up to even more than 100 per cent. The OADR65 shows a similar trend. In the Europop2004 scenario, the ratio rises from some 16 per cent to 26 per cent in 2030. After 2035, it stays more or less constant. In contrast, Europop2008 increases rapidly to a level of 31 per cent in 2030 and continues rising up to a value of 37 per cent in 2050. Compared to 2006, the OADR65 will rise by 87 per cent up to 2030, respectively 120 per cent in 2050. The impact of the demographic change on the public pension system in the Netherlands will be demonstrated in the following chapter.

4.3.2   Results

We apply a constant per-capita wage growth rate of 1.5 per cent and a constant discount rate of 3.0 per cent, both in real terms. The results of our calculations are depicted in Table 73.

Table 73: Open-system net liabilities of the Dutch social security pension scheme in 2006

Demographic scenarios	Open-system net liabilities	
	in bn EUR	in % of GDP 2006
Europop2004	959.76	177.8 %
Europop2008	1,355.54	251.1 %

Source: Own calculations

The main outcome of our calculations is that the public pension system of the Netherlands is not at all sustainable in both demographic scenarios. However, due to different underlying assumptions the extent to which the system misses sustainability varies considerably. Europop2004 indicates open-system net liabilities (OSNL) amounting to 959.755 bn. EUR, corresponding to some 178 per cent of GDP in 2006. By contrast, the Europop2008 scenario shows OSNL of 1,355.54 bn. EUR, corresponding to about 251 per cent of GDP. Accordingly the liabilities of the Europop2008 scenario come off 42 per cent higher than the respective liabilities from the Europop2004 scenario. This remarkable difference can mainly be ascribed to the varying course of the old-age dependency ration demonstrated in the previous section.

The next question to be raised refers to the future pension level in the Netherlands. It is worth mentioning at this point that the AOW is one of the few pension systems in Western Europe which has not experienced a reform cutting down the future pension level. From this it follows that pension will stay constantly in relation to corresponding per-capita wages. Figure 65 illustrates this development:

Figure 65: Future gross pension level in the Netherlands 2006 to 2070
indexed to 100 in 2006

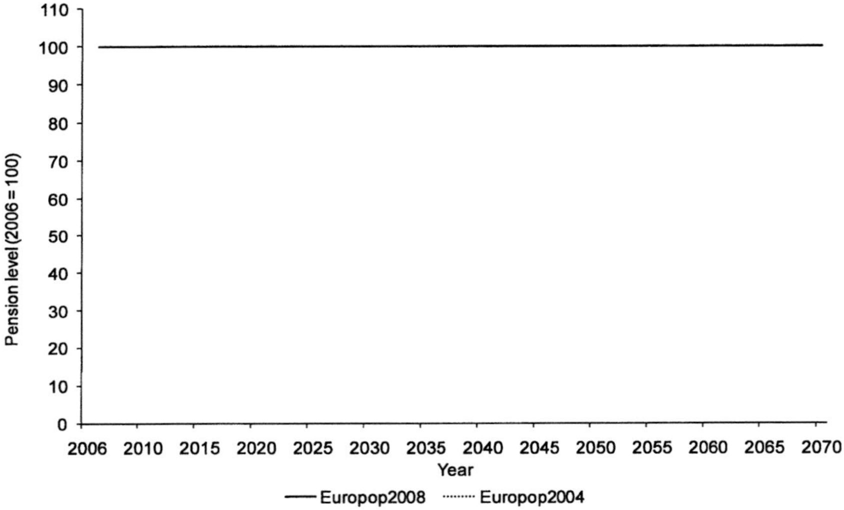

Source: Own calculations

Admittedly, the explanatory power of Figure 65 is quite limited. Nevertheless, from our point of view it is useful to visualize the fact that the Dutch public pension represents the only scheme where future pensions grow in line with future wages. It is straightforward that this setup will have some consequences on the future development of contributions. Therefore, we revise the assumption of constant pension contribution rates and calculate endogenous contribution rates necessary to balance the future increase of total pension expenditures. Figure 66 illustrates the course of endogenous contribution rates.

As expected, endogenous contribution rates will rise substantially over time. Moreover, the Europop2008 scenario shows a considerably higher growth path. In this scenario, the contribution rate increases from 17.9 per cent to a value of 29.0 per cent until 2030 and even further to 32.9 per cent. In other words, contributions in 2050 will be about 84 per cent higher than in the base year 2006. Due to assumed higher net migration and lower gains in life expectancy, the Europop2004 scenario shows a rather modest development of endogenous contribution rates. Nevertheless, rates will rise from 17.9 per cent to 25.1 per cent in 2030. Thereafter, they will stay constant over time and reach a value of 25.1 per cent in 2050. Compared to the base year 2006, this accounts for an increase of 40 per cent.

Figure 66: Future endogenous pension contribution rates in the Netherlands, 2006 to 2070

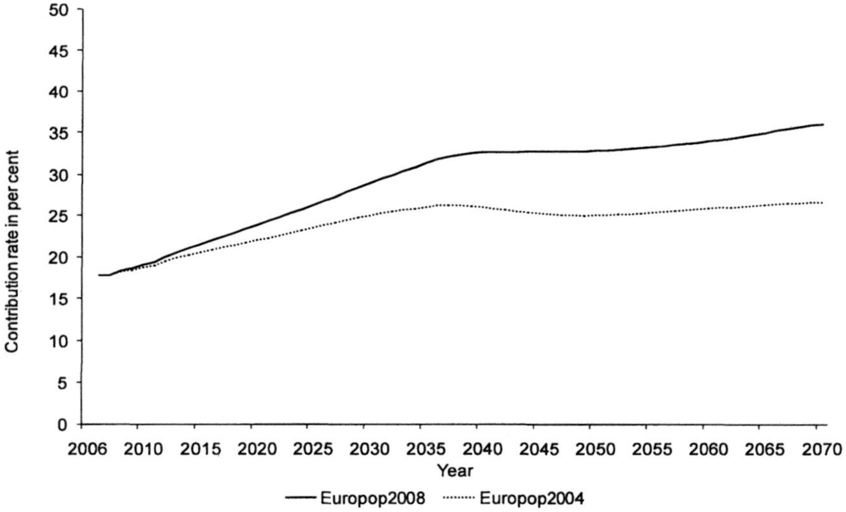

Source: Own calculations

Summing up it can be stated that despite rather low pension expenditures in the base year in relation to GDP the Dutch public pension system will impose an extensive burden on future contributors. This can only be avoided by a pension reform which slows down the growth of future pension expenditures. The calculations between our two demographic scenarios differ substantially from each other but since Europop2008 as Eurostat's current population projection probably represents the more realistic scenario, its outcomes should be regarded as more reliable than the results of the rather optimistic (and out-dated) Europop2004 scenario.

4.4 SE – Sweden

Contributions to the Swedish pension scheme are earnings-related and directed partly to notional accounts (NDC) and partly to financial accounts (financially funded).[219] However, in our study merely the NDC part of the pension scheme will be taken into consideration. Furthermore, we put a focus on old-age pensions simply because disability and survivor pensions are not integrated in the system and financed out of tax revenues. The old-age pension expenditures in 2006 amounted to 176.13 bn. SEK.[220] Corresponding revenues arose from contributions adding up to 166.12 bn. SEK and tax-financed subsidies covering extraneous insurance benefits amounting to 19.93 bn. SEK.[221, 222] Hence, the pension scheme showed a surplus of 9.92 bn. SEK in 2006. This can be ascribed to the fact that the entitlements earned by private households exceeded the pension benefits due in that year. The profiles which have been applied for distributing the aggregate sums to the age cohorts in the base year can be found in the appendix of this study.[223]

4.4.1 Future demographic development

The future demographic development of a country plays a crucial role for its PAYG-financed pension scheme. Analogous to the previous sections of this chapter, we chose two projection scenarios which are based on the assumptions of the last two official population projections from Eurostat, namely Europop2004 and Europop2008. The central assumptions of these scenarios for the Swedish population are indicated in Table 74.

Both scenarios expect constant total fertility rates in the future. Life expectancy is assumed to increase; in the Europop2004 scenario, female life expectancy rises from 83.1 years to 86.5 years while male life expectancy grows from 78.8 years to 83.3

---

[219] For a detailed description of the Swedish public pension system see section 3.17.2 of this study.

[220] This number differs from the number we applied for calculation the accrued-to-date liabilities of the Swedish public pension scheme in section 3.17. The reason for this is the fact that in this section we consider old-age pensions only while in section 3.17 we included disability and survivor pensions. We excluded disability and survivor pensions in this section because they are not directly part of the NDC scheme.

[221] Data source: Statistics Sweden, Michael Wolf.

[222] Tax-financed subsidies are generally paid for years of military service, years of study and years of child care.

[223] See Figure 102 and Figure 103.

years. In the corresponding Europop2008 scenario women born in 2050 can expect to live for 88.3 years while their male counterparts face a life expectancy of 84.3 years. Both scenarios assume a drop in future net migration compared to 2006. However, the difference between both scenarios makes up for around 5,000 net migrants; Europop2004 indicates a net migration of 21,343 in 2050 while Europop2008 displays a net migration of 16,690.

Table 74: Central assumptions of the Swedish population projection

Parameter	Year	Scenarios	
		Europop2004	Europop2008
Total fertility rate	2006	1.85	1.85
	2050	1.85	1.85
Life expectancy at birth for females/males in years	2006	83.1/ 78.8	83.1/ 78.8
	2050	86.5/ 83.3	88.3/ 84.3
Net migration	2006	50,842	50,842
	2050	21,343	16,690

Source: Eurostat (2009)

As mentioned before, when it comes to future developments of pension schemes set up on a PAYG basis, it is the future age structure and not the total number of inhabitants which drives the results. The Swedish population structure in 2006 has been described in-depth in section 3.17.1, thus we now focus on the future age structure. Figure 67 illustrates the age structure for the years 2006 and 2005, applying both Europop2004 and Europop2008.

The cohorts up to the age of 50 years do not show considerable changes in structure which is due to relatively high constant fertility rates. However, cohort sizes from the age of 50 upwards in 2006 are by far outnumbered by their counterparts in 2050. The differences between our two demographic scenarios are rather modest, since the assumptions of both scenarios differ only slightly from each other. The structural change between 2006 and 2050 gives rise to the assumption that the old-age dependency ratio (OADR) will increase over time. Figure 68 quantifies this development:

Figure 67: Population structure of Sweden (2006 and 2050)

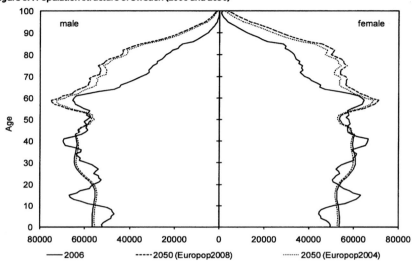

Source: Own calculations based on Eurostat (2009)

The image above demonstrates that the rather small differences of our demographic assumptions result in similar courses of the old age dependency ratio (OADR). Beginning with the OADR60[224], the ratio rises from a level of some 31 per cent to nearly 41 per cent in the Europop2008 and the Europop2004 scenario. Thereafter, the growth paths slightly differ from each other; in 2050 the ratio reaches a level of nearly 47 per cent in the Europop2008 scenario while the Europop2004 scenario indicates a value of almost 45 per cent in 2050. Regarding the OADR65, the growth paths of our two scenarios correspond to each other for even a longer period. The ratio shows a value of close to 30 per cent in 2030 for both scenarios compared to 21 per cent in the base year 2006. In 2050, Europop2008 indicates a level of some 34 per cent while in Europop2004 the ration comes up to nearly 33 per cent. Thereafter the OADR65 grows a little faster in the Europop2008 scenario due to higher life expectancy and lower net migration. Summarizing, it has to be pointed out that the old-age dependency ratio will rise by between 44 to 65 per cent, depending on the demographic scenario and the chosen age dependency ratio.

---

[224] See footnote 206 for an explanation of this abbreviation.

Figure 68: Development of the old-age dependency ratio in Sweden until 2070

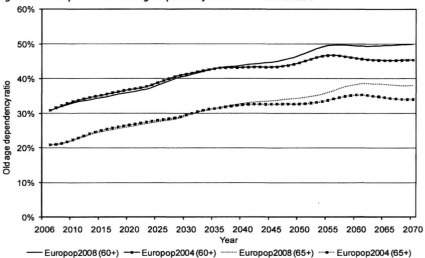

Source: Own calculations based on Eurostat (2009)

4.4.2   Results

Before presenting the results of our calculations it is worth emphasizing that NDC pension schemes are in theory sustainable. In other words, open-system net liabilities (OSNL) should amount to zero since the catch of a NDC scheme lies in its capacity to automatically react on demographic or economic changes. For example, if life expectancy rises the pensions of those cohorts who enjoy a longer life are reduced accordingly without discretionary intervention of policy makers. Given the wage sum growth drops down, the automatic balance mechanism (ABM) accordingly adjusts the indexation of pensions.[225] Analogous to our previous calculations, we apply a constant per-capita wage growth of 1.5 per cent and a constant discount rate of 3.0 per cent, both in real terms. Table 75 indicates if the theoretical sustainability of the Swedish public pension scheme holds in practice:

---

[225] For a closer look on the functioning of the Swedish NDC pension scheme see Settergren (2001).

Open-system net liabilities of four selected countries

Table 75: Open-system net liabilities of the Swedish social security pension scheme in 2006

Demographic scenarios	Open-system net liabilities	
	in bn SEK	in % of GDP 2006
Europop2004	192.65	6.6 %
Europop2008	790.24	27.3 %

Source: Own calculations

It can be stated that in both demographic scenarios the Swedish NDC pension scheme faces a situation close to sustainability. In the Europop2004 scenario the OSNL amount to some six per cent of GDP in 2006, while in the Europop2008 scenario they amount to around 27 per cent of GDP. The discrepancy of our calculations to a situation of perfect sustainability (OSNL to equal zero) can be explained the following fact: As long as the balances of expenditures and revenues will not equal zero in every future year, there is obviously only one discount rate which leads to OSNL of zero. As said previously, pensions are adjusted automatically (but with a time lag) to altering conditions. Therefore it is worthwhile examining the future level of pensions which is illustrated in Figure 69.

Figure 69: Future gross pension level in Sweden 2006 to 2070
indexed to 100 in 2006

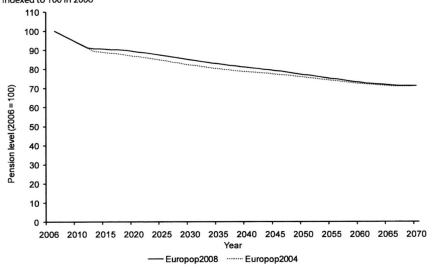

Source: Own calculations

As a result of the automatic mechanisms of the Swedish pension scheme, pensions are reduced. We set the pension level in 2006 to 100 and measure the future pension level in relation to the per-capita average wage of the corresponding year. Applying the Europop2008 scenario, pensions in 2030 will have reached a level of 85 per cent compared to the pension level in 2006. The corresponding Europop2004 scenario indicates a level of some 82 per cent in relation to the pension level of 2006. Afterwards the pension level continues to decrease; in 2050 it comes up to 77 per cent, respectively 75 per cent (Europop2008/ Europop2004). The decrease of pension levels can generally be traced back to rising life expectancies and decreasing wage sum growth, caused by slightly smaller age groups in the future labour force.

Being a pension scheme of the defined contribution type, pension contribution rates in Sweden should generally be expected to stay constant over time. However, to demonstrate the difference between a perfectly sustainable situation and our outcomes, in an experiment we estimated contribution rates which in every given future year compensate the possible deficits or surpluses. Figure 70 shows the course of the endogenous contribution rates.

Figure 70: Future endogenous pension contribution rates in Sweden, 2006 to 2070

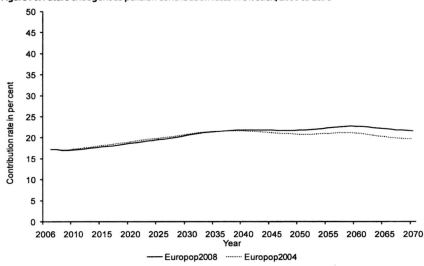

Source: Own calculations

In contrast to the endogenous contribution rates of the countries examined previously in this chapter, Figure 70 clearly indicates that endogenous pension contribution rates in Sweden stay constant by and large. However, starting on a level of 17.2 per cent, after a short decline in the first years the rate comes up to 20.6 per cent and respectively 20.8 per cent (Europop2008/ Europop2004 scenario). In 2050, Eurostat2008 indicates a rate of 21.8 per cent while in the Eurostat2004 scenario the rate amounts to 20.8 per cent. However, as the differences to the initial contribution rate can be considered as negligible, our experiment regarding endogenous contribution rates also approves the sustainability of the pension scheme.

In summary, it can be said that the Swedish pension system is well prepared for the prospective demographic challenges. Admittedly, pensions from the NDC scheme will decrease over time in relation to wages; however, this decrease will to some extent be compensated by benefits paid out of the newly established funded part of the pension scheme, which is not included in our calculations.

4.5 Cross-country comparison of open-system net liabilities

After having calculated the open-system net liabilities (OSNL) for the public pension schemes of four selected countries, we now take a closer look at the differences between the liabilities of the corresponding public pension schemes. We start by examining the major differences in demographic developments as one of the main determining factors of the OSNL. We hereby focus on the Europop2008 scenario as a benchmark since it is the current population projection scenario of Eurostat and probably represents a more realistic approximation than the out-dated Europop2004 scenario. Nevertheless, wherever it seems convenient we also consider the Europop2004 scenario for comparison purposes.

4.5.1 Comparison of future demographic developments

As well known among demographers, there are three main factors which determine the future size and structure of a population; fertility, migration and mortality. Hence, we will now compare the corresponding determinants of the four countries examined, beginning with the total fertility rate. The expected future development of fertility in Germany, Lithuania, the Netherlands and Sweden is presented in Figure 71.

Figure 71: Cross-country comparison of future total fertility rates (Europop2008)

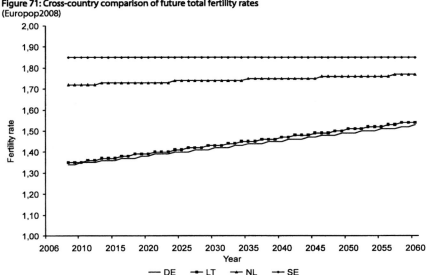

Source: Eurostat (2009)

It can be seen that Sweden shows the highest initial fertility rate, followed by the Netherlands. Germany and Lithuania face almost the same fertility rate in 2006 which lies slightly below 1.4 children per woman. As Europop2008 represents a convergence scenario, fertility in Sweden is supposed to stay constant over time while in the Netherlands it is expected to rise modestly from a rate of 1.72 in 2006 up to 1.77 in 2060.[226] In contrast to that, fertility rates in Lithuania are assumed to increase considerably between 2006 and 2060. In Lithuania, an increase from a value of 1.35 in 2006 up to 1.54 in 2060 is expected whereas Germany is assumed to face a fertility rate of 1.53 in 2060 compared to 1.34 in 2006. To sum up, the ranking in terms of fertility is expected to stay constant until 2060; however, low fertility rates in Lithuania and Germany are supposed to convert to the Dutch and Swedish ones. All countries examined are expected to stay below the replacement level of 2.1 children per woman.

When comparing the net migration in different countries, it is logical that migration should not be assessed in absolute terms but rather in relation to the total population of the respective country. The reason for this is twofold: On the one hand, it is straightforward that net migration into a country in absolute terms depends – among other factors – on the size of the initial population. On the other hand, the impact of net migration in absolute terms substantially depends on the total size of the population. For these reasons, we refrained from presenting a comparison of net migration in absolute terms but rather calculated the development of net migration rates in relation to initial population in 2006, based on Europop2008 assumptions. The corresponding outcomes are depicted in Figure 72.

As one can see, Sweden initially faces the highest net migration relative to its population, followed by Germany and the Netherlands. The initial net migration of Lithuania even shows a negative net migration rate. Due to the convergence process assumed in Europop2008 net migration rates assimilate over time. The German and the Swedish net migration rates are assumed to follow roughly the same growth path from 2030 on. The Dutch net migration is expected to develop constantly while in Lithuania net migration is supposed to slightly increase until it reaches a considerable but only temporary surplus between 2045 and 2060. After 2060 it is assumed to be close to zero. What we can learn from this figure is that according to Europop2008 future net migration will to a certain degree be levelled among countries so that this determining factor does not seem to play a crucial role

---

[226] The assumptions of Europop2008 reach as far as the year 2060 while Europop2004 assumptions stop at the year 2050. As we focus on the Europop2008 scenario in this section, the numbers in the images used are shown until 2060.

regarding the explanatory power of the different amount of liabilities among countries.

Figure 72: Cross-country comparison of future net migration
(in per cent of total population in 2006)

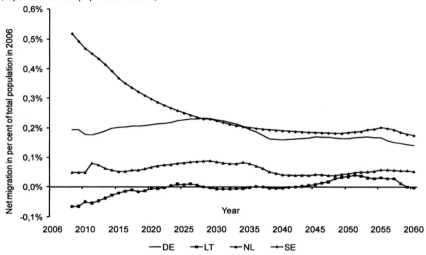

Source: Eurostat (2009)

Regarding the initial life expectancy of the different population, Germany, the Netherlands and Sweden face quite similar conditions. On the male side, Sweden shows the highest life expectancy (78.8 years), closely followed by the Netherlands (77.7 years) and Germany (77.2 years). Female life expectancy also turns out to be the highest in Sweden (83.1 years), followed by Germany (82.4 years) and the Netherlands (82.0). However, Lithuania clearly gets out of the line in this regard. This counts for female life expectancy (77.0 years in 2006), but a good deal more for Lithuanian men who face a life expectancy 11.7 years lower than women from their country and around twelve years lower than their male counterparts from the other countries mentioned. Figure 73 illustrates how life expectancy will change until 2060 according to Europop2008.

It can be seen that the absolute gains in life expectancy until 2060 turn out to be quite similar. However, Lithuania again represents an exception in this context as especially male life expectancy is supposed to be subject to a considerable increase of more than 15 years. Female life expectancy will rise by nearly ten years whereas the increases in the other countries range between six and eight years. The excep-

233

tional rise of Lithuanian male life expectancy can again be ascribed to the convergence assumptions of Europop2008. Summing up it can be stated that mortality in the examined countries develops almost uniformly, with the notable exception of Lithuania.

Figure 73: Cross-country comparison of life expectancy at birth in 2006 and 2060 (Europop2008)

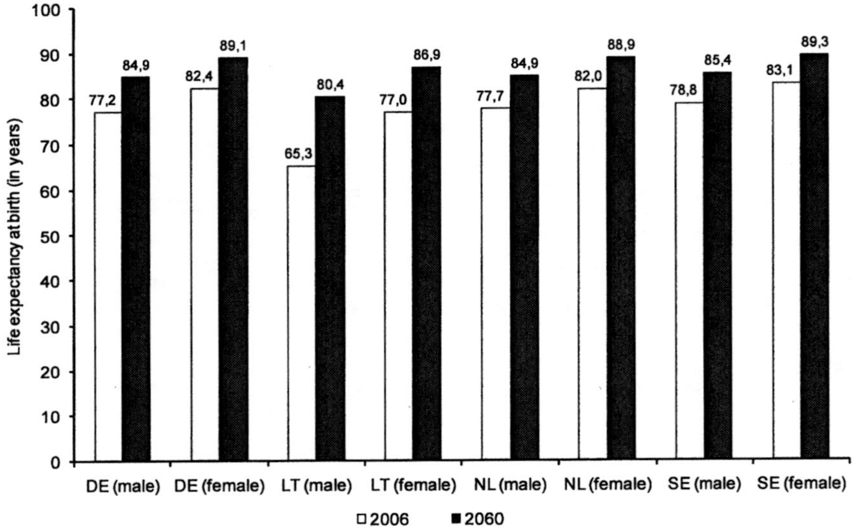

Source: Eurostat (2009)

Previously it has been emphasized that the most important demographic key driver of future developments of PAYG finances pension schemes is the ratio of retirees to contributors which can be approximated by the old-age dependency ratio (OADR). Hence, Figure 74 provides a cross-country comparison of the OADR65 from 2006 to 2060.

As one can see, Germany faces the oldest population of all four countries. Indeed this is only valid until the year 2055 when Lithuania will show an even higher ratio than Germany. The Netherlands initially show the lowest value; however, the ratio rises considerably up to 2040 when the growth path slows down and develops nearly constantly. On first thought it could be stated that Germany as the "old man of Europe" will experience the most alarming development in terms of an ageing society. But when it comes to sustainability one has to bear in mind that the differences between the future and the base year are most crucial and not the development of absolute figures or indicators like the OADR. In other words, if one the sustainability of a PAYG pension scheme, not the absolute figure of the OADR should be regarded but the future change relative to the base year.

Figure 74: Cross-country comparison of future old-age dependency ratios (65+), 2006 to 2060

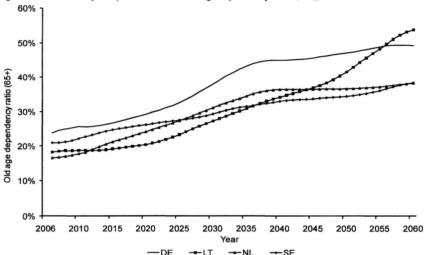

Source: Own calculations based on Eurostat (2009)

It appears that the OADR65 in Sweden shows the lowest increase amounting to some 84 per cent growth between 2006 and 2060. The German OADR65 in 2060 indicates an increase of around 108 per cent relative to 2006, the Dutch society faces an enhancement of 130 per cent and Lithuania represents the country which faces the biggest ageing with an increase of the OADR65 until 2060 of nearly 195 per cent in relation to 2006. Expressed differently, the ratio of old people to members of the labour force in 2060 will be almost three times as high as it was in 2006.

4.5.2 Sustainability of social security pension schemes

After having compared the future demographic situations of the four countries examined in this chapter, in this section we will test if the outcomes of our sustainability analysis follow the same rankings as the demographic developments. Figure 75 provides a comparison of the open-system net liabilities of all four countries.

235

Open-system net liabilities of four selected countries

Figure 75: Cross-country comparison of open-system net liabilities in 2006
in per cent of GDP of the respective country

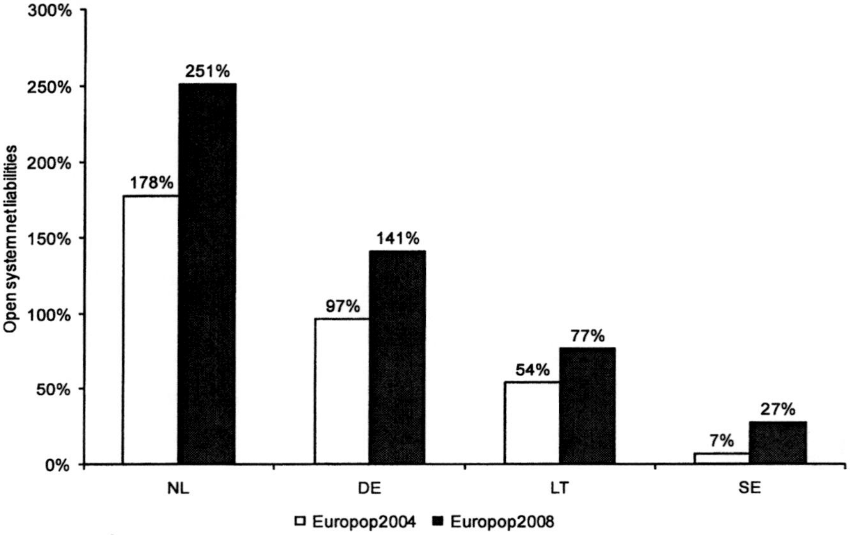

Source: Own calculations

The Dutch public pension scheme features the highest amount of OSNL in relation to GDP, followed by Germany, Lithuania and Sweden.[227] Despite its more unfavourable demographic future, Lithuania clearly ranks below the Netherlands. This can be ascribed to the fact that the Dutch pension scheme has so far not been adjusted to future demographic challenges. In contrast, the Lithuanian pension scheme has undergone a partly shift from PAYG financing to capitalized funding. Moreover, it can be seen that in spite of substantial pension reforms in recent years, the public pension scheme in Germany still shows fairly high liabilities. However, as the initial level of pension expenditures in Germany is also quite high (especially compared to Lithuania), this can be explained quite easily. Sweden as the representative of a pension scheme automatically responding to demographic and economic changes finds itself in a practically sustainable situation.

---

[227] Admittedly, the comparison is limited to some extent as the OSNL for Sweden only include old age pensions while the OSNL for Germany, Lithuania and the Netherlands are based on old age pensions, disability pensions and survivor pensions.

At this point it is worth mentioning that the indicator of open-system net liabilities expressed in relation to GDP certainly has a weakness. Since it is related merely to the GDP of the base year it does not take into consideration the question how many contributors, or – more generally spoken– how many people of the labour force will be burdened.

The endogenous contribution rates explained in-depth in the corresponding country sections of this chapter represent an indicator which takes into account the varying sizes of future labour force. In a fictitious sustainable situation contribution rates do not have to be adjusted which means that they stay constant over time. The deviation of future endogenous contribution rates to the initial rate of the base year illustrates the extent to which the respective pension scheme misses sustainability. Figure 76 supplies a comparison of the endogenous contribution rates in the various pension schemes.

Figure 76: Cross-country comparison of endogenous pension contribution rates (Europop2008)

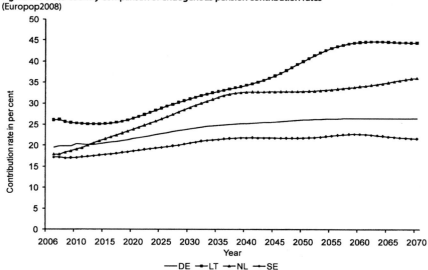

Source: Own calculations

One can see that the ranking demonstrated in Figure 75 significantly changes. The highest increase of contribution rates can be found in the Lithuanian pension scheme due to the fact that the labour force in Lithuania will decrease considerably in the future. In other words, despite the fact that the Lithuanian pension scheme has undergone a partly shift to funding, the contribution rate will have to increase if no further pension reforms will be decided. The Netherlands rank second in terms of endogenous contribution rates. Except for the Lithuanian case, this outcome corresponds to the ranking of the OSNL.

It is worth noticing that the contribution rates of Germany and Sweden follow the same growth path. This is no surprise, as many experts are of the opinion that the German public pension scheme de facto resembles a NDC system like Sweden to a high degree.[228] This is justified with reforms like the increase of the legal retirement age as a response to rising life expectancy or the so-called sustainability factor which reduces the growth of pensions in accordance with the share of retirees to contributors. Admittedly, most changes of the public pension system in Germany have to be decided discretionarily, mostly accompanied by long public controversies, while in Sweden no action has to be made to adjust the system to changing conditions. However, when it comes to the impact of those reforms on the sustainability of the respective pension scheme, no big difference between the German and the Swedish system can be discovered.

---

[228] See for example Börsch-Supan and Wilke (2005).

4.6 Cross-country comparison of accrued-to-date and open-system net liabilities

In chapter 3, the accrued-to-date liabilities (ADL) of public pension schemes of 19 EU countries have been estimated. This chapter contains an analysis of the open-system net liabilities (OSNL) of public pension schemes of four EU countries. In this section we will present a short comparison of the ADL and the OSNL for Germany, Lithuania, the Netherlands and Sweden. Before doing this, we will briefly describe the main differences of both approaches.

Section 2.1 includes definitions of the various approaches to measure public pension liabilities. According to these definitions, the main differences between ADL and OSNL are given by the different time horizons (finite at ADL versus infinite at OSNL) and the question if revenues like contributions are to be included (OSNL) or not (ADL). However, there is at least one more difference between the two approaches which is worth noticing. It refers to the legal status quo which is applied to when estimating pension liabilities for a certain base year. While the ADL approach applies the status quo of the respective base year, the OSNL approach relates to the time when the calculation takes place.

Let us suppose that in the year 2009 the liabilities of a country's public pension scheme are to be estimated. The relevant data shall be based on the year 2006. If in 2007 a pension reform was enforced, the impact of this reform would be taken into account in the OSNL approach, but not in the ADL approach. The reason for this differing treatment is the character of ADL. They are generally seen as a statistical number which is supposed to express households' entitlements at a specific date. As these households cannot anticipate any future pension reforms, these are not taken into consideration.[229] In contrast to this, the OSNL are estimated to provide an indication of how a pension scheme will develop in the future. Hence, all relevant information available up to the time of calculation is applied.

Let us now take a look at the results of the cross-country comparison of ADL and OSNL for Germany, Lithuania, the Netherlands and Sweden. These are illustrated in Figure 77:

---

[229] The statistical character of ADL especially refers to the cases where ADL are included in the supplementary table of the system of national accounts (SNA, see section 2.5). See Eurostat/ECB Task Force (2008), p. 11 et sqq. for further details.

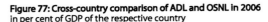

Figure 77: Cross-country comparison of ADL and OSNL in 2006
in per cent of GDP of the respective country

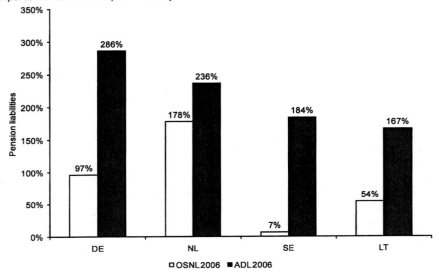

Source: Own calculations

First of all, it is worth mentioning that the outcomes of ADL and OSNL have totally different meanings. While the OSNL of a pension scheme could possibly turn out be zero or even negative, such an outcome is not imaginable for the ADL of a pension scheme. In case a pension scheme shows OSNL of zero per cent of GDP, this implies that the pension scheme is financed in a sustainable way. A negative outcome of OSNL would stand for a situation where the present value of future revenues exceeds the present value of future expenditures. Consequently, such a pension scheme would allow for either increases of future pension benefits, decreases of future contribution rates, or a combination of both. In contrast, an outcome of zero per cent of GDP for ADL would imply that members of that scheme do not dispose of any pension entitlements at all. This is only feasible for a pension scheme which has just been established. However, all pension schemes examined in this survey are matured by now. Thus, they show ADL exceeding zero.

Figure 78: Liabilities and assets of the German statutory pension insurance 2006
in per cent of GDP

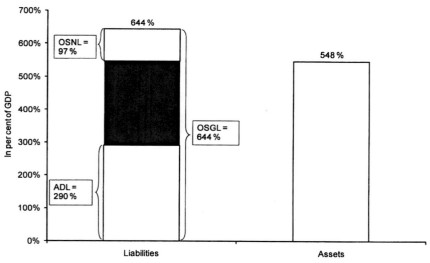

Source: Own calculations

As Figure 77 illustrates, Germany shows the highest ADL in per cent of GDP, followed by the Netherlands, Sweden and Lithuania.[230] However, looking at the OSNL the ranking changes completely.[231] Interestingly enough, this time the Netherlands show the highest liabilities followed by Germany, Lithuania and Sweden. The rationale for this ranking is the fact that all countries except the Netherlands have undergone substantial pension reforms in recent years. Figure 77 clearly shows that there is no link at all between the ADL and the OSNL of a pension scheme. In other words, the extent of accrued-to-date liabilities provides no indication of the fiscal

---

[230] All the ADL figures are expressed in PBO terms. The ADL figures for Germany and Sweden differ from the ones presented in chapter 3 due to the fact that different budget figures have been employed. This was done to ensure an adequate comparability between the ADL and OSNL of the respective pension schemes. In the case of Germany, only the benefits from the German statutory pension insurance scheme (GRV) have been taken into account. This leads to a drop of about 52 percentage points compared to the figure presented in section 3.20. In the case of Sweden, only old-age pensions have been included (compare section 4.4) which leads to a decline of close to 100 percentage points compared to the figure presented in section 3.20.

[231] The OSNL calculations presented here are – just like the ADL calculations – based on the EURO-POP2004 population projection.

sustainability of that pension scheme. In contrast, as Figure 78 exemplarily shows for the German statutory pension insurance, the ADL form only a part of the open-system gross liabilities (OSGL). The OSNL are then calculated by confronting the OSGL with the assets of the pension scheme (future contributions plus federal subsidies plus financial reserves). Summarizing, after a theoretical discussion in section 2.1 this section empirically shows the non-existent correlation between ADL and sustainability.

5 Conclusion and outlook

The goal of this study was twofold: First of all, our aim was to classify the different kinds of public pension liabilities by showing the corresponding ranges of application. We demonstrated that both acrued-to-date liabilities and open-system net liabilities can be useful indicators for the pros and cons of political decisions regarding the burden of public pensions. Secondly, the accrued-to-date pension liabilities of 19 member countries of the European Union were to be calculated. Eleven of these belong to the Euro area and the remaining eight do not (yet). Eight countries have been excluded from our calculations due to insufficient data sources. However, the countries examined cover more than 90 per cent of the EU population.

Accrued-to-date liabilities (ADL) serve as the only reasonable indicator when it comes to the assessment of what a termination of a pension scheme would cost the government. They show the necessary capital stock to meet all entitlements, given a pension scheme's financing was to be shifted from PAYG to funded principle. Furthermore, when assessing the savings of private households one should include the corresponding ADL as these can be regarded as assets of private households.

Open system net liabilities (OSNL) do not give an indication for the entitlements of private households. They rather serve as an indicator for the question of fiscal sustainability of a public pension scheme. The reason why this question can only be answered by OSNL and not by ADL is twofold: The first one is the fact that in the concept of ADL only those pension rights are taken into account which have been earned up to today. Using a broader concept of liabilities, OSNL include the future pension rights earned by current and future workers as well. Secondly, the absence of contributions in the concept of ADL makes it impossible to offer a statement regarding the sustainability of a pension scheme. Imagine for instance a country like France with high fertility rates. Although it features a pension scheme showing considerable accrued-to date liabilities, these liabiities could possibly be balanced by future contributions. In general, accrued-to-date liabilities only take into account a fraction of the future demographic development which is the numerical change of retirees; the evolution of future contributors is fully ignored.

Chapter 2 explained the framework of generational accounting and the Freiburg model. Moreover, the basic assumptions and data are described. In the recent past, the method of generational accounting has been applied to a wide variety of purposes including the calculations of OSNL. We modified this method in order to meet the concept of ADL. As chapter 3 showed, this framework – the Freiburg model – represents a valuable instrument to calculate ADL for various countries on a relatively small data base. However, like any other model it has some limitations which were also explained in chapter 2. The chapter finished with an introduction of the supplementary table which was developed by the Task Force in order to show the flows and stocks of public pension schemes in the national accounts.

In chapter 3, the findings of our ADL calculations for 19 countries were presented. Certain countries feature a general government employer pension scheme as well as a social security pension scheme (e.g. France, Germany or Poland), others only show a social security pension scheme – in some cases civil servants are integrated in the general social security (e.g. Czech Republic, Hungary or Sweden); in other cases pension schemes may not be classified in non-core national accounts (e.g. Netherlands or Spain). The country chapters were all structured in the same way; first the demographic features were described, afterwards the characteristics of the pension system and recent reforms were briefly discussed. Each chapter finished with a presentation of our findings, shown in the supplementary table.

Finally we compared our findings from the particular country chapters. The ADL in per cent of the corresponding country's GDP reach from 90 per cent to a maximum of more than 360 per cent of GDP. The highest ADL can be found in France, Poland, Austria, Germany and Italy, with all countries showing a value well above 300 per cent of GDP. In contrast, Bulgaria, the Czech Republic, Lithuania, Latvia and the United Kingdom as the country ranked last in this comparison show ADL close to or even well below 200 per cent of GDP. It turned out that the main determining factor for the level of public pension liabilities is the initial level of pension expenditures in the base year. However, there are certainly more factors which have an impact on the level of pension liabilities. One important determinant is the development of elderly persons which defines the number of potential future retirees. This figure varies considerably between the countries examined. Other relevant factors are given by the level of pension indexation and the dimension of recent pension reforms. In summary, it can be stated that the ranking of pension liabilities of the various countries follows the ranking of pension expenditures quite closely. Thus, the initial level of pension expenditures has a strong impact on the size of pension liabilities.

As a useful spin-off product, chapter 3 provides an overview of the design of the various public pension systems and the varying demographic developments among European countries. While all countries have a rising life expectancy in common, there is a huge spread regarding the pace of increase. Moreover, fertility rates across Europe reach values from 1.2 as a minimum to almost 2.0 children per woman. Thus, the ageing process in Europe will considerable vary across countries.

As stated before, ADL features a wide variety of applications excluding fiscal sustainanability. Thus, we pursued this particular matter by calculating the OSNL for four selected countries in chapter 4: Germany, Lithuania, the Netherlands and Sweden. These countries cover a considerable range of different features regarding diverging designs of the corresponding public pension schemes as well as demographic peculiarities in Europe. According to our OSNL calculations, the public pension scheme of the Netherlands shows the largest sustainable disorder, followed by Germany, Lithuania and Sweden. However, the situation changes when the future development of contribution rates is considered; in this thought experiment the Netherlands and Lithuania show considerable increases of contribution rates while the development in Germany and Sweden can be classified as rather modest. At the end of this chapter we demonstrated that there is indeed no correlation between the ADL and the sustainability of a pension scheme.

What did we learn from this study? Admittedly, the explanatory power of the isolated value of a pension scheme's ADL is rather limited. Given a pension scheme shows ADL amounting to 300 per cent of the country's GDP, you cannot really judge if the pension scheme is in a comfortable situation from a fiscal point of view or not. It is not even possible to deduce the future pension level from the ADL of a pension scheme. However, there is no doubt that ADL express entitlements of private households against the government. In a cross-country comparison of ADL it becomes evident that different countries show different levels of public pension expenditures. In other words, varying levels of ADL provide an indication of differing political decisions concerning the necessary level of social security pensions. Furthermore, if the ADL of a country's public pension scheme are regarded in combination with the household saving rates, an assessment of the saving behaviour and the portfolio allocation of households becomes possible.

Although they cannot be put on the same level as explicit public debt, we showed that there are several good reasons why ADL should be visualized in official statistics. Certainly, precaution is recommended when publishing new statistical figures like ADL; as the past has shown that the media tends to mix up facts quite easily, one has to make clear which issues should be addressed with ADL and which should not.

We also learned from this study that ADL should not be utilized as an indicator for the sustainability of a pension scheme. However, we introduced the concept of OSNL as an indicator for this issue and applied this concept for the pension schemes of four selected countries.

We strongly recommend to continuously update the calculations of this study. In fact, the relevant authorities have asked all national statistical bodies of the EU to carry out ADL calculations on an annually basis. The outcomes will enter the national accounts via the supplementary table developed by the Task Force. As soon as time series for the ADL of all countries examined in this study are available, one approach could consist of a cross-country comparison of ADL and household saving rates over time. In this way one could – besides other issues – assess the impact of a pension reform on the saving behaviour of individuals.

References

Auerbach, A., J. Gokhale and L. Kotlikoff (1994), Generational accounts: a meaningful way to evaluate fiscal policy, The Journal of Economic Perspectives, 8 (1), 73-94.

Auerbach, A., J. Gokhale and L. Kotlikoff (1992), Social security and medicare policy from the perspective of generational accounting, Tax Policy and the Economy, 6, 129-145.

Auerbach, A., J. Gokhale and L. Kotlikoff (1991), Generational accounts: a meaningful alternative to deficit accounting, Tax Policy and the Economy, 5, 55-110.

Banco de Portugal (Central Bank Portugal, 2008), Questionnaire on the statistical measurement of the assets and liabilities of pension schemes in general government of EU countries.

Bank of Italy (2006), Survey on household income and wealth (SHIW) 2006.

Banque de France (Central Bank France, 2008), Questionnaire on the statistical measurement of the assets and liabilities of pension schemes in general government of EU countries.

Barro, R. J. and X. Sala-i-Martin (2003), Economic growth, 2nd ed., MIT Press, Cambridge, MA.

Benz, T., C. Hagist and B. Raffelhüschen (2009), Reformszenarien und Ausgabenpro-jektion der Beamtenversorgung in Baden-Württemberg (reform scenarios and ex-penditure projections for the civil service pension scheme in Baden-Württemberg), survey by order of the Finanzwissenschaftliches Instituts des Bundes der Steuerzahler (BdSt) Baden-Württemberg e. V., No.7.

Berkel, B. and A. Börsch-Supan (2004), Pension reform in Germany: The impact on retirement decisions, FinanzArchiv, 60 (3), 393-421.

Besendorfer, D., E. P. Dang and B. Raffelhüschen (2006), Die Schulden und Versor-gungsverpflichtungen der Länder: Was ist und was kommt (present and future pen-sion obligations of German federal states), Wirtschaftsdienst, 86 (9), 572-579.

Blake, D. (2006), Pension economics, Wiley, Chichester.

Bonin, H. (2001), Generational accounting: Theory and application, Berlin.

Börsch-Supan, A. (2007), Rational pension reform, Discussion Paper Series Mannheim Research Institute for the Economics of Aging, No. 132.

References

Börsch-Supan, A. and C. B. Wilke (2006), The German public pension system: How it will become an NDC system look-alike; Holzmann, R. and E. Palmer (eds.), Pension reform – issues and prospects for non-financial defined contribution (NDC) schemes, World Bank, Washington, D.C., 573-610.

Braakmann, A., J. Gruetz and T. Haug (2008), Civil servant pensions in national accounts – methodology and preliminary results, paper prepared for the 30th general conference of the International Association for Research in Income and Wealth in Portoroz, Slovenia.

Braakmann, A., J. Gruetz and T. Haug (2007), Das Renten- und Pensionsvermögen in den Volkswirtschaftlichen Gesamtrechnungen (pension wealth in national accounts), Statistisches Bundesamt, Wirtschaft und Statistik, 12.

Buchanan, J.M. (1968), Social insurance in a growing economy: a proposal for radical reform, National Tax Journal, 21(4), 386-395.

Bundesministerium des Innern (2005), Dritter Versorgungsbericht der Bundesregierung, Berlin.

Campos M. M. and M. C. Pereira (2008), Impact of the recent reform of the Portuguese public employees' pension system, Economic Bulletin, Banco de Portugal, 14(2).

Carone, G., C. Denis, K. Mc Morrow, G. Mourre and W. Röger (2006), Long-term labour productivity and GDP projections for the EU25 Member States: a production function framework, Economic Papers 253, European Commission, Brussels.

Chlón-Dominczak, A. and M. Góra (2006), The NDC system in Poland: Assessment after five years; Holzmann, R. and E. Palmer (eds.), Pension reform – issues and prospects for non-financial defined contribution (NDC) schemes, World Bank, Washington, D.C., 425-447.

Czech Statistical Office (2007), Questionnaire on the statistical measurement of the assets and liabilities of pension schemes in general government of EU countries.

Department for Work and Pensions (2008), DWPs tabulation tool, http://83.244.183.180/100pc/sp/tabtool_sp.html, December 16th, 2008.

Deutsche Rentenversicherung Bund (2008), Versicherte 2005/2006 (insured persons 2005/2006), Statistik der Deutschen Rentenversicherung, 165.

Deutsche Rentenversicherung Bund (2007a), Rentenzugang 2006 (pensions awarded within 2006), Statistik der Deutschen Rentenversicherung, 163.

248

Deutsche Rentenversicherung Bund (2007b), Rentenbestand am 31. Dezember 2006 (pensions in payment on December 31st, 2006), Statistik der Deutschen Rentenversicherung, 162.

Disney, R. (2001), How should we measure pension liabilities in EU countries; Boeri, T., A. Börsch-Supan, A. Brugiavini, R. Disney, A. Kapteyn and F. Peracchi (eds.), Pensions: more information, less ideology, Kluwer Academic Publishers, Boston, 95-111.

Durant, D. and L. Frey (2007), An initial assessment of pension entitlements of French households, IFC Bulletin No. 28, 210-223.

Durant, D. and M. Reinsdorf (2008), Implicit social security and pension wealth in households' assets in the US and France , paper prepared for the 30th general conference of the International Association for Research in Income and Wealth in Portoroz, Slovenia.

Ehrentraut, O. and M. Heidler (2008), Zur nachhaltigen Finanzierung der GRV: Der Beitrag der Altersgrenzenanhebung im Rentenreformprozess (sustainable financing of the GRV: The impact of the increase of the retirement age), Perspektiven der Wirtschaftspolitik, 9(4), 424-445.

Ehrentraut, O. (2006), Alterung und Altersvorsorge: Das deutsche Drei-Säulen-System der Alterssicherung vor dem Hintergrund des demografischen Wandels (Ageing and old-age provision: The German three-pillar system of old age security against the background of the demograpic change), Peter Lang, Frankfurt.

European Commission (2007), Pension schemes and projection models in EU-25 member states, European Economy, Occasional Papers, 35.

European Commission (1999), Generational accounting in Europe, European Economy, Reports and Studies, 6.

Eurostat (2009), Database, http://epp.eurostat.ec.europa.eu.

Eurostat/ECB Contact Group (2009), Report of the Eurostat/ECB Contact Group on the statistical measurement of the assets and liabilities of pension schemes in general government to the CMFB, Luxembourg, forthcoming.

Eurostat/ECB Task Force (2008), Final report of the Eurostat/ECB Task Force on the statistical measurement of the assets and liabilities of pension schemes in general government to the CMFB, Luxembourg.

Feldstein, M. (1996), Social security and saving: New time series evidence, National Tax Journal, 49(2), 151-164.

Feldstein, M. (1974), Social security, induced retirement, and aggregate capital accumulation, Journal of Political Economy, 82, 905-926.

Franco, D. and N. Sartor (2006), NDCs in Italy: Unsatisfactory present, uncertain future; Holzmann, R. and E. Palmer (eds.), Pension reform – issues and prospects for non-financial defined contribution (NDC) schemes, World Bank, Washington, D.C., 467-492.

Franco, D., M. R. Marino and S. Zotteri (2004), Pension expenditure projections, pension liabilities and European Union fiscal rules, Paper presented in the international workshop on the balance sheet of social security pensions, Hitotsubashi University, Tokyo, 1-2 November 2004.

Franco, D. (1995), Pension liabilities – their use and misuse in the assessment of fiscal policies, Economic Papers, European Commission, 110.

Fredriksen, N. K. (2001), Fiscal sustainability in the OECD. A simple method and some preliminary results, Finansministeriet Working Paper, No. 3/2001.

Hagemann, R. P. and G. Nicoletti (1989), Ageing populations: economic effects and implications for public finance, OECD Department of Economics and Statistics Working Paper, No. 61.

Hagist, C. (2008), Demography and social health insurance – an international comparison using generational accounting, Nomos, Baden-Baden.

Hauptverband der österreichischen Sozialversicherungsträger (2008), Pensionsversicherung – Jahresstatistik 2006 (pension insurance – annual statistics 2006), Vienna.

Heidler, M. (2009), Reformen der Gesetzlichen Rentenversicherung: Politisches Risiko und intergenerative Umverteilung (reforms of the German statutory pension scheme: political risk and intergenerational redistribution), Peter Lang, Frankfurt.

Heidler, M., C. Müller and O. Weddige (2009), Measuring accrued-to-date liabilities of public pension systems – method, data and publications, Discussion Paper Series Forschungszentrum Generationenverträge, No. 37.

Heidler, M., B. Raffelhüschen and O. Weddige (2008), Final report of the statistical measurement of the liabilities of pension schemes in general government, survey by order of the European Central Bank (ECB), Freiburg.

Heidler, M. and B. Raffelhüschen (2005), How risky is the German pension system? The volatility of the internal rates of return, Discussion Paper Series Forschungszentrum Generationenverträge, No. 6.

Holzmann, R., R. Palacios and A. Zviniene (2004), Implicit pension debt: issues, measurement and scope in international perspective, Social Protection Discussion Paper Series, World Bank, No. 0403.

Holzmann, R. (1998), Financing the transition to multipillar, Social Protection Discussion Paper Series, World Bank, No. 9809.

Instituto Nacional de Estadística (INE, National Statistics Institute Spain, 2008), Questionnaire on the statistical measurement of the assets and liabilities of pension schemes in general government of EU countries.

Kane, C. and R. Palacios (1997), Reporting the implicit pension debt, World Bank, mimeo.

Könberg, B., E. Palmer and A. Sundén (2006), The NDC reform in Sweden: The 1994 legislation to the present; Holzmann, R. and E. Palmer (eds.), Pension reform – issues and prospects for non-financial defined contribution (NDC) schemes, World Bank, Washington, D.C., 449-466.

Kotlikoff, L.J. (1986), Deficit delusion, Public Interest, 84, 53-65.

Kuné, J. B., W. F. M. Petit and A. J. H. Pinxt (1993), The hidden liabilities of basic pension systems in the European Community, CEPS Working Document, No. 80, November.

Lassila, J. and T. Valkonen (2006), The Finnish pension reform of 2005, The Research Institute of the Finnish Economy, Discussion Paper No. 1000.

Latvijas Statistika (Statistics Latvia, 2008), Questionnaire on the statistical measurement of the assets and liabilities of pension schemes in general government of EU countries.

Leetmaa, P., H. Rennie and B. Thiry (2009), Household saving rate higher in the EU than in the USA despite lower income, Statistics in Focus, Eurostat, 29/2009.

Magyar Nemzeti Bank (Central Bank Hungary, 2008), Questionnaire on the statistical measurement of the assets and liabilities of pension schemes in general government of EU countries.

Mankiw, N. G., D. Romer and D. N. Weil (1992), A contribution to the empirics of economic growth, The quarterly journal of Economics, 107 (2), 407-437.

Mink, R. and P. Rother (2006), The statistical recording of implicit pension liabilities and its impact on household wealth and general government obligations, IFC Bulletin, No. 25, 241-251.

Ministry of Labour and Social Affairs Spain (2008), Update of the Spanish pension reform – new law on social security measures (December 2007), http://ec.europa.eu/employment_social/spsi/docs/social_inclusion/2006/nap/spain _update_en.pdf.

Ministry of Social Security and Labour (2007), Social report 2006-2007, Vilnius.

MISSOC – Mutual Information System on Social Protection (2009), Database of the European Commission, http://ec.europa.eu/employment_social/missoc/db/public/ compareTables.do?lang=en.

Müller, C., B. Raffelhüschen and O. Weddige (2009), Pension obligations of government employer pension schemes and social security pension schemes established in EU countries, survey by order of the European Central Bank (ECB), Freiburg.

Narodna banka Slovenska (Central Bank Slovakia, 2008), Questionnaire on the statistical measurement of the assets and liabilities of pension schemes in general government of EU countries.

Narodowy Bank Polski (Central Bank Poland, 2008), Questionnaire on the statistical measurement of the assets and liabilities of pension schemes in general government of EU countries.

National Statistical Institute Bulgaria (2008), Questionnaire on the statistical measurement of the assets and liabilities of pension schemes in general government of EU countries.

National Statistics Office Malta (2008), Questionnaire on the statistical measurement of the assets and liabilities of pension schemes in general government of EU countries.

OECD (2007), Pensions at a glance: Public policies across OECD countries, OECD Publications, Paris.

Oksanen, H. (2009), Using pension data for policy-making, presentation at the Eurostat/ECB workshop on pensions, April 29th and 30th, 2009, Frankfurt.

Palmer, E. (2006), What is NDC?, Holzmann, R. and E. Palmer (eds.), Pension reform – issues and prospectsfor non-financial defined contribution (NDC) schemes, World Bank, Washington D.C., 17-34.

Palmer, E., S. Stabina, I. Svensson and I. Vanovska (2006), NDC strategy in Latvia: Implementation and prospects for the future; Holzmann, R. and E. Palmer (eds.), Pension reform – issues and prospects for non-financial defined contribution (NDC) schemes, World Bank, Washington, D.C., 397-424.

Pflaumer, P. (1988), Methoden der Bevölkerungsvorausschätzung unter besonderer Berücksichtigung der Unsicherheit (concepts for population projections with special regard to uncertainty), Volkswirtschaftliche Schriften, Vol. 377, Berlin.

Queisser, M. and E. Whitehouse (2006), Neutral or fair? Actuarial concepts and pension-system design, OECD Social, Employment and Migration Working Papers, No. 40.

Raffelhüschen, B. (1999), Generational accounting: method, data, and limitations, European Economy, Reports and Studies, 6, 17-28.

Semeraro, G. (2007), Should financial accounts include future pension liabilities?, IFC Bulletin, No. 25 (1), 179-198.

Settergren, O. (2001), The automatic balance mechanism of the Swedish pension system, Working Papers in Social Insurance, The National Insurance Board, Sweden.

Statistics Finland (2008), Questionnaire on the statistical measurement of the assets and liabilities of pension schemes in general government of EU countries.

Statistics Greece (2008), Questionnaire on the statistical measurement of the assets and liabilities of pension schemes in general government of EU countries.

Statistics Italy (2008), Questionnaire on the statistical measurement of the assets and liabilities of pension schemes in general government of EU countries.

Statistics Lithuania (2008), Questionnaire on the statistical measurement of the assets and liabilities of pension schemes in general government of EU countries.

Statistics Sweden (2008), Questionnaire on the statistical measurement of the assets and liabilities of pension schemes in general government of EU countries.

Statistik Austria (2008), Questionnaire on the statistical measurement of the assets and liabilities of pension schemes in general government of EU countries.

Statistisches Bundesamt (2008), Volkswirtschaftliche Gesamtrechnungen 2007 (national accounts 2007), Fachserie 18, Reihe 1.4, Wiesbaden.

Statistisches Bundesamt (2007a), Finanzen und Steuern – Personal des öffentlichen Dienstes (finances and taxes – civil servants), Fachserie 14, Reihe 6.

Statistisches Bundesamt (2007b), Finanzen und Steuern – Versorgungsempfänger des öffentlichen Dienstes (finances and taxes – recipients of civil service pensions), Fachserie 14, Reihe 6.

Statistisches Bundesamt (2006a), Finanzen und Steuern – Personal des öffentlichen Dienstes (finances and taxes – civil servants), Fachserie 14, Reihe 6.

Statistisches Bundesamt (2006b), Finanzen und Steuern – Versorgungsempfänger des öffentlichen Dienstes (finances and taxes – recipients of civil service pensions), Fachserie 14, Reihe 6.1.

Statistisches Bundesamt (2005a), Finanzen und Steuern – Personal des öffentlichen Dienstes (finances and taxes – civil servants), Fachserie 14, Reihe 6.

Statistisches Bundesamt (2005b), Finanzen und Steuern – Versorgungsempfänger des öffentlichen Dienstes (finances and taxes – recipients of civil service pensions), Fachserie 14, Reihe 6.1.

SVR – Sachverständigenrat zur Begutachtung der gesamtwirtschaftlichen Entwicklung (The German Council of Economic Experts, 2007), Jahresgutachten 2007/08 – Das Erreichte nicht verspielen (Annual Report 2007/08 – the gains must not be squandered), Metzler-Poeschel, Wiesbaden.

Van den Noord, P. and R. Herd (1993), Pension liabilities in the seven major economies, OECD, Economics Department Working Papers, No. 142.

Versorgungsanstalt des Bundes und der Länder (VBL; supplementary pension scheme for public employees not being civil servants, 2008), Geschäftsbericht 2007 (business report 2007).

Versorgungsanstalt des Bundes und der Länder (2007), Geschäftsbericht 2006 (business report 2006).

Versorgungsanstalt des Bundes und der Länder (2006), Geschäftsbericht 2005 (business report 2005).

Werding, M. (2006), Implicit pension debt and the role of public pensions for human capital accumulation: An assessment for Germany, PIE Discussion Paper No. 283, www.ier.hit-u.ac.jp/pie/Japanese/discussionpaper/dp2005/dp283/text.pdf.

Appendix
Data sources

Table 76: Data sources for age-sex-specific pension profiles

Country	Data source
AT – Austria	Hauptverband der österreichischen Sozialversicherungsträger (2008)
BG – Bulgaria	National Statistical Institute Bulgaria (2008)
CZ – Czech Republic	Czech Statistical Office (2007)
DE – Germany	DRV (German statutory pension administration, 2007a and 2007b), Bundesministerium des Innern (Ministry of the interior, 2005)
ES – Spain	INE (National Statistics Institute Spain, 2008)
FI – Finland	Statistics Finland (2008)
FR – France	Banque de France (Central Bank France, 2008)
GR – Greece	Statistics Greece (2008)
HU – Hungary	Magyar Nemzeti Bank (Central Bank Hungary, 2008)
IT – Italy	Bank of Italy (2006)
LT – Lithuania	Statistics Lithuania (2008)
LV – Latvia	Latvijas Statistika (Statistics Latvia, 2008)
MT – Malta	National Statistics Office Malta (2008)
NL – Netherlands	Statistics Netherlands (2008)
PL – Poland	Narodowy Bank Polski (Central Bank Poland, 2008)
PT – Portugal	Banco de Portugal (Central Bank Portugal, 2008)
SE – Sweden	Statistics Sweden (2008)
SK – Slovakia	Narodna banka Slovenska (Central Bank Slovakia, 2008)
UK – United Kingdom	Department for Work and Pensions (2008)

Table 77: Data sources for pension budgets

Country	Data source
AT – Austria	Statistik Austria (2008)
BG – Bulgaria	National Statistical Institute Bulgaria (2008)
CZ – Czech Republic	Czech Statistical Office (2007)
DE – Germany	Statistisches Bundesamt (Federal Statistical Office Germany, 2008), Versorgungsanstalt des Bundes und der Länder (2008, 2007, 2006)
ES – Spain	INE (National Statistics Institute Spain, 2008)
FI – Finland	Statistics Finland (2008)
FR – France	Banque de France (Central Bank France, 2008)
GR – Greece	Statistics Greece (2008)
HU – Hungary	Magyar Nemzeti Bank (Central Bank Hungary, 2008)
IT – Italy	Statistics Italy (2008)
LT – Lithuania	Statistics Lithuania (2008)
LV – Latvia	Latvijas Statistika (Statistics Latvia, 2008)
MT – Malta	National Statistics Office Malta (2008)
NL – Netherlands	Statistics Netherlands (2008)
PL – Poland	Narodowy Bank Polski (Central Bank Poland, 2008)
PT – Portugal	Banco de Portugal (Central Bank Portugal, 2008)
SE – Sweden	Statistics Sweden (2008)
SK – Slovakia	Narodna banka Slovenska (Central Bank Slovakia, 2008)
UK – United Kingdom	Department for Work and Pensions (2008)

Supplementary tables 2007[232]

Table 78: Supplementary table Bulgaria 2007 PBO

			Non-core national accounts (figures in bn. BGN)	
			General Government	Social Security
			G	H
		Opening Balance Sheet		
	1	Pension entitlements		99.62
		Changes in pension entitlements due to transactions		
Sum 2.1 to 2.4	2	Increase in pension entitlements due to social contributions	0.00	5.50
	2.1	*Employer actual social contributions*		
	2.2	*Employer imputed social contributions*	0.00	
	2.3	*Household actual social contributions*		
	2.4	*Household social contribution supplements*	0.00	5.50
	3	Other (actuarial) increase of pension entitlements		19.91
	4	Reduction in pension entitlements due to payment of pension benefits		4.68
2 + 3 - 4	5	Change in pension entitlements due to social contributions and pension benefits	0.00	20.73
	6	Transfers of entitlements between schemes	0.00	0.00
	7	Changes in pension entitlements due to other transactions	0.00	0.00
		Changes in pension entitlements due to other economic flows		
	8	Changes in entitlements due to revaluations	0.00	0.00
	9	Changes in entitlements due to other changes in volume	0.00	0.00
		Closing Balance Sheet		
	10	Pension entitlements		120.36
		Pension entitlements (% of GDP 2007)		212.95
	11	Output		
	12	Assets held at the end of the period to meet pensions		

---

[232] All supplementary tables displayed are subject to our own calculations.

Appendix

Table 79 Supplementary table Bulgaria 2007 ABO

			Non-core national accounts (figures in bn. BGN)	
			General Government	Social Security
			G	H
		Opening Balance Sheet		
	1	Pension entitlements		88.87
		Changes in pension entitlements due to transactions		
Sum 2.1 to 2.4	2	Increase in pension entitlements due to social contributions	0.00	4.90
	2.1	*Employer actual social contributions*		0.00
	2.2	*Employer imputed social contributions*	0.00	
	2.3	*Household actual social contributions*	■	0.00
	2.4	*Household social contribution supplements*	0.00	4.90
	3	Other (actuarial) increase of pension entitlements	■	18.03
	4	Reduction in pension entitlements due to payment of pension benefits		4.68
2 + 3 - 4	5	Change in pension entitlements due to social contributions and pension benefits	0.00	18.25
	6	Transfers of entitlements between schemes		0.00
	7	Changes in pension entitlements due to other transactions		0.00
		Changes in pension entitlements due to other economic flows		
	8	Changes in entitlements due to revaluations	0.00	0.00
	9	Changes in entitlements due to other changes in volume	0.00	0.00
		Closing Balance Sheet		
	10	Pension entitlements		107.12
		Pension entitlements (% of GDP 2007)		189.53
	11	Output		
	12	Assets held at the end of the period to meet pensions		

Table 80: Supplementary table Germany 2007 PBO

			Non-core national accounts (figures in bn. EUR)	
			General Government	Social Security
			G	H
		Opening Balance Sheet		
	1	Pension entitlements	1129.18	6,730.99
		Changes in pension entitlements due to transactions		
Sum 2.1 to 2.4	2	Increase in pension entitlements due to social contributions	51.17	498.05
	2.1	*Employer actual social contributions*	0.00	78.21
	2.2	*Employer imputed social contributions*	-5.41	■
	2.3	*Household actual social contributions*	0.00	84.89
	2.4	*Household social contribution supplements*	56.58	334.95
	3	Other (actuarial) increase of pension entitlements	■	-156.34
	4	Reduction in pension entitlements due to payment of pension benefits	46.52	234.87
2 + 3 - 4	5	Change in pension entitlements due to social contributions and pension benefits	4.65	106.84
	6	Transfers of entitlements between schemes	0.00	0.00
	7	Changes in pension entitlements due to other transactions	0.00	-170.86
		Changes in pension entitlements due to other economic flows		
	8	Changes in entitlements due to revaluations	0.00	0.00
	9	Changes in entitlements due to other changes in volume	0.00	0.00
		Closing Balance Sheet		
	10	Pension entitlements	1133.83	6,666.96
		Pension entitlements (% of GDP 2007)	46.80	287.18
	11	Output		
	12	Assets held at the end of the period to meet pensions		

Table 81: Supplementary table Germany 2007 ABO

			Non-core national accounts (figures in bn. EUR)	
			General Government	Social Security
			G	H
		Opening Balance Sheet		
	1	Pension entitlements	1012.54	6,093.13
		Changes in pension entitlements due to transactions		
Sum 2.1 to 2.4	2	Increase in pension entitlements due to social contributions	51.69	466.16
	2.1	Employer actual social contributions	0.00	78.21
	2.2	Employer imputed social contributions	0.94	
	2.3	Household actual social contributions	0.00	84.89
	2.4	Household social contribution supplements	50.76	303.06
	3	Other (actuarial) increase of pension entitlements		-154.22
	4	Reduction in pension entitlements due to payment of pension benefits	46.52	234.87
2 + 3 - 4	5	Change in pension entitlements due to social contributions and pension benefits	5.17	77.07
	6	Transfers of entitlements between schemes	0.00	0.00
	7	Changes in pension entitlements due to other transactions	0.00	-140.76
		Changes in pension entitlements due to other economic flows		
	8	Changes in entitlements due to revaluations	0.00	0.00
	9	Changes in entitlements due to other changes in volume	0.00	0.00
		Closing Balance Sheet		
	10	Pension entitlements	1017.72	6,029.43
		Pension entitlements (% of GDP 2007)	42.00	259.72
	11	Output		
	12	Assets held at the end of the period to meet pensions		

Table 82: Supplementary table Spain 2007 PBO

			Non-core national accounts (figures in bn. EUR)	
			General Government	Social Security
			G	H
		Opening Balance Sheet		
	1	Pension entitlements		2,006.01
		Changes in pension entitlements due to transactions		
Sum 2.1 to 2.4	2	Increase in pension entitlements due to social contributions		104.53
	2.1	Employer actual social contributions		
	2.2	Employer imputed social contributions		
	2.3	Household actual social contributions		
	2.4	Household social contribution supplements		104.53
	3	Other (actuarial) increase of pension entitlements		144.53
	4	Reduction in pension entitlements due to payment of pension benefits		79.81
2 + 3 - 4	5	Change in pension entitlements due to social contributions and pension benefits		169.26
	6	Transfers of entitlements between schemes		0.00
	7	Changes in pension entitlements due to other transactions		0.00
		Changes in pension entitlements due to other economic flows		
	8	Changes in entitlements due to revaluations		0.00
	9	Changes in entitlements due to other changes in volume		0.00
		Closing Balance Sheet		
	10	Pension entitlements		2,175.28
		Pension entitlements (% of GDP 2007)		207.05
	11	Output		
	12	Assets held at the end of the period to meet pensions		

Appendix

Table 83: Supplementary table Spain 2007 ABO

			Non-core national accounts (figures in bn. EUR)	
			General Government G	Social Security H
		Opening Balance Sheet		
	1	Pension entitlements		*1,739.40*
		Changes in pension entitlements due to transactions		
Sum 2.1 to 2.4	2	**Increase in pension entitlements due to social contributions**		**90.63**
	2.1	*Employer actual social contributions*		0.00
	2.2	*Employer imputed social contributions*		█████
	2.3	*Household actual social contributions*		0.00
	2.4	*Household social contribution supplements*		90.63
	3	Other (actuarial) increase of pension entitlements		135.48
	4	Reduction in pension entitlements due to payment of pension benefits		79.81
2 + 3 - 4	5	**Change in pension entitlements due to social contributions and pension benefits**		**146.31**
	6	Transfers of entitlements between schemes		*0.00*
	7	Changes in pension entitlements due to other transactions		*0.00*
		Changes in pension entitlements due to other economic flows		
	8	Changes in entitlements due to revaluations		*0.00*
	9	Changes in entitlements due to other changes in volume		*0.00*
		Closing Balance Sheet		
	10	Pension entitlements		*1,885.70*
		Pension entitlements (% of GDP 2007)		*179.49*
	11	Output		
	12	Assets held at the end of the period to meet pensions		

Table 84: Supplementary table Finland 2007 PBO

			Non-core national accounts (figures in bn. EUR)	
			General Government G	Social Security H
		Opening Balance Sheet		
	1	Pension entitlements		*503.52*
		Changes in pension entitlements due to transactions		
Sum 2.1 to 2.4	2	**Increase in pension entitlements due to social contributions**		**41.47**
	2.1	*Employer actual social contributions*		11.87
	2.2	*Employer imputed social contributions*		█████
	2.3	*Household actual social contributions*		3.76
	2.4	*Household social contribution supplements*		25.84
	3	Other (actuarial) increase of pension entitlements		0.36
	4	Reduction in pension entitlements due to payment of pension benefits		15.10
2 + 3 - 4	5	**Change in pension entitlements due to social contributions and pension benefits**		**26.73**
	6	Transfers of entitlements between schemes		*0.00*
	7	Changes in pension entitlements due to other transactions		*0.00*
		Changes in pension entitlements due to other economic flows		
	8	Changes in entitlements due to revaluations		*0.00*
	9	Changes in entitlements due to other changes in volume		*0.00*
		Closing Balance Sheet		
	10	Pension entitlements		*530.26*
		Pension entitlements (% of GDP 2007)		*295.02*
	11	Output		
	12	Assets held at the end of the period to meet pensions		

Table 85: Supplementary table Finland 2007 ABO

				Non-core national accounts (figures in bn. EUR)	
				General Government	Social Security
				G	H
			Opening Balance Sheet		
	1	Pension entitlements			401.89
			Changes in pension entitlements due to transactions		
Sum 2.1 to 2.4	2	Increase in pension entitlements due to social contributions			36.26
	2.1	*Employer actual social contributions*			11.87
	2.2	*Employer imputed social contributions*			▰
	2.3	*Household actual social contributions*			3.76
	2.4	*Household social contribution supplements*			20.63
	3	Other (actuarial) increase of pension entitlements			0.36
	4	Reduction in pension entitlements due to payment of pension benefits			15.10
2 + 3 - 4	5	Change in pension entitlements due to social contributions and pension benefits			21.52
	6	Transfers of entitlements between schemes			0.00
	7	Changes in pension entitlements due to other transactions			0.00
			Changes in pension entitlements due to other economic flows		
	8	Changes in entitlements due to revaluations			0.00
	9	Changes in entitlements due to other changes in volume			0.00
			Closing Balance Sheet		
	10	Pension entitlements			423.41
		Pension entitlements (% of GDP 2007)			235.57
	11	Output			
	12	Assets held at the end of the period to meet pensions			

Table 86: Supplementary table France 2007 PBO

				Non-core national accounts (figures in bn. EUR)	
				General Government	Social Security
				G	H
			Opening Balance Sheet		
	1	Pension entitlements		1101.69	5,444.16
			Changes in pension entitlements due to transactions		
Sum 2.1 to 2.4	2	Increase in pension entitlements due to social contributions		66.68	420.19
	2.1	*Employer actual social contributions*		18.00	146.00
	2.2	*Employer imputed social contributions*		-11.08	▰
	2.3	*Household actual social contributions*		4.00	
	2.4	*Household social contribution supplements*		55.76	274.19
	3	Other (actuarial) increase of pension entitlements			-151.93
	4	Reduction in pension entitlements due to payment of pension benefits		39.80	188.83
2 + 3 - 4	5	Change in pension entitlements due to social contributions and pension benefits		26.88	79.43
	6	Transfers of entitlements between schemes		0.00	0.00
	7	Changes in pension entitlements due to other transactions		0.00	0.00
			Changes in pension entitlements due to other economic flows		
	8	Changes in entitlements due to revaluations		0.00	0.00
	9	Changes in entitlements due to other changes in volume		0.00	0.00
			Closing Balance Sheet		
	10	Pension entitlements		1128.56	5,523.58
		Pension entitlements (% of GDP 2007)		59.64	291.91
	11	Output			
	12	Assets held at the end of the period to meet pensions			

Appendix

Table 87: Supplementary table France 2007 ABO

				Non-core national accounts	
				(figures in bn. EUR)	
				General Government	Social Security
				G	H
			Opening Balance Sheet		
		1	Pension entitlements	*909.30*	*4,595.06*
			Changes in pension entitlements due to transactions		
Sum 2.1 to 2.4		2	**Increase in pension entitlements due to social contributions**	*67.44*	*377.89*
		2 1	*Employer actual social contributions*	18.00	146.00
		2.2	*Employer imputed social contributions*	*-0.71*	■
		2.3	*Household actual social contributions*	4.00	0.00
		2.4	*Household social contribution supplements*	46.16	231.89
		3	Other (actuarial) increase of pension entitlements	■	-103.77
		4	Reduction in pension entitlements due to payment of pension benefits	39.80	188.83
2 + 3 - 4		5	**Change in pension entitlements due to social contributions and pension benefits**	*27.64*	*85.28*
		6	Transfers of entitlements between schemes	*0.00*	*0.00*
		7	Changes in pension entitlements due to other transactions	*0.00*	*0.00*
			Changes in pension entitlements due to other economic flows		
		8	Changes in entitlements due to revaluations	*0.00*	*0.00*
		9	Changes in entitlements due to other changes in volume	*0.00*	*0.00*
			Closing Balance Sheet		
		10	Pension entitlements	*936.94*	*4,680.34*
			Pension entitlements (% of GDP 2007)	*49.52*	*247.34*
		11	Output		
		12	Assets held at the end of the period to meet pensions		

Table 88: Supplementary table Greece 2007 PBO

				Non-core national accounts	
				(figures in bn. EUR)	
				General Government	Social Security
				G	H
			Opening Balance Sheet		
		1	Pension entitlements		*491.95*
			Changes in pension entitlements due to transactions		
Sum 2.1 to 2.4		2	**Increase in pension entitlements due to social contributions**		*44.69*
		2.1	*Employer actual social contributions*		9.38
		2 2	*Employer imputed social contributions*		■
		2 3	*Household actual social contributions*		9.65
		2.4	*Household social contribution supplements*		25.66
		3	Other (actuarial) increase of pension entitlements		18.01
		4	Reduction in pension entitlements due to payment of pension benefits		20.26
2 + 3 - 4		5	**Change in pension entitlements due to social contributions and pension benefits**		*42.44*
		6	Transfers of entitlements between schemes		*0.00*
		7	Changes in pension entitlements due to other transactions		*0.00*
			Changes in pension entitlements due to other economic flows		
		8	Changes in entitlements due to revaluations		*0.00*
		9	Changes in entitlements due to other changes in volume		*0.00*
			Closing Balance Sheet		
		10	Pension entitlements		*534.39*
			Pension entitlements (% of GDP 2007)		*234.19*
		11	Output		
		12	Assets held at the end of the period to meet pensions		

Table 89: Supplementary table Greece 2007 ABO

				Non-core national accounts (figures in bn. EUR)	
				General Government	Social Security
				G	H
			Opening Balance Sheet		
		1	Pension entitlements		463.24
			Changes in pension entitlements due to transactions		
Sum 2.1 to 2.4		2	Increase in pension entitlements due to social contributions		43.19
	2.1		*Employer actual social contributions*		9.38
	2.2		*Employer imputed social contributions*		▮
	2.3		*Household actual social contributions*		9.65
	2.4		*Household social contribution supplements*		24.16
		3	Other (actuarial) increase of pension entitlements	▮	17.01
		4	Reduction in pension entitlements due to payment of pension benefits		20.26
2 + 3 - 4		5	Change in pension entitlements due to social contributions and pension benefits		39.94
		6	Transfers of entitlements between schemes		0.00
		7	Changes in pension entitlements due to other transactions		0.00
			Changes in pension entitlements due to other economic flows		
		8	Changes in entitlements due to revaluations		0.00
		9	Changes in entitlements due to other changes in volume		0.00
			Closing Balance Sheet		
		10	Pension entitlements		503.19
			Pension entitlements (% of GDP 2007)		220.52
		11	Output		
		12	Assets held at the end of the period to meet pensions		

Table 90: Supplementary table Hungary 2007 PBO

				Non-core national accounts (figures in bn. HUF)	
				General Government	Social Security
				G	H
			Opening Balance Sheet		
		1	Pension entitlements		61,236.23
			Changes in pension entitlements due to transactions		
Sum 2.1 to 2.4		2	Increase in pension entitlements due to social contributions		3,186.13
	2.1		*Employer actual social contributions*		
	2.2		*Employer imputed social contributions*		▮
	2.3		*Household actual social contributions*		
	2.4		*Household social contribution supplements*		3,186.13
		3	Other (actuarial) increase of pension entitlements	▮	4,306.44
		4	Reduction in pension entitlements due to payment of pension benefits		2,520.00
2 + 3 - 4		5	Change in pension entitlements due to social contributions and pension benefits		4,972.57
		6	Transfers of entitlements between schemes		0.00
		7	Changes in pension entitlements due to other transactions		0.00
			Changes in pension entitlements due to other economic flows		
		8	Changes in entitlements due to revaluations		0.00
		9	Changes in entitlements due to other changes in volume		0.00
			Closing Balance Sheet		
		10	Pension entitlements		66,208.80
			Pension entitlements (% of GDP 2007)		260.47
		11	Output		
		12	Assets held at the end of the period to meet pensions		

Appendix

Table 91: Supplementary table Hungary 2007 ABO

			Non-core national accounts	
			(figures in bn. HUF)	
			General Government	Social Security
			G	H
		Opening Balance Sheet		
	1	Pension entitlements		53,066.85
		Changes in pension entitlements due to transactions		
Sum 2.1 to 2.4	2	**Increase in pension entitlements due to social contributions**		2,762.52
	2.1	*Employer actual social contributions*		0.00
	2.2	*Employer imputed social contributions*		■
	2.3	*Household actual social contributions*		0.00
	2.4	*Household social contribution supplements*		2,762.52
	3	Other (actuarial) increase of pension entitlements	■	4,124.66
	4	Reduction in pension entitlements due to payment of pension benefits		2,520.00
2 + 3 - 4	5	**Change in pension entitlements due to social contributions and pension benefits**		4,367.18
	6	Transfers of entitlements between schemes		0.00
	7	Changes in pension entitlements due to other transactions		0.00
		Changes in pension entitlements due to other economic flows		
	8	Changes in entitlements due to revaluations		0.00
	9	Changes in entitlements due to other changes in volume		0.00
		Closing Balance Sheet		
	10	Pension entitlements		57,434.03
		Pension entitlements (% of GDP 2007)		225.95
	11	Output		
	12	Assets held at the end of the period to meet pensions		

Table 92: Supplementary table Lithuania 2007 PBO

			Non-core national accounts	
			(figures in bn. EUR)	
			General Government	Social Security
			G	H
		Opening Balance Sheet		
	1	Pension entitlements	3.25	40.03
		Changes in pension entitlements due to transactions		
Sum 2.1 to 2.4	2	**Increase in pension entitlements due to social contributions**	0.68	4.42
	2.1	*Employer actual social contributions*		1.87
	2.2	*Employer imputed social contributions*	0.50	■
	2.3	*Household actual social contributions*		0.20
	2.4	*Household social contribution supplements*	0.18	2.35
	3	Other (actuarial) increase of pension entitlements	■	11.60
	4	Reduction in pension entitlements due to payment of pension benefits	0.14	2.07
2 + 3 - 4	5	**Change in pension entitlements due to social contributions and pension benefits**	0.54	13.95
	6	Transfers of entitlements between schemes	0.00	0.00
	7	Changes in pension entitlements due to other transactions	0.00	0.00
		Changes in pension entitlements due to other economic flows		
	8	Changes in entitlements due to revaluations	0.00	0.00
	9	Changes in entitlements due to other changes in volume	0.00	0.00
		Closing Balance Sheet		
	10	Pension entitlements	3.79	53.98
		Pension entitlements (% of GDP 2007)	13.33	189.92
	11	Output		
	12	Assets held at the end of the period to meet pensions		

Table 93: Supplementary table Lithuania 2007 ABO

			Non-core national accounts (figures in bn. EUR)	
			General Government	Social Security
			G	H
		Opening Balance Sheet		
	1	Pension entitlements	2.83	35.01
		Changes in pension entitlements due to transactions		
Sum 2.1 to 2.4	2	Increase in pension entitlements due to social contributions	0.44	4.12
	2.1	*Employer actual social contributions*		1.87
	2.2	*Employer imputed social contributions*	0.29	
	2.3	*Household actual social contributions*		0.20
	2.4	*Household social contribution supplements*	0.15	2.05
	3	Other (actuarial) increase of pension entitlements		9.80
	4	Reduction in pension entitlements due to payment of pension benefits		2.07
2 + 3 - 4	5	Change in pension entitlements due to social contributions and pension benefits	0.44	11.85
	6	Transfers of entitlements between schemes		0.00
	7	Changes in pension entitlements due to other transactions		0.00
		Changes in pension entitlements due to other economic flows		
	8	Changes in entitlements due to revaluations	0.00	0.00
	9	Changes in entitlements due to other changes in volume		0.00
		Closing Balance Sheet		
	10	Pension entitlements	3.27	46.86
		Pension entitlements (% of GDP 2007)	11.50	164.86
	11	Output		
	12	Assets held at the end of the period to meet pensions		

Table 94: Supplementary table Latvia 2007 PBO

			Non-core national accounts (figures in bn. LVL)	
			General Government	Social Security
			G	H
		Opening Balance Sheet		
	1	Pension entitlements		13.95
		Changes in pension entitlements due to transactions		
Sum 2.1 to 2.4	2	Increase in pension entitlements due to social contributions		2.83
	2.1	*Employer actual social contributions*		2.08
	2.2	*Employer imputed social contributions*		
	2.3	*Household actual social contributions*		
	2.4	*Household social contribution supplements*		0.75
	3	Other (actuarial) increase of pension entitlements		-0.02
	4	Reduction in pension entitlements due to payment of pension benefits		0.75
2 + 3 - 4	5	Change in pension entitlements due to social contributions and pension benefits		2.06
	6	Transfers of entitlements between schemes		0.00
	7	Changes in pension entitlements due to other transactions		0.00
		Changes in pension entitlements due to other economic flows		
	8	Changes in entitlements due to revaluations		0.00
	9	Changes in entitlements due to other changes in volume		0.00
		Closing Balance Sheet		
	10	Pension entitlements		16.01
		Pension entitlements (% of GDP 2007)		114.69
	11	Output		
	12	Assets held at the end of the period to meet pensions		

Table 95: Supplementary table Latvia 2007 ABO

				Non-core national accounts	
				(figures in bn. LVL)	
				General Government	Social Security
				G	H
			Opening Balance Sheet		
		1	Pension entitlements		11.99
			Changes in pension entitlements due to transactions		
Sum 2.1 to 2.4		2	Increase in pension entitlements due to social contributions		2.72
	2.1		Employer actual social contributions		2.08
	2.2		Employer imputed social contributions		
	2.3		Household actual social contributions		0.00
	2.4		Household social contribution supplements		0.64
		3	Other (actuanal) increase of pension entitlements		-0.24
		4	Reduction in pension entitlements due to payment of pension benefits		0.75
2 + 3 - 4		5	Change in pension entitlements due to social contributions and pension benefits		1.73
		6	Transfers of entitlements between schemes		0.00
		7	Changes in pension entitlements due to other transactions		0.00
			Changes in pension entitlements due to other economic flows		
		8	Changes in entitlements due to revaluations		0.00
		9	Changes in entitlements due to other changes in volume		0.00
			Closing Balance Sheet		
		10	Pension entitlements		13.72
			Pension entitlements (% of GDP 2007)		98.30
		11	Output		
		12	Assets held at the end of the period to meet pensions		

Table 96: Supplementary table Malta 2007 PBO

				Non-core national accounts	
				(figures in bn. EUR)	
				General Government	Social Security
				G	H
			Opening Balance Sheet		
		1	Pension entitlements	2.18	11.53
			Changes in pension entitlements due to transactions		
Sum 2.1 to 2.4		2	Increase in pension entitlements due to social contributions	0.14	0.88
	2.1		Employer actual social contributions		0.14
	2.2		Employer imputed social contributions	0.03	
	2.3		Household actual social contributions		0.14
	2.4		Household social contribution supplements	0.11	0.59
		3	Other (actuanal) increase of pension entitlements		0.12
		4	Reduction in pension entitlements due to payment of pension benefits	0.08	0.39
2 + 3 - 4		5	Change in pension entitlements due to social contributions and pension benefits	0.06	0.61
		6	Transfers of entitlements between schemes	0.00	0.00
		7	Changes in pension entitlements due to other transactions	0.00	0.00
			Changes in pension entitlements due to other economic flows		
		8	Changes in entitlements due to revaluations	0.00	0.00
		9	Changes in entitlements due to other changes in volume	0.00	0.00
			Closing Balance Sheet		
		10	Pension entitlements	2.24	12.14
			Pension entitlements (% of GDP 2007)	41.34	224.17
		11	Output		
		12	Assets held at the end of the period to meet pensions		

Table 97: Supplementary table Malta 2007 ABO

			Non-core national accounts (figures in bn. EUR)	
			General Government	Social Security
			G	H
		Opening Balance Sheet		
	1	Pension entitlements	2.10	10.37
		Changes in pension entitlements due to transactions		
Sum 2.1 to 2.4	2	Increase in pension entitlements due to social contributions	0.06	0.82
	2.1	*Employer actual social contributions*		0.14
	2.2	*Employer imputed social contributions*	-0.04	
	2.3	*Household actual social contributions*		0.14
	2.4	*Household social contribution supplements*	0.10	0.53
	3	Other (actuarial) increase of pension entitlements		0.12
	4	Reduction in pension entitlements due to payment of pension benefits	0.08	0.39
2 + 3 - 4	5	Change in pension entitlements due to social contributions and pension benefits	-0.02	0.55
	6	Transfers of entitlements between schemes		0.00
	7	Changes in pension entitlements due to other transactions		0.00
		Changes in pension entitlements due to other economic flows		
	8	Changes in entitlements due to revaluations	0.00	0.00
	9	Changes in entitlements due to other changes in volume		0.00
		Closing Balance Sheet		
	10	Pension entitlements	2.08	10.92
		Pension entitlements (% of GDP 2007)	38.47	201.60
	11	Output		
	12	Assets held at the end of the period to meet pensions		

Table 98: Supplementary table Netherlands 2007 ABO and PBO

			Non-core national accounts (figures in bn. EUR)	
			General Government	Social Security
			G	H
		Opening Balance Sheet		
	1	Pension entitlements		1,275.64
		Changes in pension entitlements due to transactions		
Sum 2.1 to 2.4	2	Increase in pension entitlements due to social contributions		83.46
	2.1	*Employer actual social contributions*		
	2.2	*Employer imputed social contributions*		
	2.3	*Household actual social contributions*		17.64
	2.4	*Household social contribution supplements*		65.83
	3	Other (actuarial) increase of pension entitlements		34.27
	4	Reduction in pension entitlements due to payment of pension benefits		35.96
2 + 3 - 4	5	Change in pension entitlements due to social contributions and pension benefits		81.77
	6	Transfers of entitlements between schemes		0.00
	7	Changes in pension entitlements due to other transactions		0.00
		Changes in pension entitlements due to other economic flows		
	8	Changes in entitlements due to revaluations		0.00
	9	Changes in entitlements due to other changes in volume		0.00
		Closing Balance Sheet		
	10	Pension entitlements		1,357.42
		Pension entitlements (% of GDP 2007)		239.38
	11	Output		
	12	Assets held at the end of the period to meet pensions		

Table 99: Supplementary table Poland 2007 PBO

| | | | | Non-core national accounts (figures in bn. PLN) | |
				General Government G	Social Security H
			Opening Balance Sheet		
		1	Pension entitlements	*289.50*	*3,538.42*
			Changes in pension entitlements due to transactions		
Sum 2.1 to 2.4		2	**Increase in pension entitlements due to social contributions**	*26.97*	*177.81*
	2.1		*Employer actual social contributions*		
	2.2		*Employer imputed social contributions*	12.08	▉
	2.3		*Household actual social contributions*		
	2.4		*Household social contribution supplements*	14.89	177.81
		3	Other (actuarial) increase of pension entitlements	▉	-20.73
		4	Reduction in pension entitlements due to payment of pension benefits	10.39	121.38
2 + 3 - 4		5	**Change in pension entitlements due to social contributions and pension benefits**	*16.58*	*35.71*
		6	Transfers of entitlements between schemes	*0.00*	*0.00*
		7	Changes in pension entitlements due to other transactions	*0.00*	*0.00*
			Changes in pension entitlements due to other economic flows		
		8	Changes in entitlements due to revaluations	*0.00*	*0.00*
		9	Changes in entitlements due to other changes in volume	*0.00*	*0.00*
			Closing Balance Sheet		
		10	Pension entitlements	*306.08*	*3,574.13*
			Pension entitlements (% of GDP 2007)	*26.21*	*306.06*
		11	Output		
		12	Assets held at the end of the period to meet pensions		

Table 100: Supplementary table Poland 2007 ABO

| | | | | Non-core national accounts (figures in bn. PLN) | |
				General Government G	Social Security H
			Opening Balance Sheet		
		1	Pension entitlements	*253.64*	*3,100.20*
			Changes in pension entitlements due to transactions		
Sum 2.1 to 2.4		2	**Increase in pension entitlements due to social contributions**	*25.84*	*156.06*
	2.1		*Employer actual social contributions*	0.00	0.00
	2.2		*Employer imputed social contributions*	12.77	▉
	2.3		*Household actual social contributions*	0.00	0.00
	2.4		*Household social contribution supplements*	13.07	156.06
		3	Other (actuarial) increase of pension entitlements	▉	7.33
		4	Reduction in pension entitlements due to payment of pension benefits	10.39	121.38
2 + 3 - 4		5	**Change in pension entitlements due to social contributions and pension benefits**	*15.45*	*42.02*
		6	Transfers of entitlements between schemes		*0.00*
		7	Changes in pension entitlements due to other transactions		*0.00*
			Changes in pension entitlements due to other economic flows		
		8	Changes in entitlements due to revaluations	*0.00*	*0.00*
		9	Changes in entitlements due to other changes in volume	*0.00*	*0.00*
			Closing Balance Sheet		
		10	Pension entitlements	*269.09*	*3,142.22*
			Pension entitlements (% of GDP 2007)	*23.04*	*269.07*
		11	Output		
		12	Assets held at the end of the period to meet pensions		

Table 101: Supplementary table Portugal 2007 PBO

			General Government	Social Security
			Non-core national accounts	
			(figures in bn. EUR)	
			H	*I*
		Opening Balance Sheet		
	1	Pension entitlements		463.75
		Changes in pension entitlements due to transactions		
Sum 2.1 to 2.4	2	**Increase in pension entitlements due to social contributions**		42.84
	2.1	*Employer actual social contributions*		12.44
	2.2	*Employer imputed social contributions*		
	2.3	*Household actual social contributions*		6.42
	2.4	*Household social contribution supplements*		23.98
	3	Other (actuarial) increase of pension entitlements		6.55
	4	Reduction in pension entitlements due to payment of pension benefits		17.67
2 + 3 - 4	5	**Change in pension entitlements due to social contributions and pension benefits**		31.73
	6	Transfers of entitlements between schemes		0.00
	7	Changes in pension entitlements due to other transactions		0.00
		Changes in pension entitlements due to other economic flows		
	8	Changes in entitlements due to revaluations		0.00
	9	Changes in entitlements due to other changes in volume		0.00
		Closing Balance Sheet		
	10	Pension entitlements		495.48
		Pension entitlements (% of GDP 2007)		303.82
	11	Output		
	12	Assets held at the end of the period to meet pensions		

Table 102: Supplementary table Portugal 2007 ABO

			General Government	Social Security
			Non-core national accounts	
			(figures in bn. EUR)	
			H	*I*
		Opening Balance Sheet		
	1	Pension entitlements		391.93
		Changes in pension entitlements due to transactions		
Sum 2.1 to 2.4	2	**Increase in pension entitlements due to social contributions**		39.11
	2.1	*Employer actual social contributions*		12.44
	2.2	*Employer imputed social contributions*		
	2.3	*Household actual social contributions*		6.42
	2.4	*Household social contribution supplements*		20.25
	3	Other (actuarial) increase of pension entitlements		4.66
	4	Reduction in pension entitlements due to payment of pension benefits		17.67
2 + 3 - 4	5	**Change in pension entitlements due to social contributions and pension benefits**		26.10
	6	Transfers of entitlements between schemes		0.00
	7	Changes in pension entitlements due to other transactions		0.00
	8	Changes in entitlements due to revaluations		0.00
	9	Changes in entitlements due to other changes in volume		0.00
		Closing Balance Sheet		
	10	Pension entitlements		418.03
		Pension entitlements (% of GDP 2007)		256.33
	11	Output		
	12	Assets held at the end of the period to meet pensions		

Appendix

Table 103: Supplementary table Sweden 2007 PBO

			Non-core national accounts (figures in bn. SEK)	
			General Government	Social Security
			G	H
		Opening Balance Sheet		
	1	Pension entitlements		**8,249.32**
		Changes in pension entitlements due to transactions		
Sum 2.1 to 2.4	2	**Increase in pension entitlements due to social contributions**		**600.79**
	2.1	*Employer actual social contributions*		190.42
	2.2	*Employer imputed social contributions*		■
	2.3	*Household actual social contributions*		
	2.4	*Household social contribution supplements*		410.37
	3	Other (actuarial) increase of pension entitlements	■	-402.91
	4	Reduction in pension entitlements due to payment of pension benefits		281.65
2 + 3 - 4	5	**Change in pension entitlements due to social contributions and pension benefits**		**-83.78**
	6	Transfers of entitlements between schemes		**0.00**
	7	Changes in pension entitlements due to other transactions		**0.00**
		Changes in pension entitlements due to other economic flows		
	8	Changes in entitlements due to revaluations		**0.00**
	9	Changes in entitlements due to other changes in volume		**0.00**
		Closing Balance Sheet		
	10	Pension entitlements		**8,165.54**
		Pension entitlements (% of GDP 2007)		**265.93**
	11	Output		
	12	Assets held at the end of the period to meet pensions		

Table 104: Supplementary table Sweden 2007 ABO

			Non-core national accounts (figures in bn. SEK)	
			General Government	Social Security
			G	H
		Opening Balance Sheet		
	1	Pension entitlements		**7,141.32**
		Changes in pension entitlements due to transactions		
Sum 2.1 to 2.4	2	**Increase in pension entitlements due to social contributions**		**546.61**
	2.1	*Employer actual social contributions*		190.42
	2.2	*Employer imputed social contributions*		■
	2.3	*Household actual social contributions*		0.00
	2.4	*Household social contribution supplements*		356.19
	3	Other (actuarial) increase of pension entitlements	■	-299.85
	4	Reduction in pension entitlements due to payment of pension benefits		281.65
2 + 3 - 4	5	**Change in pension entitlements due to social contributions and pension benefits**		**-34.89**
	6	Transfers of entitlements between schemes		**0.00**
	7	Changes in pension entitlements due to other transactions		**0.00**
		Changes in pension entitlements due to other economic flows		
	8	Changes in entitlements due to revaluations		**0.00**
	9	Changes in entitlements due to other changes in volume		**0.00**
		Closing Balance Sheet		
	10	Pension entitlements		**7,106.44**
		Pension entitlements (% of GDP 2007)		**231.44**
	11	Output		
	12	Assets held at the end of the period to meet pensions		

Table 105: Supplementary table Slovakia 2007 PBO

			Non-core national accounts (figures in bn. SKK)	
			General Government	Social Security
			G	H
		Opening Balance Sheet		
	1	Pension entitlements	*157.04*	*3,336.06*
		Changes in pension entitlements due to transactions		
Sum 2.1 to 2.4	2	Increase in pension entitlements due to social contributions	*16.15*	*338.92*
	2.1	*Employer actual social contributions*	2.08	114.52
	2.2	*Employer imputed social contributions*	5.14	
	2.3	*Household actual social contributions*	0.80	50.31
	2.4	*Household social contribution supplements*	8.12	174.09
	3	Other (actuarial) increase of pension entitlements		79.04
	4	Reduction in pension entitlements due to payment of pension benefits	5.24	126.52
2 + 3 - 4	5	Change in pension entitlements due to social contributions and pension benefits	*10.91*	*291.43*
	6	Transfers of entitlements between schemes	*0.00*	*0.00*
	7	Changes in pension entitlements due to other transactions	*0.00*	*0.00*
		Changes in pension entitlements due to other economic flows		
	8	Changes in entitlements due to revaluations	*0.00*	*0.00*
	9	Changes in entitlements due to other changes in volume	*0.00*	*0.00*
		Closing Balance Sheet		
	10	Pension entitlements	*167.94*	*3,627.49*
		Pension entitlements (% of GDP 2007)	*9.06*	*195.76*
	11	Output		
	12	Assets held at the end of the period to meet pensions		

Table 106: Supplementary table Slovakia 2007 ABO

			Non-core national accounts (figures in bn. SKK)	
			General Government	Social Security
			G	H
		Opening Balance Sheet		
	1	Pension entitlements	*140.40*	*2,971.75*
		Changes in pension entitlements due to transactions		
Sum 2.1 to 2.4	2	Increase in pension entitlements due to social contributions	*15.51*	*319.99*
	2.1	*Employer actual social contributions*	2.08	114.52
	2.2	*Employer imputed social contributions*	5.36	
	2.3	*Household actual social contributions*	0.80	50.31
	2.4	*Household social contribution supplements*	7.28	155.16
	3	Other (actuarial) increase of pension entitlements		69.27
	4	Reduction in pension entitlements due to payment of pension benefits	5.24	126.52
2 + 3 - 4	5	Change in pension entitlements due to social contributions and pension benefits	*10.27*	*262.73*
	6	Transfers of entitlements between schemes		*0.00*
	7	Changes in pension entitlements due to other transactions		*0.00*
		Changes in pension entitlements due to other economic flows		
	8	Changes in entitlements due to revaluations	*0.00*	*0.00*
	9	Changes in entitlements due to other changes in volume	*0.00*	*0.00*
		Closing Balance Sheet		
	10	Pension entitlements	*150.67*	*3,234.48*
		Pension entitlements (% of GDP 2007)	*8.13*	*174.55*
	11	Output		
	12	Assets held at the end of the period to meet pensions		

Table 107: Supplementary table UK 2007 PBO

			Non-core national accounts	
			(figures in bn. GBP)	
			General Government	Social Security
			G	H
		Opening Balance Sheet		
	1	Pension entitlements		*1,205.14*
		Changes in pension entitlements due to transactions		
Sum 2.1 to 2.4	2	**Increase in pension entitlements due to social contributions**		*61.72*
	2.1	*Employer actual social contributions*		
	2.2	*Employer imputed social contributions*		▮
	2.3	*Household actual social contributions*		
	2.4	*Household social contribution supplements*		*61.72*
	3	Other (actuarial) increase of pension entitlements	▮	*57.99*
	4	Reduction in pension entitlements due to payment of pension benefits		*57.25*
2 + 3 - 4	5	**Change in pension entitlements due to social contributions and pension benefits**		*62.46*
	6	Transfers of entitlements between schemes		*0.00*
	7	Changes in pension entitlements due to other transactions		*-4.00*
		Changes in pension entitlements due to other economic flows		
	8	Changes in entitlements due to revaluations		*0.00*
	9	Changes in entitlements due to other changes in volume		*0.00*
		Closing Balance Sheet		
	10	Pension entitlements		*1,263.60*
		Pension entitlements (% of GDP 2007)		*90.19*
	11	Output		
	12	Assets held at the end of the period to meet pensions		

Profiles[233]

Figure 79: Public pension profile Austria: Average benefit per resident (2006, in EUR)

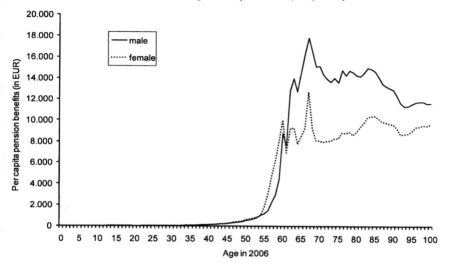

---

[233] The data sources for all profiles shown in this section can be found in Table 76.

Figure 80: Public pension profile Bulgaria: Average benefit per resident (2006, in BGN)

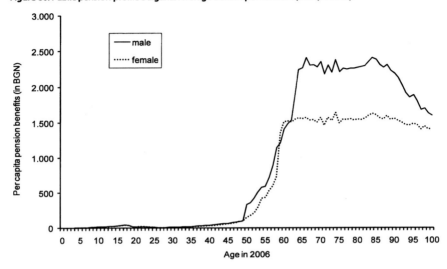

Figure 81: Public pension profile Czech Republic: Average benefit per resident (2006, in CZK)

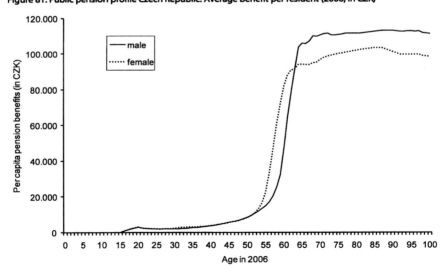

Figure 82: Social security pension profile Germany: Average benefit per resident (2006, in EUR)

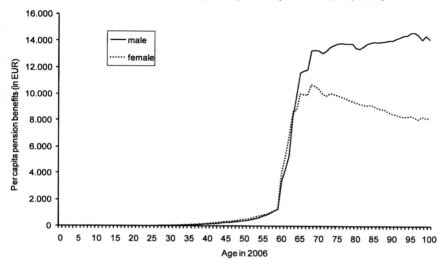

Figure 83: Social security contribution profile Germany: Average contribution per resident (2006, in EUR)

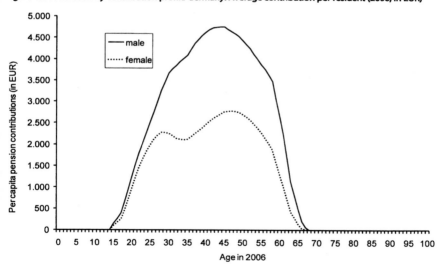

Figure 84: Government employer pension profile Germany: Average benefit per member of civil servants' population (2006, in EUR)[234]

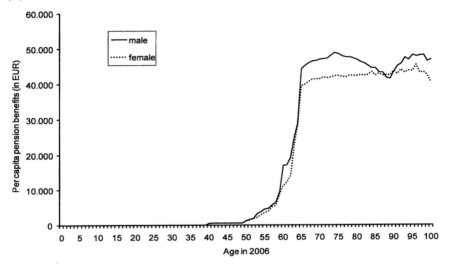

Figure 85: Public pension profile Spain: Average benefit per resident (2006, in EUR)

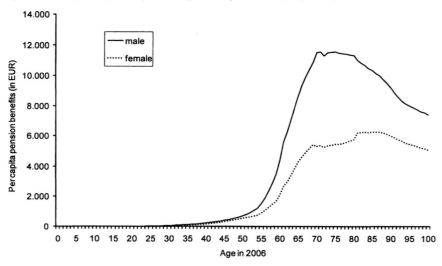

Figure 86: Public pension profile Finland (private sector): Average benefit per resident (2006, in EUR)

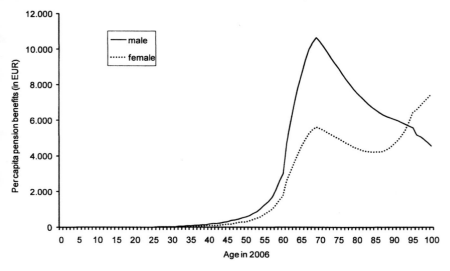

Figure 87: Public pension profile Finland (VaEL scheme): Average benefit per resident (2006, in EUR)

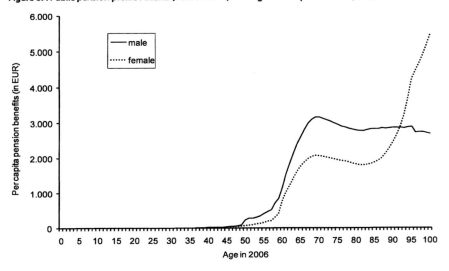

Figure 88; Public pension profile Finland (public sector except VaEL scheme): Average benefit per resident (2006, in EUR)

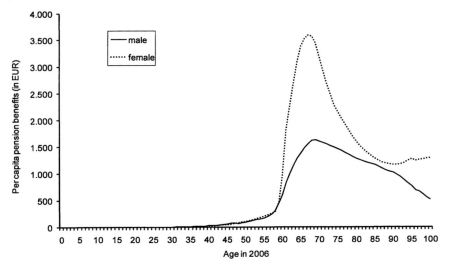

Figure 89: Public pension profile France: Average benefit per resident (2006, in EUR)

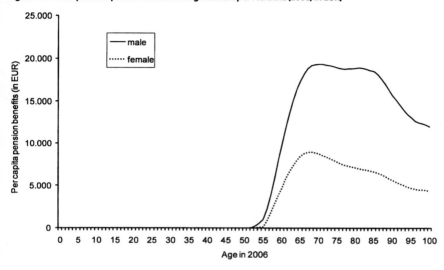

Figure 90: Public pension profile Greece: Average benefit per resident (2006, in EUR)

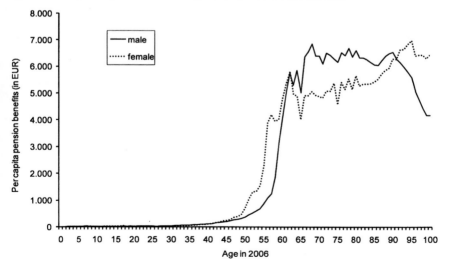

279

Figure 91: Public pension profile Hungary: Average benefit per resident (2006, In HUF)

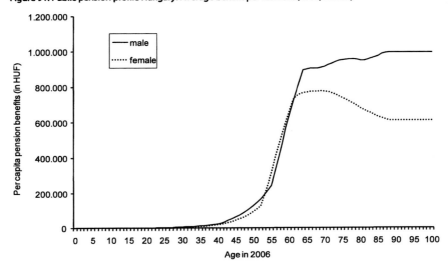

Figure 92: Public pension profile Italy: Average benefit per resident (2006, In EUR)

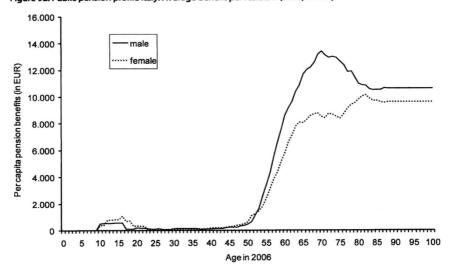

Figure 93: Public pension profile Lithuania: Average benefit per resident (2006, in EUR)

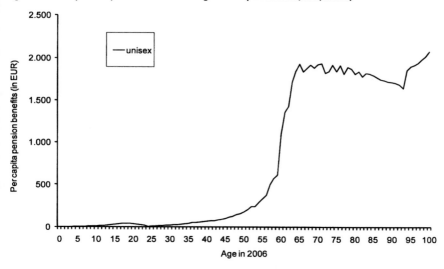

Figure 94: Public pension contribution profile Lithuania: Average contribution per resident (2006, in EUR)

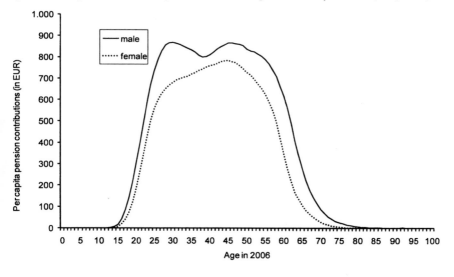

Figure 95: Public pension profile Latvia: Average benefit per resident (2006, in LVL)

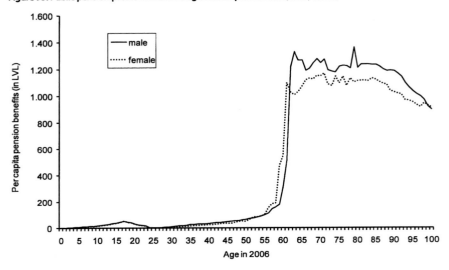

Figure 96: Public pension profile Malta: Average benefit per resident (2006, in EUR)

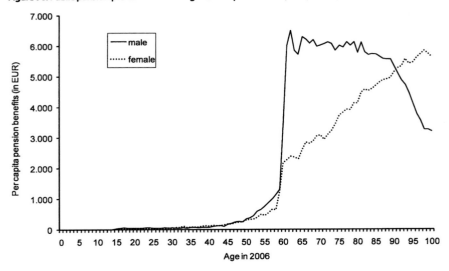

Figure 97: Public pension profile Netherlands: Average benefit per resident (2006, in EUR)

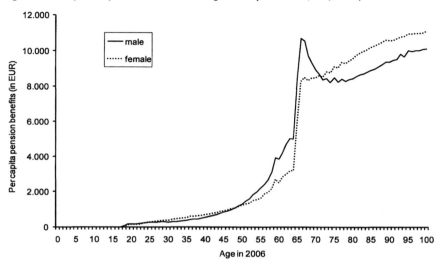

Figure 98: Public pension contribution profile Netherlands: Average contribution per resident (2006, in EUR)

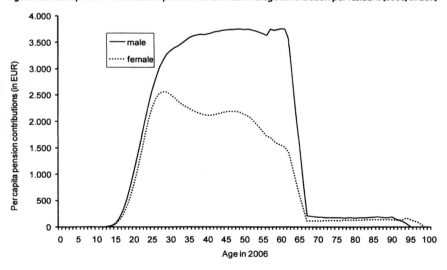

Figure 99: Public pension profile Poland: Average benefit per resident (2006, in PLN)

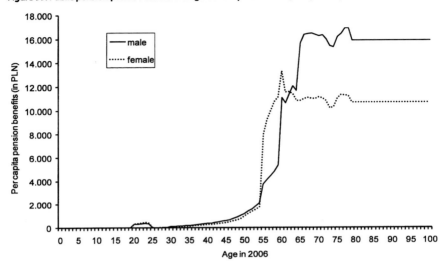

Figure 100: Public pension profile Portugal (general system): Average benefit per resident (2006, in EUR)

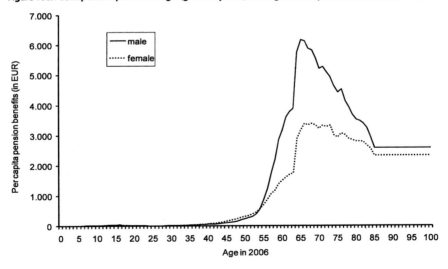

Figure 101: Public pension profile Portugal (CGA): Average benefit per resident (2006, in EUR)

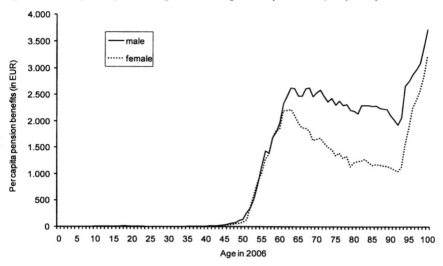

Figure 102: Public pension profile Sweden: Average benefit per resident (2006, in SEK)

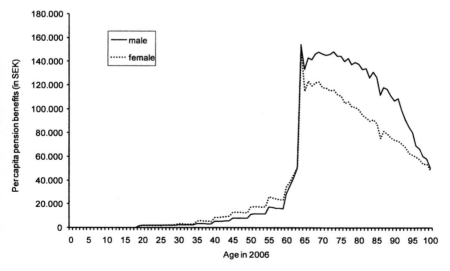

Figure 103: Public pension contribution profile Sweden: Average contribution per resident (2006, in SEK)

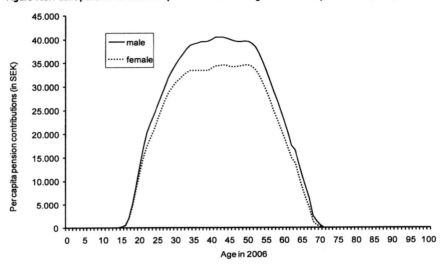

Figure 104: Social security pension profile Slovakia: Average benefit per resident (2006, in SKK)

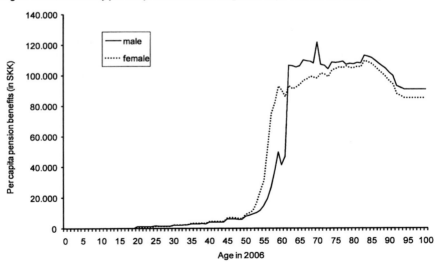

Figure 105: Government employer pension profile Slovakia: Average benefit per resident (2006, in SKK)

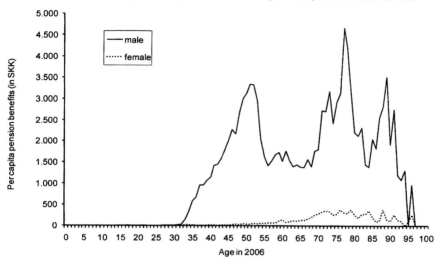

Figure 106: Public pension profile United Kingdom: Average benefit per resident (2006, in GBP)

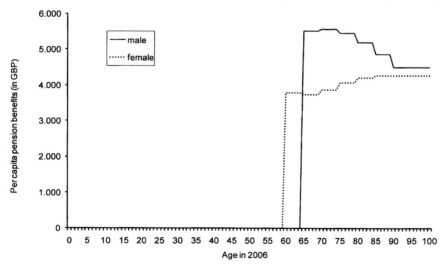

Sensitivity analyses

Table 108: Sensitivity analysis social security pension scheme Austria 2006 (in bn. EUR)

Parameters		ABO	Difference to standard scenario	PBO	Difference to standard scenario
r	g				
1.0%	1.0%	825.95	39.7%	937.55	39.3%
1.0%	1.5%	825.95	39.7%	976.56	45.1%
1.0%	2.0%	825.95	39.7%	1019.30	51.5%
2.0%	1.0%	692.75	17.2%	774.18	15.1%
2.0%	1.5%	692.75	17.2%	802.72	19.3%
2.0%	2.0%	692.75	17.2%	833.88	23.9%
3.0%	1.0%	591.20	0.0%	651.65	-3.2%
3.0%	1.5%	591.20	0.0%	672.90	0.0%
3.0%	2.0%	591.20	0.0%	696.04	3.4%
4.0%	1.0%	512.28	-13.3%	557.89	-17.1%
4.0%	1.5%	512.28	-13.3%	574.00	-14.7%
4.0%	2.0%	512.28	-13.3%	591.47	-12.1%
5.0%	1.0%	449.88	-23.9%	484.82	-28.0%
5.0%	1.5%	449.88	-23.9%	497.22	-26.1%
5.0%	2.0%	449.88	-23.9%	510.63	-24.1%

Table 109: Sensitivity analysis government employer pension scheme Austria 2006 (in bn. EUR)

Parameters		ABO	Difference to standard scenario	PBO	Difference to standard scenario
r	g				
1.0%	1.0%	310.82	39.7%	352.82	39.3%
1.0%	1.5%	310.82	39.7%	367.50	45.1%
1.0%	2.0%	310.82	39.7%	383.58	51.5%
2.0%	1.0%	260.70	17.2%	291.34	15.1%
2.0%	1.5%	260.70	17.2%	302.08	19.3%
2.0%	2.0%	260.70	17.2%	313.81	23.9%
3.0%	1.0%	222.48	0.0%	245.23	-3.2%
3.0%	1.5%	222.48	0.0%	253.23	0.0%
3.0%	2.0%	222.48	0.0%	261.93	3.4%
4.0%	1.0%	192.78	-13.3%	209.94	-17.1%
4.0%	1.5%	192.78	-13.3%	216.01	-14.7%
4.0%	2.0%	192.78	-13.3%	222.58	-12.1%
5.0%	1.0%	169.30	-23.9%	182.45	-28.0%
5.0%	1.5%	169.30	-23.9%	187.12	-26.1%
5.0%	2.0%	169.30	-23.9%	192.16	-24.1%

Table 110: Sensitivity analysis social security pension scheme Bulgaria 2006 (in bn. BGN)

Parameters		ABO	Difference to standard scenario	PBO	Difference to standard scenario
r	g				
1.0%	1.0%	120.77	35.9%	134.99	35.5%
1.0%	1.5%	124.58	40.2%	145.06	45.6%
1.0%	2.0%	128.59	44.7%	156.36	57.0%
2.0%	1.0%	101.30	14.0%	111.52	11.9%
2.0%	1.5%	104.21	17.3%	118.91	19.4%
2.0%	2.0%	107.26	20.7%	127.14	27.6%
3.0%	1.0%	86.59	-2.6%	94.07	-5.6%
3.0%	1.5%	88.87	0.0%	99.62	0.0%
3.0%	2.0%	91.25	2.7%	105.76	6.2%
4.0%	1.0%	75.23	-15.3%	80.80	-18.9%
4.0%	1.5%	77.04	-13.3%	85.07	-14.6%
4.0%	2.0%	78.94	-11.2%	89.75	-9.9%
5.0%	1.0%	66.27	-25.4%	70.50	-29.2%
5.0%	1.5%	67.75	-23.8%	73.84	-25.9%
5.0%	2.0%	69.29	-22.0%	77.48	-22.2%

Table 111: Sensitivity analysis social security pension scheme Czech Republic 2006 (in bn. CZK)

Parameters		ABO	Difference to standard scenario	PBO	Difference to standard scenario
r	g				
1.0%	1.0%	6916.30	29.6%	8472.03	30.9%
1.0%	1.5%	7056.00	32.2%	8859.81	36.8%
1.0%	2.0%	7200.23	34.9%	9277.46	43.3%
2.0%	1.0%	5985.47	12.1%	7216.97	11.5%
2.0%	1.5%	6096.96	14.2%	7518.46	16.1%
2.0%	2.0%	6211.84	16.4%	7841.98	21.1%
3.0%	1.0%	5248.10	-1.7%	6236.38	-3.7%
3.0%	1.5%	5338.48	0.0%	6474.35	0.0%
3.0%	2.0%	5431.46	1.7%	6728.81	3.9%
4.0%	1.0%	4655.16	-12.8%	5458.49	-15.7%
4.0%	1.5%	4729.49	-11.4%	5649.00	-12.7%
4.0%	2.0%	4805.83	-10.0%	5852.02	-9.6%
5.0%	1.0%	4171.74	-21.9%	4832.61	-25.4%
5.0%	1.5%	4233.68	-20.7%	4987.15	-23.0%
5.0%	2.0%	4297.20	-19.5%	5151.30	-20.4%

Table 112: Sensitivity analysis social security pension scheme Germany 2006 (in bn. EUR)

Parameters		ABO	Difference to standard scenario	PBO	Difference to standard scenario
r	g				
1.0%	1.0%	8209.89	**34.7%**	8978.11	**33.4%**
1.0%	1.5%	8736.94	**43.4%**	9994.17	**48.5%**
1.0%	2.0%	9317.85	**52.9%**	11181.17	**66.1%**
2.0%	1.0%	6824.20	**12.0%**	7363.65	**9.4%**
2.0%	1.5%	7225.22	**18.6%**	8112.39	**20.5%**
2.0%	2.0%	7664.59	**25.8%**	8978.11	**33.4%**
3.0%	1.0%	5781.18	**-5.1%**	6166.64	**-8.4%**
3.0%	**1.5%**	**6093.12**	**0.0%**	**6730.99**	**0.0%**
3.0%	2.0%	6433.02	**5.6%**	7377.20	**9.6%**
4.0%	1.0%	5270.16	**-13.5%**	5259.79	**-21.9%**
4.0%	1.5%	5227.45	**-14.2%**	5694.14	**-15.4%**
4.0%	2.0%	5495.83	**-9.8%**	6186.99	**-8.1%**
5.0%	1.0%	4352.68	**-28.6%**	4558.97	**-32.3%**
5.0%	1.5%	4552.72	**-25.3%**	4899.75	**-27.2%**
5.0%	2.0%	4768.57	**-21.7%**	5283.19	**-21.5%**

Table 113: Sensitivity analysis government employer pension scheme Germany 2006 (in bn. EUR)

Parameters		ABO	Difference to standard scenario	PBO	Difference to standard scenario
r	g				
1.0%	1.0%	310.82	**39.7%**	352.82	**39.3%**
1.0%	1.5%	310.82	**39.7%**	367.50	**45.1%**
1.0%	2.0%	310.82	**39.7%**	383.58	**51.5%**
2.0%	1.0%	260.70	**17.2%**	291.34	**15.1%**
2.0%	1.5%	260.70	**17.2%**	302.08	**19.3%**
2.0%	2.0%	260.70	**17.2%**	313.81	**23.9%**
3.0%	1.0%	222.48	**0.0%**	245.23	**-3.2%**
3.0%	**1.5%**	**222.48**	**0.0%**	**253.23**	**0.0%**
3.0%	2.0%	222.48	**0.0%**	261.93	**3.4%**
4.0%	1.0%	192.78	**-13.3%**	209.94	**-17.1%**
4.0%	1.5%	192.78	**-13.3%**	216.01	**-14.7%**
4.0%	2.0%	192.78	**-13.3%**	222.58	**-12.1%**
5.0%	1.0%	169.30	**-23.9%**	182.45	**-28.0%**
5.0%	1.5%	169.30	**-23.9%**	187.12	**-26.1%**
5.0%	2.0%	169.30	**-23.9%**	192.16	**-24.1%**

Table 114: Sensitivity analysis social security pension scheme Spain 2006 (in bn. EUR)

Parameters		ABO	Difference to standard scenario	PBO	Difference to standard scenario
r	g				
1.0%	1.0%	2438.28	40.2%	2808.06	40.0%
1.0%	1.5%	2438.28	40.2%	2928.13	46.0%
1.0%	2.0%	2438.28	40.2%	3059.21	52.5%
2.0%	1.0%	2041.18	17.4%	2311.26	15.2%
2.0%	1.5%	2041.18	17.4%	2399.41	19.6%
2.0%	2.0%	2041.18	17.4%	2495.38	24.4%
3.0%	1.0%	1739.40	0.0%	1940.15	-3.3%
3.0%	1.5%	1739.40	0.0%	2006.01	0.0%
3.0%	2.0%	1739.40	0.0%	2077.53	3.6%
4.0%	1.0%	1505.60	-13.4%	1657.31	-17.4%
4.0%	1.5%	1505.60	-13.4%	1707.33	-14.9%
4.0%	2.0%	1505.60	-13.4%	1761.50	-12.2%
5.0%	1.0%	1321.27	-24.0%	1437.69	-28.3%
5.0%	1.5%	1321.27	-24.0%	1476.28	-26.4%
5.0%	2.0%	1321.27	-24.0%	1517.94	-24.3%

Table 115: Sensitivity analysis social security pension scheme Finland 2006 (in bn. EUR)

Parameters		ABO	Difference to standard scenario	PBO	Difference to standard scenario
r	g				
1.0%	1.0%	568.68	41.5%	718.59	42.7%
1.0%	1.5%	575.47	43.2%	769.42	52.8%
1.0%	2.0%	582.37	44.9%	826.62	64.2%
2.0%	1.0%	471.09	17.2%	578.89	15.0%
2.0%	1.5%	476.28	18.5%	615.03	22.1%
2.0%	2.0%	481.56	19.8%	655.39	30.2%
3.0%	1.0%	397.83	-1.0%	477.21	-5.2%
3.0%	1.5%	401.89	0.0%	503.52	0.0%
3.0%	2.0%	406.02	1.0%	532.71	5.8%
4.0%	1.0%	341.65	-15.0%	401.41	-20.3%
4.0%	1.5%	344.89	-14.2%	421.00	-16.4%
4.0%	2.0%	348.18	-13.4%	442.59	-12.1%
5.0%	1.0%	297.74	-25.9%	343.65	-31.8%
5.0%	1.5%	300.37	-25.3%	358.54	-28.8%
5.0%	2.0%	303.03	-24.6%	374.84	-25.6%

Appendix

Table 116: Sensitivity analysis social security pension scheme France 2006 (in bn. EUR)

Parameters		ABO	Difference to standard scenario	PBO	Difference to standard scenario
r	g				
1.0%	1.0%	6518.74	41.9%	7748.90	42.3%
1.0%	1.5%	6518.74	41.9%	8105.35	48.9%
1.0%	2.0%	6518.74	41.9%	8497.84	56.1%
2.0%	1.0%	5421.02	18.0%	6314.55	16.0%
2.0%	1.5%	5421.02	18.0%	6569.74	20.7%
2.0%	2.0%	5421.02	18.0%	6849.58	25.8%
3.0%	1.0%	4595.06	0.0%	5257.57	-3.4%
3.0%	1.5%	4595.06	0.0%	5444.16	0.0%
3.0%	2.0%	4595.06	0.0%	5647.94	3.7%
4.0%	1.0%	3960.56	-13.8%	4461.30	-18.1%
4.0%	1.5%	3960.56	-13.8%	4600.45	-15.5%
4.0%	2.0%	3960.56	-13.8%	4751.82	-12.7%
5.0%	1.0%	3463.76	-24.6%	3849.06	-29.3%
5.0%	1.5%	3463.76	-24.6%	3954.77	-27.4%
5.0%	2.0%	3463.76	-24.6%	4069.32	-25.3%

Table 117: Sensitivity analysis government employer pension scheme France 2006 (in bn. EUR)

Parameters		ABO	Difference to standard scenario	PBO	Difference to standard scenario
r	g				
1.0%	1.0%	1274.61	40.2%	1556.80	41.3%
1.0%	1.5%	1274.61	40.2%	1627.32	47.7%
1.0%	2.0%	1274.61	40.2%	1705.02	54.8%
2.0%	1.0%	1066.87	17.3%	1274.02	15.6%
2.0%	1.5%	1066.87	17.3%	1324.72	20.2%
2.0%	2.0%	1066.87	17.3%	1380.35	25.3%
3.0%	1.0%	909.30	0.0%	1064.50	-3.4%
3.0%	1.5%	909.30	0.0%	1101.69	0.0%
3.0%	2.0%	909.30	0.0%	1142.33	3.7%
4.0%	1.0%	787.41	-13.4%	905.93	-17.8%
4.0%	1.5%	787.41	-13.4%	933.73	-15.2%
4.0%	2.0%	787.41	-13.4%	964.00	-12.5%
5.0%	1.0%	691.39	-24.0%	783.53	-28.9%
5.0%	1.5%	691.39	-24.0%	804.69	-27.0%
5.0%	2.0%	691.39	-24.0%	827.64	-24.9%

Table 118: Sensitivity analysis social security pension scheme Greece 2006 (in bn. EUR)

Parameters		ABO	Difference to standard scenario	PBO	Difference to standard scenario
r	g				
1.0%	1.0%	656.07	**41.6%**	686.73	**39.6%**
1.0%	1.5%	656.07	**41.6%**	716.86	**45.7%**
1.0%	2.0%	656.07	**41.6%**	750.11	**52.5%**
2.0%	1.0%	546.24	**17.9%**	565.92	**15.0%**
2.0%	1.5%	546.24	**17.9%**	587.66	**19.5%**
2.0%	2.0%	546.24	**17.9%**	611.56	**24.3%**
3.0%	1.0%	463.24	**0.0%**	475.95	**-3.3%**
3.0%	1.5%	**463.24**	**0.0%**	**491.95**	**0.0%**
3.0%	2.0%	463.24	**0.0%**	509.46	**3.6%**
4.0%	1.0%	399.28	**-13.8%**	407.47	**-17.2%**
4.0%	1.5%	399.28	**-13.8%**	419.47	**-14.7%**
4.0%	2.0%	399.28	**-13.8%**	432.55	**-12.1%**
5.0%	1.0%	349.07	**-24.6%**	354.33	**-28.0%**
5.0%	1.5%	349.07	**-24.6%**	363.48	**-26.1%**
5.0%	2.0%	349.07	**-24.6%**	373.41	**-24.1%**

Table 119: Sensitivity analysis social security pension scheme Hungary 2006 (in bn. HUF)

Parameters		ABO	Difference to standard scenario	PBO	Difference to standard scenario
r	g				
1.0%	1.0%	72531.95	**36.7%**	84223.52	**37.5%**
1.0%	1.5%	74879.08	**41.1%**	90908.39	**48.5%**
1.0%	2.0%	77345.87	**45.8%**	98476.52	**60.8%**
2.0%	1.0%	60625.89	**14.2%**	68908.32	**12.5%**
2.0%	1.5%	62423.86	**17.6%**	73737.32	**20.4%**
2.0%	2.0%	64308.09	**21.2%**	79157.74	**29.3%**
3.0%	1.0%	51659.48	**-2.7%**	57662.11	**-5.8%**
3.0%	1.5%	**53066.85**	**0.0%**	**61236.23**	**0.0%**
3.0%	2.0%	54537.76	**2.8%**	65215.30	**6.5%**
4.0%	1.0%	44760.62	**-15.7%**	49205.67	**-19.6%**
4.0%	1.5%	45883.98	**-13.5%**	51911.73	**-15.2%**
4.0%	2.0%	47055.08	**-11.3%**	54901.07	**-10.3%**
5.0%	1.0%	39347.67	**-25.9%**	42706.54	**-30.3%**
5.0%	1.5%	40260.23	**-24.1%**	44798.91	**-26.8%**
5.0%	2.0%	41209.33	**-22.3%**	47093.53	**-23.1%**

Table 120: Sensitivity analysis social security pension scheme Italy 2006 (in bn. EUR)

Parameters		ABO	Difference to standard scenario	PBO	Difference to standard scenario
r	g				
1.0%	1.0%	6302.73	42.6%	6702.46	40.6%
1.0%	1.5%	6302.73	42.6%	6953.08	45.9%
1.0%	2.0%	6302.73	42.6%	7227.19	51.6%
2.0%	1.0%	5224.49	18.2%	5512.24	15.7%
2.0%	1.5%	5224.49	18.2%	5693.73	19.5%
2.0%	2.0%	5224.49	18.2%	5891.60	23.6%
3.0%	1.0%	4420.08	0.0%	4631.84	-2.8%
3.0%	1.5%	4420.08	0.0%	4765.95	0.0%
3.0%	2.0%	4420.08	0.0%	4911.69	3.1%
4.0%	1.0%	3805.76	-13.9%	3964.81	-16.8%
4.0%	1.5%	3805.76	-13.9%	4065.77	-14.7%
4.0%	2.0%	3805.76	-13.9%	4175.13	-12.4%
5.0%	1.0%	3326.82	-24.7%	3448.55	-27.6%
5.0%	1.5%	3326.82	-24.7%	3525.87	-26.0%
5.0%	2.0%	3326.82	-24.7%	3609.36	-24.3%

Table 121: Sensitivity analysis social security pension scheme Lithuania 2006 (in bn. EUR)

Parameters		ABO	Difference to standard scenario	PBO	Difference to standard scenario
r	g				
1.0%	1.0%	48.05	37.3%	54.90	37.1%
1.0%	1.5%	50.40	44.0%	60.16	50.3%
1.0%	2.0%	52.95	51.2%	66.20	65.4%
2.0%	1.0%	39.80	13.7%	44.67	11.6%
2.0%	1.5%	41.55	18.7%	48.47	21.1%
2.0%	2.0%	43.42	24.0%	52.79	31.9%
3.0%	1.0%	33.67	-3.8%	37.21	-7.0%
3.0%	1.5%	35.01	0.0%	40.03	0.0%
3.0%	2.0%	36.43	4.1%	43.20	7.9%
4.0%	1.0%	29.00	-17.2%	31.63	-21.0%
4.0%	1.5%	30.05	-14.2%	33.77	-15.6%
4.0%	2.0%	31.16	-11.0%	36.15	-9.7%
5.0%	1.0%	25.37	-27.5%	27.35	-31.7%
5.0%	1.5%	26.20	-25.1%	29.01	-27.5%
5.0%	2.0%	27.09	-22.6%	30.85	-22.9%

Table 122: Sensitivity analysis government employer pension scheme Lithuania 2006 (in bn. EUR)

Parameters		ABO	Difference to standard scenario	PBO	Difference to standard scenario
r	g				
1.0%	1.0%	4.16	38.1%	4.78	37.9%
1.0%	1.5%	4.36	44.9%	5.24	51.4%
1.0%	2.0%	4.58	52.3%	5.78	66.9%
2.0%	1.0%	3.43	14.1%	3.87	11.8%
2.0%	1.5%	3.58	19.1%	4.21	21.5%
2.0%	2.0%	3.75	24.5%	4.59	32.6%
3.0%	1.0%	2.89	-3.9%	3.21	-7.2%
3.0%	1.5%	3.01	0.0%	3.46	0.0%
3.0%	2.0%	3.13	4.1%	3.74	8.1%
4.0%	1.0%	2.49	-17.4%	2.72	-21.4%
4.0%	1.5%	2.58	-14.4%	2.91	-15.9%
4.0%	2.0%	2.67	-11.3%	3.12	-9.8%
5.0%	1.0%	2.17	-28.0%	2.35	-32.2%
5.0%	1.5%	2.24	-25.6%	2.49	-28.0%
5.0%	2.0%	2.32	-23.1%	2.66	-23.3%

Table 123: Sensitivity analysis social security pension scheme Latvia 2006 (in bn. LVL)

Parameters		ABO	Difference to standard scenario	PBO	Difference to standard scenario
r	g				
1.0%	1.0%	16.06	34.0%	18.94	35.8%
1.0%	1.5%	16.31	36.0%	20.00	43.4%
1.0%	2.0%	16.56	38.1%	21.18	51.8%
2.0%	1.0%	13.66	14.0%	15.74	12.9%
2.0%	1.5%	13.85	15.6%	16.51	18.4%
2.0%	2.0%	14.04	17.2%	17.36	24.5%
3.0%	1.0%	11.84	-1.2%	13.38	-4.1%
3.0%	1.5%	11.99	0.0%	13.95	0.0%
3.0%	2.0%	12.14	1.3%	14.58	4.5%
4.0%	1.0%	10.42	-13.1%	11.57	-17.0%
4.0%	1.5%	10.53	-12.1%	12.01	-13.9%
4.0%	2.0%	10.66	-11.1%	12.49	-10.5%
5.0%	1.0%	9.28	-22.6%	10.17	-27.1%
5.0%	1.5%	9.38	-21.8%	10.51	-24.6%
5.0%	2.0%	9.48	-20.9%	10.88	-22.0%

Table 124: Sensitivity analysis social security pension scheme Malta 2006 (in bn. EUR)

Parameters		ABO	Difference to standard scenario	PBO	Difference to standard scenario
r	g				
1.0%	1.0%	13.85	33.6%	15.32	32.9%
1.0%	1.5%	14.68	41.6%	16.89	46.5%
1.0%	2.0%	15.59	50.4%	18.70	62.2%
2.0%	1.0%	11.59	11.8%	12.65	9.7%
2.0%	1.5%	12.22	17.9%	13.81	19.8%
2.0%	2.0%	12.92	24.6%	15.13	31.3%
3.0%	1.0%	9.87	-4.8%	10.65	-7.6%
3.0%	1.5%	10.37	0.0%	11.53	0.0%
3.0%	2.0%	10.91	5.2%	12.52	8.6%
4.0%	1.0%	8.54	-17.6%	9.12	-20.9%
4.0%	1.5%	8.93	-13.8%	9.80	-15.0%
4.0%	2.0%	9.36	-9.7%	10.57	-8.3%
5.0%	1.0%	7.49	-27.8%	7.93	-31.2%
5.0%	1.5%	7.81	-24.7%	8.47	-26.5%
5.0%	2.0%	8.15	-21.3%	9.07	-21.3%

Table 125: Sensitivity analysis government employer pension scheme Malta 2006 (in bn. EUR)

Parameters		ABO	Difference to standard scenario	PBO	Difference to standard scenario
r	g				
1.0%	1.0%	2.86	36.1%	2.95	35.6%
1.0%	1.5%	3.04	45.0%	3.28	50.4%
1.0%	2.0%	3.25	54.8%	3.65	67.8%
2.0%	1.0%	2.36	12.5%	2.40	10.4%
2.0%	1.5%	2.50	19.2%	2.64	21.2%
2.0%	2.0%	2.66	26.5%	2.91	33.7%
3.0%	1.0%	1.99	-5.1%	2.00	-8.1%
3.0%	1.5%	2.10	0.0%	2.18	0.0%
3.0%	2.0%	2.22	5.6%	2.38	9.2%
4.0%	1.0%	1.71	-18.6%	1.70	-22.0%
4.0%	1.5%	1.79	-14.6%	1.83	-15.8%
4.0%	2.0%	1.88	-10.2%	1.98	-8.9%
5.0%	1.0%	1.49	-29.1%	1.47	-32.7%
5.0%	1.5%	1.56	-25.9%	1.57	-27.9%
5.0%	2.0%	1.63	-22.4%	1.69	-22.5%

Table 126: Sensitivity analysis social security pension scheme Netherlands 2006 (in bn. EUR)

Parameters		ABO	Difference to standard scenario	PBO	Difference to standard scenario
r	g				
1.0%	1.0%	1802.92	41.3%	1802.92	41.3%
1.0%	1.5%	2054.61	61.1%	2054.61	61.1%
1.0%	2.0%	2358.49	84.9%	2358.49	84.9%
2.0%	1.0%	1419.84	11.3%	1419.84	11.3%
2.0%	1.5%	1594.86	25.0%	1594.86	25.0%
2.0%	2.0%	1802.92	41.3%	1802.92	41.3%
3.0%	1.0%	1149.97	-9.9%	1149.97	-9.9%
3.0%	1.5%	1275.64	0.0%	1275.64	0.0%
3.0%	2.0%	1422.96	11.5%	1422.96	11.5%
4.0%	1.0%	954.12	-25.2%	954.12	-25.2%
4.0%	1.5%	1046.97	-17.9%	1046.97	-17.9%
4.0%	2.0%	1154.45	-9.5%	1154.45	-9.5%
5.0%	1.0%	808.16	-36.6%	808.16	-36.6%
5.0%	1.5%	878.53	-31.1%	878.53	-31.1%
5.0%	2.0%	959.07	-24.8%	959.07	-24.8%

Table 127: Sensitivity analysis social security pension scheme Poland 2006 (in bn. PLN)

Parameters		ABO	Difference to standard scenario	PBO	Difference to standard scenario
r	g				
1.0%	1.0%	4336.08	39.9%	4944.08	39.7%
1.0%	1.5%	4393.33	41.7%	5220.53	47.5%
1.0%	2.0%	4451.78	43.6%	5525.99	56.2%
2.0%	1.0%	3612.36	16.5%	4050.50	14.5%
2.0%	1.5%	3655.95	17.9%	4251.18	20.1%
2.0%	2.0%	3700.40	19.4%	4471.52	26.4%
3.0%	1.0%	3066.26	-1.1%	3389.29	-4.2%
3.0%	1.5%	3100.20	0.0%	3538.42	0.0%
3.0%	2.0%	3134.77	1.1%	3701.19	4.6%
4.0%	1.0%	2645.38	-14.7%	2888.60	-18.4%
4.0%	1.5%	2672.33	-13.8%	3001.84	-15.2%
4.0%	2.0%	2699.75	-12.9%	3124.73	-11.7%
5.0%	1.0%	2314.75	-25.3%	2501.47	-29.3%
5.0%	1.5%	2336.54	-24.6%	2589.16	-26.8%
5.0%	2.0%	2358.68	-23.9%	2683.84	-24.2%

Table 128: Sensitivity analysis government employer pension scheme Poland 2006 (in bn. PLN)

Parameters		ABO	Difference to standard scenario	PBO	Difference to standard scenario
r	g				
1.0%	1.0%	354.76	39.9%	404.50	39.7%
1.0%	1.5%	359.44	41.7%	427.12	47.5%
1.0%	2.0%	364.22	43.6%	452.11	56.2%
2.0%	1.0%	295.55	16.5%	331.39	14.5%
2.0%	1.5%	299.11	17.9%	347.81	20.1%
2.0%	2.0%	302.75	19.4%	365.84	26.4%
3.0%	1.0%	250.87	-1.1%	277.30	-4.2%
3.0%	1.5%	253.64	0.0%	289.50	0.0%
3.0%	2.0%	256.47	1.1%	302.81	4.6%
4.0%	1.0%	216.43	-14.7%	236.33	-18.4%
4.0%	1.5%	218.64	-13.8%	245.60	-15.2%
4.0%	2.0%	220.88	-12.9%	255.65	-11.7%
5.0%	1.0%	189.38	-25.3%	204.66	-29.3%
5.0%	1.5%	191.16	-24.6%	211.83	-26.8%
5.0%	2.0%	192.98	-23.9%	219.58	-24.2%

Table 129: Sensitivity analysis social security pension scheme Portugal 2006 (in bn. EUR)

Parameters		ABO	Difference to standard scenario	PBO	Difference to standard scenario
r	g				
1.0%	1.0%	540.41	37.9%	646.09	39.3%
1.0%	1.5%	540.41	37.9%	673.44	45.2%
1.0%	2.0%	540.41	37.9%	703.49	51.7%
2.0%	1.0%	456.45	16.5%	533.37	15.0%
2.0%	1.5%	456.45	16.5%	553.26	19.3%
2.0%	2.0%	456.45	16.5%	575.04	24.0%
3.0%	1.0%	391.93	0.0%	449.00	-3.2%
3.0%	1.5%	391.93	0.0%	463.75	0.0%
3.0%	2.0%	391.93	0.0%	479.84	3.5%
4.0%	1.0%	341.41	-12.9%	384.53	-17.1%
4.0%	1.5%	341.41	-12.9%	395.66	-14.7%
4.0%	2.0%	341.41	-12.9%	407.76	-12.1%
5.0%	1.0%	301.18	-23.2%	334.31	-27.9%
5.0%	1.5%	301.18	-23.2%	342.86	-26.1%
5.0%	2.0%	301.18	-23.2%	352.12	-24.1%

Table 130: Sensitivity analysis social security pension scheme Sweden 2006 (in bn. SEK)

Parameters		ABO	Difference to standard scenario	PBO	Difference to standard scenario
r	g				
1.0%	1.0%	10317.15	44.5%	12026.04	45.8%
1.0%	1.5%	10317.15	44.5%	12708.38	54.1%
1.0%	2.0%	10317.15	44.5%	13478.51	63.4%
2.0%	1.0%	8492.00	18.9%	9630.04	16.7%
2.0%	1.5%	8492.00	18.9%	10099.33	22.4%
2.0%	2.0%	8492.00	18.9%	10625.70	28.8%
3.0%	1.0%	7141.32	0.0%	7917.99	-4.0%
3.0%	1.5%	7141.32	0.0%	8249.32	0.0%
3.0%	2.0%	7141.32	0.0%	8618.67	4.5%
4.0%	1.0%	6117.21	-14.3%	6659.40	-19.3%
4.0%	1.5%	6117.21	-14.3%	6899.06	-16.4%
4.0%	2.0%	6117.21	-14.3%	7164.62	-13.1%
5.0%	1.0%	5323.70	-25.5%	5710.22	-30.8%
5.0%	1.5%	5323.70	-25.5%	5887.48	-28.6%
5.0%	2.0%	5323.70	-25.5%	6082.78	-26.3%

Table 131: Sensitivity analysis social security pension scheme Slovakia 2006 (in bn. SKK)

Parameters		ABO	Difference to standard scenario	PBO	Difference to standard scenario
r	g				
1.0%	1.0%	4104.27	38.1%	4581.09	37.3%
1.0%	1.5%	4243.99	42.8%	4932.46	47.9%
1.0%	2.0%	4392.00	47.8%	5326.63	59.7%
2.0%	1.0%	3410.89	14.8%	3754.50	12.5%
2.0%	1.5%	3515.86	18.3%	4011.63	20.3%
2.0%	2.0%	3626.36	22.0%	4297.78	28.8%
3.0%	1.0%	2890.65	-2.7%	3143.25	-5.8%
3.0%	1.5%	2971.75	0.0%	3336.06	0.0%
3.0%	2.0%	3056.76	2.9%	3549.10	6.4%
4.0%	1.0%	2491.26	-16.2%	2680.43	-19.7%
4.0%	1.5%	2555.34	-14.0%	2828.12	-15.2%
4.0%	2.0%	2622.29	-11.8%	2990.25	-10.4%
5.0%	1.0%	2178.52	-26.7%	2322.63	-30.4%
5.0%	1.5%	2230.14	-25.0%	2437.97	-26.9%
5.0%	2.0%	2283.90	-23.1%	2563.80	-23.1%

Table 132: Sensitivity analysis government employer pension scheme Slovakia 2006 (in bn. SKK)

Parameters		ABO	Difference to standard scenario	PBO	Difference to standard scenario
r	g				
1.0%	1.0%	201.13	43.3%	223.92	42.6%
1.0%	1.5%	209.34	49.1%	242.47	54.4%
1.0%	2.0%	218.08	55.3%	263.40	67.7%
2.0%	1.0%	163.43	16.4%	179.42	14.3%
2.0%	1.5%	169.44	20.7%	192.63	22.7%
2.0%	2.0%	175.81	25.2%	207.40	32.1%
3.0%	1.0%	139.45	-0.7%	147.38	-6.1%
3.0%	1.5%	140.40	0.0%	157.04	0.0%
3.0%	2.0%	145.17	3.4%	167.75	6.8%
4.0%	1.0%	115.25	-17.9%	123.70	-21.2%
4.0%	1.5%	118.72	-15.4%	130.94	-16.6%
4.0%	2.0%	122.38	-12.8%	138.91	-11.5%
5.0%	1.0%	99.44	-29.2%	105.78	-32.6%
5.0%	1.5%	102.17	-27.2%	111.33	-29.1%
5.0%	2.0%	105.04	-25.2%	117.39	-25.2%

Table 133: Sensitivity analysis social security pension scheme UK 2006 (in bn. GBP)[235]

Parameters		ABO	Difference to standard scenario	PBO	Difference to standard scenario
r	g				
1.0%	1.0%			1625.44	34.9%
1.0%	1.5%			1625.44	34.9%
1.0%	2.0%			1625.44	34.9%
2.0%	1.0%			1390.09	15.3%
2.0%	1.5%			1390.09	15.3%
2.0%	2.0%			1390.09	15.3%
3.0%	1.0%			1205.14	0.0%
3.0%	1.5%			1205.14	0.0%
3.0%	2.0%			1205.14	0.0%
4.0%	1.0%			1057.69	-12.2%
4.0%	1.5%			1057.69	-12.2%
4.0%	2.0%			1057.69	-12.2%
5.0%	1.0%			938.56	-22.1%
5.0%	1.5%			938.56	-22.1%
5.0%	2.0%			938.56	-22.1%

---

[235] For the social security pension scheme of the UK, only PBO calculations were carried out.

SOZIALÖKONOMISCHE SCHRIFTEN

Herausgegeben von Professor Dr. Dr. h.c. Bert Rürup und
Professor Dr. Werner Sesselmeier

Band 41 Nicolas Gatzke: Public Private Partnerships und öffentliche Verschuldung. PPP-Modelle im Licht deutscher und europäischer Verschuldungsregeln und ihre Transparenz in den öffentlichen Haushalten. 2010.

Band 42 Olaf Weddige: Measuring Public Pension Liabilities in the European Union. 2011.

www.peterlang.de